Don Green

Latecomers

Children of Parents Over 35

Andrew L. Yarrow

THE FREE PRESS
A Division of Macmillan, Inc.
NEW YORK

Collier Macmillan Canada
TORONTO

Maxwell Macmillan International
NEW YORK   OXFORD   SINGAPORE   SYDNEY

The Free Press
A Division of Macmillan, Inc.
866 Third Avenue, New York, N.Y. 10022

Collier Macmillan Canada, Inc.
1200 Eglinton Avenue East
Suite 200
Don Mills, Ontario M3C 3N1

Printed in the United States of America

printing number
1   2   3   4   5   6   7   8   9   10

Library of Congress Cataloging-in-Publication Data

Yarrow, Andrew L.
　　Latecomers : children of parents over 35 / Andrew L. Yarrow.
　　　　p.　cm.
　　ISBN 0-02-935685-7
　　1. Children of parents over 35—United States.　2. Parent and child—United States.　I. Title.
　　HQ777.95.Y37　1991
　　306.874—dc20
　　　　　　　　　　　　　　　　　　　　　　　　　90-45944
　　　　　　　　　　　　　　　　　　　　　　　　　CIP

Contents

Preface

As a reporter for the *New York Times*, I have become somewhat accustomed to the powerful effects an article can have. But never in my experience has a story struck such a responsive chord in so many people as a feature I wrote in January 1987 on children of older parents.[1]

My parents were in their late thirties when I was born, but I only really began to explore the subject while writing that article. To my surprise it elicited many letters and phone calls, which ultimately led me to write this book.

The response, however, hardly prepared me for what happened a year later when I started to work on it. I had interviewed dozens of now-adult children of older parents, primarily in the northeastern United States. I also had surveyed two student samples, at Hunter College in New York City and Michigan State University in East Lansing. But I felt that I needed to broaden my sample to include people from different geographical and demographic backgrounds. So I placed notices in three very different publications—one with a broad, national audience, the *New York Times Book Review;* one a professional journal with a relatively small, specialized national readership, the *Family Therapy Networker;* and another with a sizable circulation in a large, Middle American city, the *Milwaukee Journal.*

Much to my astonishment, letters began to pour in by the hundreds. Day after day for months, letters arrived from every corner of the United States and Canada, as well as a smattering from Europe, the Caribbean, and the Orient. Scores of people called; my answering machine would often have a dozen new messages each day from various, far-flung children of older parents. All told, about eight-hundred responded. They came from forty-seven states, five Canadian provinces, and nine other countries.

Initially I had intended to interview most, if not all, of those who responded, but because of the volume of responses, I had to reconsider. I did interview about seventy people, and I replied to most of the others who had written or called me, sending them a four-page questionnaire, with multiple-choice

v

and open-ended questions about the effects and meanings of having older parents. Again, to my surprise, more than 80 percent filled out and returned the questionnaires in the self-addressed stamped envelopes I provided. At least half the respondents added pages of text, reflecting, reminiscing, explaining, and evaluating what it meant to them at different times in their lives to have older parents.

Women accounted for roughly three-fourths of those who responded. Respondents ranged in age from an eleven-year-old girl and a few teenagers to a man and woman in their nineties. Every intervening age group was well represented. Not only were there people from towns, cities, and suburbs throughout the country, but they came from every walk of life—students, homemakers, professionals, and service and blue-collar workers. Nineteen percent were only children; another 7 percent were other firstborns; 12 percent were "middle" children; and 62 percent were last-born children.

When these "children" were born, their mothers' average age was 38.5; nearly 40 percent of mothers were in their forties; and the oldest was fifty-one when her child was born. The average age for fathers was 43.4, and 71 percent were forty or older when their children were born; the oldest was seventy-nine.[2]

Respondents were self-selected volunteers, and there was no control group, yet the fact that so many people were motivated to participate with such enthusiasm clearly reflects remarkably widespread and deep feelings about having older parents. As one woman correctly predicted in her letter: "When I saw your author's query in the *New York Times,* I thought, He's got to be kidding—he'll get tons of volunteers."

Most only wrote short notes, but at least two hundred of the letters ranged from one to six pages, in which writers discussed their experiences and feelings in depth. As one woman wrote: "I could go on and on about myself and about the impact that growing up with older parents had, and still has, on me." Several sent detailed family trees or photographs of themselves and their parents. Some felt so strongly about the subject that they had written poems, letters to newspapers, and even, in one case, a college-application essay about being the child of older parents.

Over and over, people declared that they had "very strong feelings about the subject of 'children of older parents,'" liberally punctuating their comments with exclamation points. Many echoed the sentiments of a man who said that he was "always fascinated with examining how my life was different from contemporaries with parents fifteen years younger."

"I have always felt that my personality was shaped more by having older parents than by any other factor," another concluded.

Since the very subject of children of older parents has been ignored for so long, many expressed gratitude that it was being addressed. Indeed, quite a few said they had long looked for books or articles on the topic, and several said that they had contemplated writing about it themselves.

Some felt, as a Los Angeles woman did, that "it would be fascinating to finally match stories with other late-in-life babies." Many who had friends or spouses whose parents also were older wondered if there were common personality traits among later-born children because of their similar life experiences.

Despite the strong, serious feelings most respondents expressed about being children of older parents, some had a sense of humor about the subject.

"Are we to be called COOPs (children of older parents)? Do we need a support group?" a Burlington, Vermont, woman wondered.

A doctor from central California mentioned that his ninety-three-year-old father had recently remarried—a seventy-five-year-old woman. "If they have children, I will really have some interesting information for your book!" he said.

And a Massachusetts woman, who asked about the book's conclusions, added: "Hopefully, it won't prove that [we] are neurotic, spoiled brats, but brilliant, sensitive, gorgeous, and witty."

Acknowledgments

Many people provided invaluable assistance of many kinds for this book.

My editors at the Free Press, Susan Milmoe and Gioia Stevens, shepherded this project to publication. My agent, Henry Dunow, launched this project with enthusiasm and unflagging support. Marian Radke-Yarrow, my mother, provided assistance in each of her roles—as an older parent, a psychologist, and a patient reader of my manuscript. Nancy Newhouse and Harold Gal, my editors in the Style department of the *New York Times*, made this book possible by publishing my original article on children of older parents. Naomi Kroger, a professor of sociology at Hunter College, administered my questionnaire to sixty-seven of her students and tabulated the results. Rose Dobrof and Pat Chartock at New York's Brookdale Center on Aging, and Robert Butler at the Mount Sinai School of Medicine, also in New York, offered helpful research perspectives, particularly with respect to geriatrics and caregiving issues. Psychologist Edith Nottelmann provided help in computing the data, and Robert Burns painstakingly entered data and tabulated the results from approximately five hundred questionnaires. Stephanie Ventura of the National Center for Health Statistics led me through a tangle of demographic data, and read portions of the manuscript. Mirca Liberti and Louise Fradkin of the support group Children of Aging Parents provided me with many subjects to interview as well as their office in Levittown, Pennsylvania, in which to interview them. Psychologist Grazyna Kochanska did secondary data analyses of her study of child-rearing and family relations, using parental age as a variable. Diane Garden and Mike Monheit at Michigan State University in East Lansing distributed my questionnaire to about two dozen students. Christine Windquist Nord provided me with information from her unpublished dissertation on later-life childbearing, drawing on data from the National Survey of Children. William Seltzer and Alice Clague of the United Nations Statistical Office provided me with the most recent international health statistics compiled by the United Nations. Others who read and commented on portions of the manuscript were Dr. Shari Targum; Ann Jackowitz; Dr. Stanley Zinberg, chairman of the obstetrics and gynecology department at New York Infirmary–Beekman Hospital Downtown; and Dr. Ilona Brandeis, clinical assistant professor of obstetrics and gynecology at New York University. George and Lois Ulmer patiently assisted me in sending questionnaires to hundreds of children of older parents.

This project, of course, would not have been possible without the contributions of time and thoughtful reflection by the eight hundred children of older parents whom I interviewed or who contacted me in response to my notices in the *New York Times Book Review*, the *Family Therapy Networker*, and the *Milwaukee Journal* and filled out my questionnaire. In addition, dozens of students at Hunter College and Michigan State University also answered the questionnaire, and many older parents and experts from various fields contributed their perspectives and knowledge.

I

Setting the Stage

1

All But Ignored

My mother colored her hair religiously and never would admit how old she really was. But I often felt a twinge of embarrassment when I saw my parents next to the other kids' at school functions. They must have been nearly fifteen years older, and they always seemed less active and more old-fashioned. I never told anyone, but I worried constantly about their health. They weren't really fragile, but I knew they would die before any of my friends' parents died.

Essentially, my parents were grown-ups when I was born. They had somehow passed that mysterious, magic age in adult life when you figure out you're mortal. The yearnings of youth have abated, and the business of your immortality— your children—is very crucial. I've always been grateful never to have borne the baggage of parents who felt my arrival curtailed their own opportunities.

These are the voices of children of older parents. Their experiences and feelings have been largely invisible to social scientists and rarely thought about by couples having children in their late thirties or forties. In fact, they have been all but ignored by everyone except those themselves born to older mothers and fathers. Yet, for many whose births came relatively late in their parents' lives, the emotional texture of their childhood and adulthood is quite different from that of children with younger parents. Indeed, most of these latecomers would agree with a woman who earnestly declared: "I can assure you that having older parents does make a difference!"

A host of studies and headlines have trumpeted the fact that growing numbers of women are delaying childbearing beyond their thirty-fifth birthdays. During the 1980s, the number

3

of children born to American women in their late thirties and early forties nearly doubled. By 1990 one in every thirteen babies in America—about three hundred thousand a year—was born to a woman at least thirty-five years old, and about one in every six was born to a father over thirty-five. And these proportions are expected to grow substantially.

Even though this means that later-born sons and daughters will occupy an ever-more-prominent place in society's demographic mix, surprisingly little attention has been paid to children of older parents. Psychologists and pundits have yet to recognize them as an identifiable group.

Divorced parents, working mothers, alcoholic parents, "absent" fathers, teenage parents, adoptive parents—the impact on children of the special circumstances of these and other parents has been extensively investigated. Similarly, the effects of birth order, sibling relationships, being an only child, and other aspects of family life have been probed.

Furthermore, "older mothers" and "postponed parenting" are often discussed as important contemporary phenomena, and "age of mother" is a variable frequently used by demographers and other social scientists. But thus far there has been virtually no real analysis of these complex social facts with their many interpersonal and developmental dimensions.

Like the other ways in which a generation is affected by the one that preceded it, parents' ages can define the life setting for children and influence them on many levels for decades. Their experiences as latecomers often leave indelible marks, shaping their personalities, life patterns, and feelings about their families long after they have grown up.

Although postponed parenthood may be perceived as a new phenomenon, childbearing after thirty-five has always occurred. In fact, the proportion of babies born to American women thirty-five or older was larger in 1960 (10 percent of all babies born that year) than in the late 1980s (7.5 percent). In the past, these late arrivals were more often last-born children in large families. But even the delaying of first births is not new: During the depression years of the 1930s, there were as many only or first-born children of older parents as there are today. Children of older parents are an even more significant minority in many countries other than the United States. In nations as different as Spain,

Israel, Sweden, and Bangladesh, approximately one in every eight children is born to a mother who is at least thirty-five.

Recent interest notwithstanding, later-life parenting has long been surrounded by stereotypes and fears and stigmatized as deviating from the accepted norms of when one should become a parent. Such attitudes have been soundly reinforced by literature, popular culture, social science, and the medical community. Mothers over thirty-five have been termed high-risk by gynecologists and obstetricians because of the higher probabilities of problem pregnancies or birth defects like Down's syndrome.

Nonetheless a demographic revolution—fueled by feminism, readily available contraception, advances in prenatal care, changing social attitudes, and the influx of women into the work force—has generated a boom in delayed first-time childbearing. As Census Bureau demographer Arthur J. Norton has proclaimed, "The most important social change [of the 1980s and 1990s] regarding parenthood is timing."[1]

With more and more women and couples choosing to put off having children until well into their thirties or beyond, midlife parenting has become almost chic in certain circles.

These present-day older mothers and fathers can be emphatic about the benefits of postponing parenthood. They stress their emotional and professional stability. Unlike people in their twenties, they say, they are less likely to be struggling to define their own identities and goals. They assert that they can give their children more and cite statistics that older couples are considerably less likely to get divorced. In short, they argue that there is no better time to have children.

"It's such a wonderful thing!" declared one forty-one-year-old first-time mother. "You cherish having a baby later in life. Everybody thinks their first child is incredibly special, but for older parents, their child is even more special. I had done so much more thinking about what it means to be a mother, and I know I pay more attention to my daughter than if I'd had her earlier."

Joining this chorus are celebrity older mothers and fathers whose glowing tales fill newspaper and magazine articles. A flurry of books, articles, television shows, and movies have focused on this new breed of older parents. And a quick perusal of a library card catalog yields a long list of alternately scary and reassuring titles such as "Up Against the Clock," "The Biological Clock," "Parenthood After 30?," "Having a Baby After 30," "Primelife Pregnancy," "Pregnancy After 35," "Women Can Wait," and "You're Not Too Old to Have a Baby."

Virtually all these books and articles have looked at postponed parenting from the perspective of the mothers and, occasionally, the fathers. They emphasize the many advantages for their audience of parents and prospective parents and vaguely imply that these advantages will inevitably be passed on to the children like a strand of DNA. Rarely is anything said about the ways in which the timing of parenthood may affect the children. Likewise, many older parents or parents-to-be just don't think about what delayed childbearing may mean for their children either in the short term or fifteen to twenty-five years down the road.

But what does it mean to be a child of older parents?

Is it a hazard, an advantage, or does it really make a difference at all? Are the latecomers' personal and interpersonal worlds different from those of children born earlier in their parents' lives? Are experiences with peers and family relationships affected? And do life's advantages and burdens add up differently?

Of course, parental age in itself has no real meaning apart from its repercussions on children as well as parents. What is the significance for a child of his or her "point of entry" into the family? And in what discernibly different ways do later-born children and older parents interact with and influence each other?

This book presents the neglected point of view of children of older parents. The fabric of their lives is woven from the remembrances, current experiences, and reflections of more than eight hundred people of all ages and backgrounds who were interviewed, responded to a questionnaire, or wrote about issues they felt were related to having older parents.

These later-born children expressed their feelings, recollections, and opinions—positive and negative, poignant and mundane—about a wide range of experiences in the development of their own identities. They spoke thoughtfully about themselves and their parents as they recounted memories of long-ago and more recent incidents. They recalled, often with remarkable candor and clarity, their family life and social worlds during childhood, adolescence, and adulthood, and they described their roles and responsibilities as children of aging parents. Individual memories, assumed to be unique, were echoed by other respondents; the details may have been different, but the themes were often the same.

They felt bitterness and gratitude, anger and joy. A considerable number blamed the fact that their parents had had them later in life for a variety of psychological and interpersonal problems. Others felt that their lives had been enriched by having more mature and financially secure parents. They also compared themselves with children of younger parents and discussed their perceived advantages and disadvantages and the many differences that cannot so neatly be characterized as either positive or negative. Not only were their experiences seen as different, but the styles and ambiance of family life were viewed as strongly influenced by the age of their parents.

The balance of advantages and disadvantages shifted at different stages in their lives. They recognized both enduring and changing constellations of age-related characteristics in their parents that they wished to emulate or avoid.

Some said that age made no difference in their lives, and that it did not seem unusual to have "older" parents. But the vast majority felt that their parents' ages had affected them, often profoundly. Indeed, many agreed with a Chicago man who wrote, "This condition and situation has influenced my entire life and behavior."

Theirs is a complex and varied story. They spoke not as a unified chorus, but as hundreds of soloists whose themes frequently harmonized, yet often sounded dissonant. As in a modern musical composition, the harmonious and dissonant parts create a whole that is both more and less than the experience of any individual child of older parents.

Their stories are told in extended case histories, and their feelings and observations are presented throughout the book.[2] Results from my questionnaire survey are included, and significant differences in experience and perspective that were associated with respondents' birth-order status, family size, age, gender, and parents' ages are also examined. Data from several studies by social scientists have provided information on how parent-child relationships are affected by parental age. Late childbearing and parenthood are also viewed in the larger contexts of history, culture, society, demography, and health. And suggestive anecdotes are drawn from the lives of famous children of older parents.

After looking closely at two contrasting latecomers in chapter 2, social attitudes concerning midlife parenting and historical and cross-cultural dimensions are examined in chapters 3 and 4. In chapter 5, I introduce the ways in which children of older parents feel "different" because of what could be called signs of age—parents looking or acting older. Chapter 6 then explores perceived differences resulting from the fact that most latecomers' extended families and the other adults with whom they interact are older than the comparable figures for children of younger parents. Part 3, which includes chapters 7 through 10, focuses on the different family contexts of being a later-born child and how these circumstances define different "types" of latecomers.

Whereas the types of differences addressed in chapters 5 and 6 in many ways cut across time, other types of differences between latecomers and "on-time" children loom large at particular stages of life. Although family and social circumstances and developmental issues are obviously interrelated, the unique developmental dimensions of being a latecomer are addressed in chapters 11 through 20. In the final part, the perspective changes, focusing on today's older mothers and fathers.

2

The Children Speak

Two Case Histories—Robert and Lynn

"All the parents on TV looked like they should be my parents' kids," said Robert, an editor in a large southern city. "I remember, in about the third or fourth grade, being struck by how much older my parents were than the parents on TV. They looked like grandparents."

Robert grew up in a middle-class neighborhood of the Bronx. His father was a salesman for a sportswear company in New York, and his mother was a housewife. He had one sister who was three years older.

So far the picture looks pretty conventional—like that of tens of millions of other American families in the 1950s, during the height of the baby boom and the halcyon days of postwar American prosperity.

But when Robert was born in 1948, his father was forty-seven years old and his mother was forty.

"On TV the image was of this young, vigorous country having children," he recalled. "But we seemed in a sort of backwater, among these older people who didn't have energy, drive, or ambition. My life seemed like a subplot to the country's."

∞

Although most Americans in the mid-twentieth century were marrying in their early twenties, Robert's father and mother—like a sizable minority of couples after World War II—did not wed until relatively advanced ages. Both had been very close to their families and had lived with their parents until they married at ages forty-three and thirty-six.

They may have taken "a long time in their lives to get going" with starting a family, as Robert put it, but once they did, they

9

became very involved parents. "It was that funny kind of involvement that you feel absolutely sure of their interest and concern in what you're doing," he said. "I never doubted at any point that I was absolutely the apple of their eye. I always felt very loved and valued by them."

Nonetheless, like most young children, Robert compared his parents to those of his friends and schoolmates. He became aware that his mother and father were different and that the biggest difference was that they were considerably older than either his peers' parents or those fictionally normative parents on "Leave it to Beaver," "Father Knows Best," and other TV series.

"When I realized they were older than other kids' parents, there were times I felt embarrassed or angry that I was deprived, that my father wasn't young or athletic, that they weren't like the parents on TV," he said.

His father seemed less energetic and less interested in playing ball with his son than did other fathers. He did play, although "it was something I sort of pushed him to do," Robert said. Even summer evenings tended to be occupied with more sedentary pleasures such as reading the newspaper and watching television.

By his later grade-school years, Robert recalled, he began feeling "self-conscious about being seen in public with my parents because they seemed old. It was embarrassing that they were older than other parents. I didn't want my friends to see me with these old codgers.

"They didn't really look older in a way the world would have noticed. But when I was ten, my father was nearly sixty and was balding. And you're so conscious as a kid of things that make you stick out in any way.

"I remember a couple of times going shopping with my father, and a salesman would say, 'Is this your grandson?' I'd stiffen, but I don't think it bothered him.

"I think my parents were proud to be older and have had kids. They felt their great achievement in life was bringing us up and providing for us."

In many ways, they did provide well, both emotionally and financially. Yet, many of the values they brought to parenting were shaped by the time in which they grew up—an era some fifteen years earlier than that of most other parents with young

children in the 1950s. Robert's parents were young adults when
the stock market crashed in 1929, and his father was among
the millions of unemployed in the early nineteen thirties.

"They were so much a product of the depression," he said.
"They didn't want to take risks, and they were very concerned
with security. My father was proud that he had never bought
anything on credit." In short, their mentality was quite different
from the pervasive ideology of the expansive, consumer-driven
economy of the 1950s. "I took for granted that they seemed to
have come from such a different era."

This sense of his family being out of step with the times,
coming from a sort of historical "backwater," was reinforced
by memories of his grandparents and other relatives. Robert never
knew his father's parents, who had died by the time he was in
kindergarten, but both of his maternal grandparents were still
alive during his childhood.

"They had both come from Russia around the turn of the
century, and they seemed of an utterly foreign world. They had
the exoticism of being from the old country. Going over to their
apartment felt like stepping back [in] to another time, with the
smells, the furnishings, the accents. That's what I assumed grandparents were—from another world and another time. But it made
me feel more special."

Robert remembered his grandfather—a tall man, "with a
full head of white hair, very elegant and very exotic"—playing
with him and making a fuss over him. He died, however, when
Robert was six.

His grandmother, on the other hand, "was very gruff, a rather
unhappy lady. She'd complain about her health and her children
not visiting enough. She died quietly just before my bar mitzvah.
Frankly, it was a relief not to make those ritual Saturday night
visits to see her."

Robert's only other close relatives were his father's sister
and brother-in-law, who were fifty and sixty years old, respectively, when he was ten. Without cousins or young aunts or
uncles, Robert found his childhood world to be ringed with
people a half century older than he was. "Early on, I got very
comfortable being with groups of adults," he remembered.

By the time Robert got to high school, his parents seemed
to become less involved in his life. "They left me more alone
in my teenage years. They just didn't have the energy to smooth

out conflicts." This perceived parental detachment made it harder to go through the normal angst of adolescent rebellion, for better or worse. He went out of his way not to provoke them, and even when he did do things that should have upset them, they responded passively.

Because his father was so much older, "he never seemed a rival in the way that someone closer to my age would have been," Robert said. This "absence of competition" he found comforting.

"My father called me 'Good Robert.' I was a kindly person who didn't make waves or get into conflicts with other people. But when I wasn't Good Robert, he'd ask me in this very mournful way where Good Robert was."

Taken together, his parents' detachment, the lack of competition, and their expectations that their son would be a trouble-free Good Robert made his adolescence unusually placid. "It was hard to be rebellious with them," he recalled. "They were sort of like grandparents, and how do you rebel against grandparents?

"And in my teen years, their health began to fail," he continued. "They were so old. They weren't people you wanted to make your adversaries. It would have been cruel."

Shortly after Robert went away to college at age sixteen, his father retired and his mother became ill. His father had developed Parkinson's disease, and his mother was diagnosed as having cancer. As her illness worsened, Robert's father devoted his time to taking care of his wife.

His parents seemed even more distant from him, Robert recalled. "They certainly had things to worry about besides me. When I was sixteen or seventeen, they were really dealing with the issues of elderly people. The fact that they had a teenage son was low on their list of priorities."

Suddenly his sister and he were thrust into the role of caring for their parents. "I felt I was being moved quickly to adulthood," he said. "I wasn't overjoyed that my parents were ill, but there was something about having more responsibility and independence that I welcomed. It set me apart from other people my age. I didn't have the illusion that there would be someone there to take care of me when I was older—which other people I met in college had to fall back on."

Robert's mother died when she was fifty-eight and he was eighteen.

"It was sort of the second blow to my father," he recalled. "His whole life had been about serving others. He'd taken care of his mother into his forties, and then he took care of his kids. Now, within the space of a few years, he didn't have a job, a wife, or kids living at home, and he wasn't in good health, as his Parkinson's became very debilitating."

When Robert went home to see his father or spent time with him on vacations, he said, "It was like meeting a new person. So many things had disappeared. He was an old man, living in a rapidly decaying area of the Bronx. It was sad."

His father had a severe heart attack just before Robert began graduate school. Soon after, he moved into an apartment complex for the elderly, and in 1976—when Robert was twenty-seven—he died.

"It was a very strange feeling, having both your parents dead when you're in your twenties," Robert reflected. "It was very sobering to know that I was on my own in the world, that there was no one I needed to account to. It was like God was dead; if I did anything horrible or scandalous, I would be the only one to suffer. There were no parents to agonize over my decisions. It was again like a push to grow up more quickly.

"It was another thing that set me apart from other people my age. People twenty or thirty years older were dealing with aging parents. And those issues were over for me."

Like his forty-three-year-old sister, Robert and his wife do not have children, and he says that he has no desire for them. "I don't know how that fits. It may be the model of our parents having kids so late in life—maybe some family legacy of delaying the decision," he pondered. "My father was forty-three when my sister was born, so I have a few years left to decide," he jokingly added.

But the enduring effect of having had older parents, Robert said, was that "the whole process of growing up got speeded up." He was around more older people as a child, and he was expected or forced to assume more adult responsibilities at an earlier age than his peers were. During his childhood, he felt unequivocal love and devotion from his parents, which he attributed to their maturity.

"The thing that stands out most about having older parents is that you become an orphan at a relatively early age," he concluded. "Death became a reality earlier. I lost my grandparents earlier, and other relatives' health failed earlier. I experienced a lot of death growing up, more than my friends. And I was confronted with the reality of being alone in the world at an early age."

Lynn

The outlines of Lynn's story may well sound familiar to children of older parents growing up in the last years of the twentieth century. Like many of today's later-born children, she was the only child of two professional parents who had followed a career track through their twenties and thirties. Her father was a doctor and her mother, the staff director for a committee in the House of Representatives, was one of very few women in her mid-1930s law school class. They married, both for the first time, when he was forty and she was thirty-seven.

Two years later Lynn was born. Her parents were already well established in their careers and thus had the money and inclination to pamper their one precious child.

"I grew up in Washington in this high-powered political atmosphere. My father had a surgery practice, and my mother helped write one of the major pieces of legislation of the 1960s," she recalled. "They always took me on business trips, and we'd stay in the best hotels. I was taken out to the finest restaurants in Washington from the time I was three, and I was schlepped to museums and galleries, which would have been great if I had been older.

"There was an overinvestment in me, and everything was done to cater to me. But emotionally my mother was afraid of me as a baby, I think, because she had never been around children. She wasn't confident of her skills at mothering, so she hired a woman who was my primary caretaker until I was ten."

Lynn's parents were hardly lacking in energy, "but it was directed away from the family," she said.

"Some of my fondest memories were going on picnics with my friends' parents. My mother never played any sports or walked much, and she was always involved in her Capitol Hill stuff. My father would take me places, but I always wished my parents were younger. I wished they were more athletic and that *they* would take me on picnics."

She regretted that they never really played with her and that her mother was never a room-mother at school. While her friends' younger parents "would learn the newest dance or fad and listen to rock and roll—which I thought was cool, to be tuned in to kids' things—my parents never did that. I think they had lost touch with the child inside them"—which Lynn attributed to their ages and the fact that their lives were focused on their careers.

In many ways, however, her parents' maturity and life experiences lessened Lynn's perception of a "generation gap" separating her from her parents during adolescence. Her mother was quite liberal in her values, she recalled, and many of Lynn's teenage friends would come to her mother to talk about their problems.

"My mother had been a bohemian in Greenwich Village" in the early 1930s, she said. "I think she had a wild, promiscuous time before I was born."

Such experiences—quite different from those of most younger suburban mothers of the 1950s and 1960s—not only set Lynn off from her peers but also accentuated the age gap between her and her mother. It was as if her mother had lived an entire lifetime before Lynn was born. "My parents very much compartmentalized their lives," she said. "Everything was kept separate. There was their life before they married, their work life, their life as a couple, and then their family life, with me."

Lynn's family life was also quite dissimilar from the family lives of her friends. Not only were her experiences with her parents and the emotional tenor of home life different, but she lacked the support of an extended family. Three of her grandparents had died before she was born, and the last—her father's mother—lived in a faraway home for the elderly. Because her parents were the only ones in their families who had gone to college, they had drifted apart from their siblings. So there were no aunts and uncles to visit or with whom to celebrate holidays.

Lynn remembered telling her mother that she wanted a brother or sister. "She told me it was out of the question. I think she was almost menopausal when I was born."

Lynn's parents sent her to a private school, provided her with piano lessons, and subliminally coached her in how to be a poised young lady who could fit into Washington society. She rebelled by not doing well in school and by refusing to follow her father's plan for her to become a doctor. She went away to college in Colorado and married at twenty, which she later realized was "a move toward independence for the wrong reasons."

Lynn divorced at twenty-two and moved back to the Washington area, close to her parents. "I really felt then that they were getting older," she said. "My mother had already had several massive coronaries. She had the first when I was ten.

"But one of the biggest tragedies in my mother's life was her retirement from Capitol Hill in 1973, when I was twenty-four. The congressman she worked for was defeated in the 1972 elections, so she left. The life that was meaningful to her had come to an end. I remember feeling so sad, and being so aware of her being much older. Her health deteriorated horribly.

"She was dependent on my father, and she protected me from having to take care of her," Lynn recalled. "I was really resistant to switching roles, though. I felt that, 'Goddammit, I'm the baby, and she put so little into taking care of me.' It's painful for me to say this, but I didn't want to take care of her." Lynn's mother died after her fifth heart attack, at age seventy-three.

Since then, Lynn has tried to patch up her rather frayed relationship with her father. He retired and "has been playing 'poor me,'" she said, "but I'm trying to get him to take courses so he doesn't sit at home and rot."

During these years Lynn remarried and had two children. Her own experience as a child of older parents was very much on her mind when she decided to have her children before she turned thirty. She is sad that her children will "miss out on the wisdom of my mother" but hopes that, with fewer years separating her from her children, she will be more on her children's "wavelength" than her parents were with her. By having children earlier, she added, she also hopes to be able to enjoy her later years, after her children are grown, in a way that her parents never could.

3

Society Knows Best?

Social Attitudes Toward Older Parents

In recent generations the American credo of parenting has been that relatively young is best; old is problematic.

The ideal mid-twentieth-century American family, defined by television situation comedies and sociologists alike, has been made up of two or three children born a few years after a couple has married but while the husband and wife are still young. Deviation from that norm—although surprisingly common—has generally been viewed as somewhat "wrong," upsetting a sort of natural order of things. Older (over thirty-five) and younger (under twenty) parents have been considered off schedule, and a social stigma has been attached to both very early and comparatively late childbearing.

"As individuals and families move through the age structure, they are made aware of whether they are early, on time, or relatively late on events by an informal system of rewards and sanctions," wrote Glen H. Elder, Jr., a sociologist at the University of North Carolina.[1] Although people of different classes and cultural backgrounds have different perceptions of the stages in their lives, studies have found that most families see themselves as being either ahead of schedule, on schedule, or behind schedule in terms of their timing of marriage and childbearing.[2]

Teenage mothers, for instance, often feel opprobrium for being unmarried and sexually active or for marrying "too soon." On the other hand, modern America's equation of "old" with "undesirable" or "ugly" also has shaped norms about the timing of parenthood. The strength of this bias favoring youthfulness may be waning in some ways, but, for generations, a mixture of fear and disapproval has surrounded later childbearing. The

17

stigma has been more likely to affect older mothers, but American society has also been ambivalent about much older fathers. The fifty- or sixty-year-old father may be secretly admired or envied by other men for his sexual prowess and fertility, yet by others he may be viewed as something of a "dirty old man."

Cultural norms, of course, are only one of several forces—including economic and demographic factors—that influence the timing of parenthood. Nonetheless, beliefs about what are good and bad ages at which to have children have exerted a subtle yet profound effect on people's childbearing behavior. This has been especially true in the last century or so, as contraceptives have made it increasingly possible for couples to choose whether and when to have children.

Social attitudes about the timing of parenting also have helped shape the context in which a child of older parents grows up. These attitudes have been defined, reinforced, and changed by a medley of social players from such fields as medicine, social science, religion, literature, and popular culture.

Traditional medical wisdom has long maintained that later-life childbearing is riskier and more difficult. Generations of medical students have been taught that childbirth is harder and more problematic for older women, especially first-time mothers. K. C. Spain, an early-twentieth-century obstetrician, wrote in 1912 that later-life childbearing is to be "dreaded both by patient and physician."[3] Some forty-four years later, R. R. Fliehr wrote in the journal *Obstetrics and Gynecology* that a first-time expectant mother in her late thirties would evoke a "feeling of dread and foreboding in the careful obstetrician."[4]

During the post–World War II baby boom in the United States, early childbearing was especially encouraged. In a 1954 symposium of the New York Academy of Sciences, "Parental Age and Characteristics of Offspring," E. V. Cowdry summarized the scientists' conclusions, declaring that "the choice of a young mother would seem to be one's best insurance for being born intact."[5]

In 1957 Alan Guttmacher, the well-known family-planning expert, proclaimed that the advantages of early childbearing should "be emblazoned on the walls of high schools and girls' colleges." And a year later, the Council of the International Federation of Gynecologists and Obstetricians recommended that first-time mothers who were thirty-five or older be labeled—with more than a hint of pejorative connotations—"elderly primigravidas."[6]

This societal bias against older parents even affected adoption agencies. For years many agencies would not place infants with couples who were over thirty-five simply because of their age, although older parents were sometimes permitted to adopt older children.

Theorists of human development have also upheld the biases against later childbearing as recently as the 1970s. One psychology text, for example, described the "developmental tasks" of "early adulthood" as marriage and childbearing. Another similarly plotted the normative life course for Americans, prescribing marriage at age twenty-one, birth of first child at twenty-two, and birth of last child at thirty.[7]

The prejudice against delayed marriage and childbearing—especially pronounced between the late 1940s and the 1970s—was illustrated by the results of a 1971 Gallup poll of American college students. Approximately 90 percent said that a woman should marry between ages twenty and twenty-five, and 95 percent believed that a man should marry between twenty-one and thirty.

Lore, Literature, and Social Attitudes

Lore about later-life parenting can be traced to the very beginnings of Western culture.

In chapter 17 of Genesis, God tells the ninety-nine-year-old Abraham that He will bless his wife, Sarah, with a son. "Abraham fell on his face and laughed, and said to himself, 'Shall a child be born to a man who is 100 years old? Shall Sarah, who is 90 years old, bear child?'"

Chapter 21 of Genesis continues: "And Sarah conceived, and bore Abraham a son in his old age at the time of which God had spoken to him." Later in chapter 21 we learn that "Abraham was 100 years old when his son Isaac was born to him." (Sarah, apparently none the worse for her experience, lived another thirty-seven years.)

Late childbearing was also explained in the Bible in terms of fertility problems, both in the First Book of Samuel and, in the New Testament, in the Gospel According to Luke. In an oblique reference to Hannah's late birth of Samuel, it was written that: "The Lord had closed her womb. So it went on year by year." And Luke tells of Zechariah and Elizabeth, who "had no child, because Elizabeth was barren, and both were advanced in years." However, Luke continues, an angel of the Lord came to Zechariah and said that Elizabeth would bear a son named John. "And Zechariah said to the angel, 'How shall I know this? For I am an old man, and my wife is advanced in years.'" Yet, by a miracle, their son, John the Baptist, was born.

In more modern times, as children and parent-child relationships became subjects of literature and popular culture, parental ages have figured in many stories. In most cases where they have appeared in literature, older parents have been depicted as either somewhat fantastic, larger-than-life figures or cruel and distant creatures who are rarely interested in their children's well-being. The children, too, tend to appear as either particularly pure and innocent or rather distorted and neurotic.

This fantasy quality about much older parents or their children appears in works as diverse as Jean Giraudoux's play *Ondine*, in which "two old people, Auguste and Eugénie" adopt the strange, young water nymph, Ondine, and Gabriel García Márquez's *One Hundred Years of Solitude*, in which remarkable ages and age differences enhance the novel's powerful dreamlike quality.

Several of nineteenth-century Russia's greatest authors also used the device of an extreme age difference between parent (usually father) and child (usually son) to stress the gap separating generations. In Turgenev's *Fathers and Sons* (1862), the elderly parents of Yevgeny Vassilyitch Bazarov dote on their son but are completely unable to understand him—an arrogant and nihilistic young revolutionary.

Dostoyevski, in *The Brothers Karamazov*, depicts Alyosha, the nineteen-year-old youngest son, as the brother most unlike his crude, cruel, and aging father. Whereas Ivan is the skeptical and ultimately guilt-stricken intellectual and Dmitri is cruel and brooding, the young Alyosha is the Christlike, spiritual son who makes peace with his father and his brothers.

Like the Russian novelists, film directors of the 1920s often made parents look particularly old to play up the current (and popular) notion that a decisive gap separated the younger generation from their elders. Some two decades later, a movie that captured the conventional mid-twentieth-century stereotype of the eccentric and tyrannical older mother (and the consequently repressed and neurotic daughter) was the 1942 Bette Davis film *Now, Voyager*. In one of her more memorable lines, the older mother declares, with cinematic flourish: "All such late children are marked."

In the novel on which the film was based, the author, Olive Higgins Prouty, drew a portrait of her main character, Charlotte Vale, tormented by her awareness of her mother's advanced age. "Her mother had been well on in her forties when she had been born," Prouty wrote.

Three boys had preceded her. "The child of my old age," she had often heard herself described when she was small. It had always filled her with a vague sense of shame, as if her existence required an explanation. . . . Several times her mother had laughingly referred to her as "my ugly duckling." She used to wonder if all "children of old age" were ugly ducklings—branded with marks of the advanced years of their parents. Her brothers were all handsome specimens. "An old-fashioned little thing" was another phrase often applied to her when she was a child. She had always felt not only apologetic to her mother, but under deep obligation to make amends for her undesired arrival.

Charlotte's father had died when she was in boarding school, and her personality was completely defined by her oppressive mother. This poor, "unwanted child of old age" tries to free herself from her mother's influence by taking an ocean voyage, on which she meets the first of several suitors. When she finally comes close to marrying, this "spinster aunt" who orders old-fashioneds in the ship's cocktail lounge, worries aloud about having a child at her advanced age.

In the book's penultimate scene, Charlotte's long-simmering unhappiness explodes during a fight with her mother. " 'I never wanted to be born,' " she exclaims. " 'And you never wanted me to be born either! It's been a calamity on both sides!' " After this outburst, Charlotte's mother has a stroke and dies, and Charlotte is committed to an asylum—although her life is ultimately salvaged, thanks to a kindly psychiatrist and her love for a child.

The seemingly freakish quality of being a child of older parents has even been reinforced by the *Guinness Book of World Records*. This popular compendium of offbeat trivia has an entry on "oldest mother," which notes "extreme but unauthenticated cases of septuagenarian mothers." While asserting that "the oldest recorded mother of whom there is satisfactory verification was Mrs. Ruth Alice Kistler," who gave birth to a daughter when she was fifty-seven, the book adds that "many very late maternities are cover-ups for illegitimate grand-children."

In films and plays, a significant age difference between a parent and child has been treated as a subject for humor. In the "Hardy Family" series of the 1930s and 1940s, for example, the conscientious and mature Judge Hardy is comically juxtaposed against the eternally adolescent Andy Hardy, played by Mickey Rooney. The title of the first of these thirteen films, *A Family Affair*, was revived in the 1960s for a television series in which the humorous potential of a large parent-child age gap was also a central premise; but at the same time the show was founded on the notion that an older man would be softened by his adopted wards, Buffy and Jody.

The presumably comedic quality of later-life parenting was even more the point of Sumner Arthur Long's 1962 Broadway comedy, *Never Too Late*. In the first act, Harry and Edith Lambert, a decidedly middle-aged couple, discover that they are going to have a baby. Harry, a sixtyish businessman, already has a live-in adult daughter and son-in-law when he learns—much to his chagrin—that his devoted wife, somewhere in the vicinity of forty, is once again expecting.

This rather unexpected turn of events prompts poor Harry to remark that when the newcomer "gets out of college I'll be going on eighty-three." And, then with a groan, he adds, "If he's smart." (To make matters worse, his daughter exclaims, "Father, how could you?")

Embarrassed and bewildered at the prospect of becoming a father again, Harry is teased mercilessly by his neighbors. In the course of the play, almost every gag about age, procreation, and parenting is dredged up, ranging from an awkward scene centered around a new bassinette to a rather tawdry, innuendo-filled pas de deux involving Harry's daughter and son-in-law, who are trying to have a baby of their own.

The basic premise of this rather thin farce is that having a child later in life, when a couple presumably should know better, is intrinsically funny. The obvious implication is that something has gone a bit awry in the normal scheme of things. Balding, curmudgeonly men and matronly women are hardly expected to be having sex, much less children. Whether or not this haplessly portrayed father-to-be and his patient wife might be better parents than, say, their selfish but age-appropriate daughter and son-in-law is, of course, never explored. And the implications for their new child are completely ignored.

Nonetheless this conformist concoction, written halfway between the publication of Sloan Wilson's novel *The Man in the Gray Flannel Suit* and Woodstock, ran for more than two years on Broadway, opened in London in 1963, and was turned into an even more insipid film in 1965 (directed by Bud Yorkin and produced by the young Norman Lear).

Changing Attitudes

The normative ideal that it is best to become a parent in one's twenties or early thirties, continued to influence values, if not behavior, well into the 1980s. A 1987 Louis Harris survey on the American family found that 60 percent disagreed with the statement that "you should work hard when you're young and put off having children until you have enough time and money to raise them properly." The caveat suggesting that when one is older, one is better able to raise a child still did not seem to convince Americans that later is better. The poll also found that 59 percent agreed that "it's best to have children early, so you can have some time to yourself after they grow up."[8]

Despite the still-widespread belief that having children in one's mid-thirties or later is not as "good" or "right" as earlier childbearing, attitudes about the proper timing of parenthood, at least in certain circles, have changed considerably. Among upper-middle-class professionals, it appears to have become a badge of status to have children fashionably late in life.

In some ways this recent change in attitudes has been dramatic. What was once frowned upon by doctors, psychologists, and the public has now become de rigueur in some parts of the population.

Women in their late thirties and forties are still considered high-risk mothers by some obstetricians, but a combination of cultural factors and new medical knowledge and procedures has led to changes in perspectives on these "elderly" thirty-five-year-olds. As delayed motherhood has become more common, and tests such as amniocentesis have been developed to assess the health of a fetus, the medical profession has altered its view of the risks of later childbearing. Many doctors have come to believe that women are healthier and seemingly younger than their counterparts of generations ago. In a recent medical journal article, the traditional description of over-thirty-five mothers as "elderly" primigravidas was condemned as "obsolete and, in fact, offensive."[9]

Even movies and television series have legitimized, if not glamorized, delayed childbearing. In the 1987 film *Baby Boom*, the main character, played by Diane Keaton, is a successful older (adoptive) mother. The premise was apparently so appealing to Hollywood producers and audiences alike that *Baby Boom* was turned into a short-lived television series. The dramatic or co-medic potential of later-life parenting was further milked in made-for-TV movies like *Maybe Baby*, a lifeless 1988 story about a hotshot thirty-nine-year-old career woman who suddenly de-cides that she and her fifty-seven-year-old husband should have a child. Another 1988 film, *A New Life*, starred Alan Alda as a man becoming a father in his fifties. And the popular TV series "thirtysomething" features new parents somewhere in their fourth decade of life.

This transformation in beliefs and stereotypes was summa-rized by one later-born child, who said: "Change-of-life babies used to be considered dreadful." But, as growing numbers of women in their late thirties and forties are having children, "it's almost become too cutesy. They have to have a Pierre Cardin snowsuit. Everything has to be designer-this, designer-that. The child becomes a status symbol. It has to go to the best day care and preschool. For women, now you have to have a high-powered job and also have a baby. If you don't you're no good. Whereas inner-city children's parents tend to be young and poor, with these older, yuppie parents, the environment is richer. A new mark of social class will be the age of the parents."

∞

Childbearing, parenting, and the family are hardly neutral subjects. Indeed, with the possible exceptions of religion, patrio-tism, or ethnic identity, there probably aren't many other topics that can so predictably elicit strong feelings and opinions. Given that, it is all the more remarkable that attitudes about the timing of childbearing have changed so dramatically in such a short time.

Beliefs and behavior generally reflect one another, although changes in norms may lag behind changes in the ways people behave—and the interplay is anything but simple.

People usually act in accord with what they believe to be "correct" or "right," but at times they may also diverge from culturally prescribed behaviors because of necessity. Such mitigating circumstances may stem from economic or demographic pressures. For example, if people can't afford to start a family as young adults—as has been true at various times in history—they may well put aside accepted norms about when to have children. Similarly, when there is a real or perceived shortage of available single men, the average age at marriage will rise, also contributing to a delay in childbearing.

Advances in obstetrics certainly play a role in reducing the perception that later childbearing is "wrong." And, as significant numbers of women have become obstetricians and gynecologists, they have undoubtedly helped shape what is accepted medical wisdom.

Ideas also have histories and complex family trees of their own. In fact, many intellectual streams usually feed into any powerful idea or norm. For instance, notions about the "proper" role of women and the importance of individual fulfillment, which are rooted in broader cultural currents, also have changed, affecting norms and values about the timing of parenthood.

Recent attitudinal changes about delayed childbearing have been most pronounced in one sector of society—upper-middle-class couples. How those changes may affect the broader population remains to be seen.

4

Nothing New

Children of Older Parents in Other Times and Places

Although the increase in childbearing among older women is widely viewed as a new, uniquely American or European phenomenon, it is a myth that older parents are an invention of the 1980s. Older parents may have been more of a rarity during the 1950s, 1960s and 1970s in America, and first-time parents over thirty-five have always been quite unusual, but at most other times in history and in most other societies today, a surprisingly large proportion of children have been born to couples in their late thirties and forties.

Indeed, children of older parents were more common in seventeenth-century Europe and colonial America, and are more common in late-twentieth-century Ireland, Spain, and most Arab and Third World countries, than in contemporary America and most of Western Europe. The principal reason for this was that women had more children over a longer span of time—stretching from their twenties or teens until menopause or death.

Cultural factors have played a significant role in the timing of childbearing. Currently the desire of many women and men to pursue careers and other nonfamily goals before having children has been much reported. But, in the past, the principal factors affecting the timing of childbearing have been economic considerations, wars and political strife, epidemic diseases, the availability and use of contraceptives, infant mortality rates, prolonged breast-feeding, and at what age marriage typically occurs.

No reliable large-scale censuses were conducted before the late eighteenth century, and birth records and statistics on population and public health are virtually nonexistent for most of human history. Yet some intrepid historical demographers and social historians studying the family have pieced together a fasci-

26

nating patchwork of data and hypotheses relating to childbearing patterns of centuries ago.

Until quite recently, childbearing was essentially a lifetime profession for most adult women. Even though the average life expectancy in most societies before the twentieth century was less than forty-five years—and the onset of menarche was later and menopause came earlier than today—most women spent at least twenty years of their short lives bearing children.

It is believed that even in the Stone Age women gave birth well into their late thirties. The !Kung San, or Bushmen, of southern Africa's Kalahari Desert provide a window on family patterns of fifty thousand years ago, according to anthropologists Nancy Howell and Richard Lee. Even though women of this hunter-gatherer tribe who survive until age fifteen have a life expectancy of only forty more years, the average !Kung woman has her last child at about thirty-nine. Some biologists have hypothesized that the late thirties served as an evolutionary upper limit for childbearing, as life expectancy would only permit a mother to survive until her own children were at least of reproductive age.[1]

In Europe, from the sixteenth century to the nineteenth century women had on average, six or seven children, according to Lawrence Stone, a Princeton University historian who has studied the history of family life. However, for reasons that are not entirely understood, childbearing did not begin early in life. Teenage marriages may have been common among the nobility, but the majority of peasants, farmers, and townspeople of Europe, from the Middle Ages to the nineteenth century, did not marry until their mid-twenties.[2]

At the top of the social ladder, people married early and generations were short. But among the masses of common people, what scholars have called the "European marriage pattern"— characterized by late marriages and small family size—was the general rule.

"Everywhere else in the world, girls have been married off early," Professor Stone says. "This was presumably true in premedieval Europe and is true in the third world today." Economic constraints on people's ability to set up their own households clearly affected this centuries-long tendency toward later marriage, but it is still something of a puzzle that poverty and economic scarcity led to later marriages and childbearing in early modern Europe but do not, for example, in underdeveloped countries today.[3]

In colonial New England, parents typically had eight to ten children, according to John Demos, a Yale University historian of the early American family. Childbearing tended to begin when women were in their mid-twenties and to continue into their forties. And "fathering might continue up to, or into, old age."[4]

Family size had a profound effect not only on parental ages but also on age differences among siblings. In eighteenth- and nineteenth-century America, the age range of children and, consequently, the gap between parents and their younger children were wider than they are today. Frequently the youngest child was starting school when the oldest was preparing for marriage.

Infant mortality—which hovered around 150 per thousand in early modern Europe—only began to decline appreciably in the twentieth century, according to historical demographer E. A. Wrigley, which led to women having fewer children and ending their childbearing earlier.[5] But it is not until the mid-twentieth century—with the development of the birth-control pill and other contraceptive technologies—that women and couples could effectively control their reproductive lives.

The average family size—and the span of childbearing years—declined gradually during the nineteenth century and through the depression years of the nineteen thirties. In 1850 American women, on average, had six children, with the last born when they were thirty-six years old.[6] At the beginning of the twentieth century, the median age at which women had their last child was 32.9.[7] Seventy years later, that figure had dropped to 29.6.

The timing of childbearing, of course, has closely reflected the timing of marriage. During the first century or so after the Declaration of Independence, the median age at marriage for men hovered around twenty-six, and for women, between twenty-three and twenty-four.[8] The average marriage age gradually declined from about the 1880s until World War II, when it began a relatively brief but precipitous drop. Between 1940 and 1950 the median age plummeted from 24.3 to 22.8 for men and 21.5 to 20.3 for women. Consequently the median age at which mothers gave birth to their first child dropped from 22.5 in 1948 to 21.1 in 1960.[9]

The long-term fertility decline was reversed only briefly during the two-decade post–World War II baby boom. During this short historical interlude, the vast majority of American men and women married and had children in their early twenties. To do otherwise in the prosperous, conformist world of postwar America was considered somewhat deviant.

Most demographers, however, agree with John Modell, a historical demographer at Carnegie-Mellon University, who called this upswing in fertility "an aberration." Since the mid-1960's, fertility rates in most developed countries have continued to fall to unprecedented levels.[10]

The decline in fertility, coupled with the increased tendency to delay marriage and use contraceptives, also ushered in a dramatic redistribution of the timing of first births. While birthrates for younger women (twenty to twenty-four years old) dropped to the lowest levels ever recorded, between 1970 and the mid-1980s, the number of American women having their first child after thirty more than tripled, and the first-birth rate for women thirty-five to thirty-nine years old went up by 110 percent. As Professor Demos said, "What's different now is not that there are people who are older parents, but that they hadn't already had children."[11]

But even the current frequency of putting off having a first child until relatively late is not entirely new. Among women born between 1912 and 1915, nearly one-third put off childbearing until their late twenties or beyond.[12] What is dramatically new today is the degree to which personal choice is determining when couples have children. As Professor Modell said, "Life courses have become much more volitional." Thus, he added, "all bets are off" as to what childbearing patterns and the timing of parenthood will be in future generations.[13]

Late Childbearing Around the World

In the late twentieth century, childbearing patterns, of course, differ considerably from country to country as a function of a complex web of seemingly disparate factors. These include rates of infant and maternal mortality; access to birth control; overall birthrates; political stability; education; the level of economic development, and religious beliefs and secular values about children, women, and the family.

Broadly speaking, the societies where later-life parenting has been increasing since the 1970s are ones where living standards are high and infant mortality and birthrates are low. They are also places where liberal and feminist ideologies affirming women's right to work and the desires of young adults to pursue nonfamilial goals and life-styles are widely accepted.

Comparative statistics derived in large part from United Nations Demographic Yearbooks show a strikingly consistent pattern of increased later-life parenting in countries like the United States, France, Great Britain, Japan, Israel, Canada, and the Scandinavian nations. In the United States, the proportion of children born to mothers thirty-five and older rose from 4.4 percent in 1977 to 7.5 percent in 1987. Between 1977 and 1985 the percentage of children born to older mothers rose in France from 5.9 to 9.1; in Sweden, from 6.2 to 11.7, and in Japan, from 4.0 to 7.1.[*]

The pattern of birthrates is equally striking. Birthrates for younger women have been leveling off or falling throughout the postindustrial world, while the rates for women between thirty-five and thirty-nine have been rising. Between 1977 and 1987 the number of births per 1,000 women between thirty-five and thirty-nine rose from 19.2 to 26.2 in the United States. During the same years, in France the rate jumped from 23.9 to 31.4, and in West Germany it increased from 18.6 to 23.8.

However, industrialized nations where values about the family, women, and birth control have been shaped by the Catholic church exhibit very different patterns. In countries like Italy, Spain, or Chile, overall birthrates generally have been higher than in Protestant and other developed non-Catholic societies. With larger families more the norm, childbearing tends to be spread out over a longer period of women's reproductive lives. Thus, both the percentage of children born to mothers thirty-five or older and the birthrates for older mothers have been higher in these nations.

But as secular values gain increasing currency and family size decreases, births to older mothers are now declining. In Italy, for example, the proportion of births to mothers thirty-five or older dropped from 10.9 percent in 1977 to 9.2 percent

---

[*] For statistics on patterns of later-life childbearing in the United States and throughout the world, see appendixes A and B.

in 1981, and the birthrate for women between thirty-five and thirty-nine fell dramatically, from 32.2 to 25.8.

A similar trend can be seen in rapidly industrializing nations like Brazil and South Korea. Although these countries have high overall birthrates, the span of childbearing years is becoming compressed, with the result that families are getting smaller and fewer children are born to women in their late thirties or forties. In South Korea, for example, the percentage of births to mothers thirty-five or older plummeted from 7.8 in 1977 to 2.6 in 1983.

In the Third World, underdevelopment is an economic code word for poverty, malnutrition, abysmal health care, and often severe overpopulation. The clichéd Hobbesian formula generally applies in much of Asia and Africa: Life is nasty, brutish, and short. This is also by and large the arena where virtually all of the late twentieth century's wars are fought. With neither economic nor political security, ideological debates about the family are practically meaningless. Religious and other cultural proscriptions on birth control also play a major role in keeping birthrates high. Consequently—as has been true in most preindustrial societies—women tend to bear many children over a period of many years, ranging from their teens to their forties.

The few statistics available indicate that the Third World has very large numbers of children of older parents. Most, undoubtedly, are born at the end of a long period of childbearing. For example, in Guatemala, 15.7 percent of all births in 1985 were to women thirty-five or older. In Bangladesh, the proportion in 1982 was 12.4 percent, and in the African nation of Rwanda, roughly one in four children was born to an older mother in 1978.

China, which is essentially a poor, Third World country with small pockets of development, is an unusual case. The legacy of Mao Tse-tung's regimented response to the nation's overwhelming population pressures has reportedly made China's birthrate among the lowest in the Third World. During the Cultural Revolution of the late 1960s, it was all but forbidden to marry before one's late twenties, and more recently the government has vigorously encouraged one-child families. Although it is estimated that only about 20 percent of Chinese families have only one child, those who do receive a monthly bonus, preferential treatment in obtaining housing and the promise of a higher pension, among other things. Chinese radio has warned that couples with large families are subject to higher taxes. This policy has probably given China one of the highest median ages for mothers in the developing world.

Some of the highest incidences of later-life parenting are found in Arab countries—most of which are economically under-developed and where religious and cultural values prescribe large families and traditional roles for women. About one in five babies are born to women thirty-five or older in countries like Libya, Iraq, and Egypt. The 1982 birthrate for women thirty-five to thirty-nine in Egypt was an astounding 177.8 per 1,000.

There have been few natality statistics for Eastern Europe, but those that are available reveal strikingly low frequencies of late childbearing. In Bulgaria only 3.4 percent of 1986 births were to women thirty-five or older, and the birthrate for women thirty-five to thirty-nine was only 10.0 per 1,000—among the lowest in the world. Conversely, in Poland—the most Catholic of these nations—7.0 percent of births in 1985 were to older mothers.

Most studies of parental age focus on mothers, and few countries have good statistics on fathers. Yet many of these inter-national patterns of later-life parenthood also apply to fathers. Since fathers throughout the world are, on average, older than mothers, the incidence of children of older fathers is naturally greater than that for children of older mothers. However, statistics on fathers' ages tend to overstate somewhat the proportion of older fathers because of incomplete records for younger fathers.

In the United States in 1984, 16.7 percent of children whose fathers' ages were known were born when their fathers were thirty-five or older. Similar numbers can be seen in other postin-dustrial nations like France (16.7 percent in 1981), Great Britain (19.5 percent in 1985), and Australia (20.1 percent in 1985).

In Catholic, developing, and less-developed nations, the percentage of children of older fathers is somewhat higher. In both Italy and Spain, for example, roughly 23 percent of babies in the early 1980s were fathered by men thirty-five or older. In Mexico and El Salvador, the proportions were even higher: 25.2 and 29.0 percent, respectively.

But the most striking statistics on older fathers come from the Arab world, where the age differences between husbands and wives are often dramatic. In Egypt, Iraq, and Kuwait, more than 40 percent of children are fathered by men thirty-five or older, and Libya holds the curious distinction of being perhaps the only country in the world where children of older fathers appear to be the norm: Nearly two-thirds of all babies born in Libya in 1977 had fathers who were thirty-five or older.

∞

The patterns of parental timing are clearly influenced by many factors. What seems new is old, and what is "normal" at one time or place is "deviant" in another. Does it follow that the meanings and effects on children of older parents are determined by the time and place in which they live? This seems likely, but it makes those meanings and influences no less salient and real.

II

A World of Difference

5
Feeling Different
Signs of Age

"During childhood I was sure my parents were the world's oldest!" exclaimed Marian, from Vancouver, British Columbia.

In the peer-oriented world of childhood and adolescence, children of older parents often say that they feel different and set off from their classmates and friends by virtue of their parents' ages. Many of those who were interviewed or surveyed described their mothers' and fathers' appearance, behavior, life-styles, and the very fact of their parents being older as things that differentiated them from their peers and made them feel self-conscious.

These latecomers frequently recalled feeling ashamed to bring friends home to meet their parents, partly out of fear that their mothers and fathers might be seen as "old" and "different." They remembered strangers mistaking their parents for their grandparents, and some felt embarrassed or hurt by people who assumed that they were "accidental" (and hence unwanted) babies.

Even though older parents are becoming more common, and some neighborhoods appear to be teeming with midlife mothers and fathers pushing baby carriages, twelve out of every thirteen babies in the United States still are born to women under thirty-five. In the larger context of American society, that thirteenth child is still likely to feel set off from his or her peers.

When someone is aware of feeling different from others, such feelings are often linked with a sense of isolation. Many later-born children spoke of feeling lonely and being especially isolated when they were young.

Many of these feelings were expressed simply yet poignantly by the youngest respondent, an eleven-year-old girl from Washington State, whose father was thirty-six when she was born.

"Most of the kids my age have dads that are from the ages of thirty-five to forty now," she wrote. "My dad's hair is starting to get gray. I'm afraid he is going to look really old when everyone else's dad still looks young. When I'm twenty years old, my dad will be fifty-six. He is going to die before everyone else's dad dies. Sometimes it embarrasses me to have such an old dad."

Another young girl from Washington, D.C., whose parents were in their forties when she was born, expressed her concerns differently but just as forcefully. "I wish my parents were younger and not so old-fashioned. They don't let me do as much as other parents. My best friend goes on biking trips with her parents; I wish I could. I told her once that my parents were a lot older, and sometimes she feels sorry for me.

"It's embarrassing if there's a parent party at school, because they're the only ones who are older," she continued. "They dress differently. They never wear jeans. My mom is really put together; everything matches. Everyone else's parents don't really care how they dress when they're around the house."

White Hair and Wrinkles

A father's white hair or a mother's wrinkles were often vividly remembered by children of older parents. In a culture where a premium has been put on looking "young," children and teenagers who are especially sensitive to any nuanced "difference" between them and their peers are likely to be all too aware of any such physically distinguishing signs of age.

"My father was bald and hard of hearing, and my mother was lined and wrinkled and prematurely graying," recalled a young New Yorker named Sarah. "As a kid you associate that with age. My mother always wanted feedback and reassurance about how she looked, and when I was angry, I was honest."

"I was surprised, as a small child, to discover that my friends' mothers were young women, when my own mother always seemed very matronly and middle-aged," added a woman from the Philippines.

Another woman recalled that her silver-haired mother "hated being older and was very hurt at being taken for my grandmother. I remember her scratching out her face on family photographs."

Parental appearance was more important as an issue during adolescence than in either childhood or adulthood. Women, looking back on their teen years, were especially negative about their mothers' appearance, as 41 percent of those surveyed said they were unhappy or embarrassed about it. Only 15 percent had positive memories.

"One of the first years I went to summer camp, I remember a friend's father who had very muscular legs," said Jane, whose own father was forty when she was born. "Since my father looked older and never wore shorts, I was baffled by the sight of this father who looked like my brother."

Another summer-camp experience was recalled by a fifty-one-year-old woman who was so self-conscious about her father looking older that she concocted a make-believe description of him. But her wishful white lie was discovered when her parents came to visit. "I was nine, and it was my first summer at camp," she recounted. "I described my father to fellow campers as young and handsome, with black hair. It must have been wishful thinking rather than an attempt to deceive, because I knew on Parents' Day the campers would see him for themselves. And, indeed, I remember one of them saying to me on that day, 'Your father's not young, and he has gray hair!'"

"When I was in high school and my mother worked at the school, there were a number of single women who were thought of as 'old ladies,' and my mother became thought of as one of them," remembered a now-middle-aged man named David. "I was very embarrassed by that. All these women were overweight and in their late fifties, and all of a sudden I was thinking of my mother in a way I didn't want her to be."

Occasionally, children may be made even more painfully aware that their parents look older by unthinking and cruel comments. Schoolmates may remark how much older a mother or father appears, and those remarks can often have a biting edge.

"Other children teased me that my mother must be my grandmother," remembered a woman from Louisiana. "They told me she was too old, with her gray hair. It embarrassed me to go to school functions with my mother, because I knew it would stir up the ridicule again."

Nell, whose mother was a thirty-nine-year-old manic depressive when she was born, also vividly recalled the taunts of her classmates: "Your mother's not only crazy but she's old!"

Parents' Lies

Embarrassment can be reinforced if older parents conceal or lie about their ages. When children learn their parents' true ages in such situations, it may be doubly painful because a bond of trust has been broken.

"Nobody talked about age in my family," said a Philadelphia woman who was adopted when her mother was forty-two and her father was thirty-eight. "It was partly because my mother was older than my father, and partly because she had been hospitalized for seventeen years with tuberculosis, which was another secret. She colored her hair and never wanted to state her age. Once, when it slipped out, she was very clear that I [was not to] tell anyone how old she was."

It was not uncommon, according to many of those who were interviewed or surveyed, that their parents (especially their mothers) lied about their ages due to embarrassment or vanity. The perceived stigma of being an older parent even led some to misrepresent their ages on their children's birth certificates. Children whose parents subtly or openly conveyed embarrassment about their ages undoubtedly are more likely to feel embarrassed themselves.

"When I was about ten, my mother said to me, 'Would you love me if I were ten years older?' " recalled Berry, a graphic designer whose mother was forty-two when she was born. "At the time, I laughed, and I guess I forgot about it. But she brought it up again a few years later, and it made me suspicious. Then my aunt told me that my mother had taken ten years off her age. I was amazed and disappointed that she had felt ashamed and had lied to me."

Indeed, parents often seemed more concerned about their ages than their children were. A young woman from Connecticut, whose mother repeatedly asked her if she felt ashamed about her older parents, said she would "try to reassure her, but I think even now she feels guilty somehow."

Several later-born children said that even now they did not know exactly how old their parents were because age was treated as a closely guarded secret. Others admitted that they only discovered their mothers' or fathers' true ages by snooping in their parents' wallets and looking at their drivers' licenses.

"Age first became important to me when my mother was

having her seventy-fifth birthday, and she said she was really eighty," an Atlanta woman remembered. "I learned I was five years closer to not having a mother."

A Massachusetts woman only learned her mother's true age after her mother died. Going through her mother's papers, the daughter discovered an old census form showing her mother as ten years older than she had always claimed to be.

Even mothers and fathers who do not lie may be more sensitive than younger parents about telling their children how old they are. They may artfully try to avoid the subject or nervously joke that they are ninety-five going on one hundred and fifty.

The Energy Crisis

When parents' ages translate into diminished vigor or physical infirmities, embarrassment and shame are likely to be overshadowed by a sense of regret that parents lack the desire or energy to play many games or sports with their children. Children of older parents may envy their friends who play tennis or touch football or go on skiing or camping trips with their families.

"I think I was a lot less athletic as a child than other people whose parents were always out doing active things," recalled a woman who was born when her mother was nearly fifty. "There was less of an emphasis on fun. Life was supposed to be serious. So I found myself reading books—scholarly nonfiction—that most normal teenagers wouldn't read. And I never really got into sports or athletics until college."

This "energy crisis" became particularly apparent during adolescence and was most acutely felt by sons of older parents. Just as they were reaching a peak in their own energy as teenagers, their parents were winding down, more inclined to think about the evening's TV schedule than to be backyard quarterbacks.

A study by psychologists K. MacDonald and Ross Parke confirmed that as parental age increased, less time was devoted to physical play. Their research also indicated that children whose fathers were less playful were less competent in relating to their peers.[1]

"My father never really played sports with me because of his health," said a man whose father was forty when he was born. "When I was in Little League, we had a coach who was probably in his twenties when my father was in his fifties. The coach was very athletic, and I remember wishing he were my father."

Almost half the men in the survey regretted or resented their fathers' relative lack of energy. Only one-fourth said that they did not perceive their fathers as less energetic than those of their friends. Furthermore, many envied classmates with younger parents who seemed more playful and fun-loving—like kids themselves.

"My parents didn't do things like serve as Scout leaders or throw birthday parties the way other kids' parents did," remembered a woman from Priest River, Idaho. "They simply lacked the energy."

Another woman recalled that her parents had been avid skiers, golfers, and tennis players when they were younger. However, the ski trips ended when she was eleven and her parents were in their early fifties. "They seemed to have run out of steam," she said.

The importance of the "energy" issue to later-born children is cast into sharp relief when they are compared to children of younger parents. Among the urban college students who were surveyed, 62 percent of the children of seventeen-to-twenty-one-year-old parents said that, during their teenage years, their fathers had a lot of energy, compared with 38 percent of children of twenty-two-to-thirty-four-year-old parents and only 25 percent of those who were born when their parents were thirty-five or older.

Although the theme of low-energy parents predominated, there were also the fifty-five-year-old dynamos who took hiking trips as Scout leaders or swirled about on skating rinks with their daughters. As a woman from San Diego said, "My parents always looked good, were healthy, and had reasonably high energy levels, so I never had any reason to think much about their actual ages." Because they were in such good shape, she added, "I was always proud to be able to say that my parents were older than someone else's."

Grandparent Syndrome

Another reason for many latecomers' negative feelings is what could be called the "grandparent syndrome." If parents are older and look older, it is almost inevitable that someone will mistake them for grandmothers or grandfathers. This may happen once or twice and be relegated to the dustheap of quirky memories, or it may occur with annoying frequency, making children excruciatingly aware that their parents are older and different. These inadvertently insensitive comments, in some cases, were not only among their least-fond memories but also what first made later-born children aware that their parents were older than the norm. For others, such remarks reinforced perceptions of their parents as being almost as old as some friends' grandparents and bolstered the feeling that their parents really looked or acted more like grandparents.

"My parents were mistaken for my grandparents all the time—in school visits and Cub Scouts," said Charles, who was born when his mother was forty-seven and father was fifty. "They acted like grandparents, and it seemed odd that my father retired when I was not yet out of high school. I was very conscious that these were old people. I was embarrassed and ashamed, and it made me feel terrible."

"I particularly recall classmates asking me during my elementary school years, when my mother wore housedresses, orthopedic shoes, and no makeup, why my grandmother walked me to school instead of my mother," wrote Nina, from Los Angeles. "This was devastating, especially since her competition was an upper-middle-class mother who had her nails and hair done several times a week, and whose biggest obligation was her standing noon appointment with the girls at the Mah-Jongg club."

Because of her embarrassment, she recalled wanting to "hide [her] older and less-glamorous parents." So, from an early age, she made an effort to do things without her family in order to conceal the "stigma of my very different parents."

Although no one mistook his father for his grandfather, a young New Jersey man remembered an incident from his childhood that made him think of his father as grandfatherly. "My father whittled a slingshot for me once, and I remember thinking that someone in the neighborhood had a grandfather who did the same thing for him." Memories like these clearly reflect a sensitivity on the part of many children of older parents to the subtle nuances of age typing in American society.

Surprising numbers of later-born children fantasized about having younger parents—ones who were more active and attractive and less obviously "different." Sometimes these mostly latent desires bubbled to the surface, as children publicly and defiantly pretended that they weren't really the offspring of these old-looking parents.

A forty-three-year-old woman from a small town in Illinois wrote at length about her "feeling of being different" because her parents were older. Although she noted "their attention, devotion, and adult conversations" as positive influences on her personality, she recalled "an incident that I clearly and guiltily remember as a blatant attempt to separate myself from my older parents." She was about ten years old and was going shopping with her parents and older sister in another town.

"I was walking far enough ahead that I hoped I would be thought of as just a wandering neighborhood child, unrelated to the three people walking together in back of me. Realizing that dress, features, and aura all spelled 'family,' I knew I'd have to break the link in another way if I didn't want the two or three other people on the street to think that the slightly heavy, gray-haired adults twenty paces behind me were actually my parents.

"It was a calculated decision, but I was going to try to pass it off as an innocent, humorous reference to my mother's slow-paced walking," she continued. "I stopped. I turned back. I called, 'Hurry up, *Grandma*.' I had done it! Now those strangers would think that somewhere I had young, beautiful parents. And my mother, I fervently hoped, would not catch on to my actual intent. How wrong I was. I was stupider and she was savvier than I thought. She caught on instantly, knew exactly what I was up to, and let me know it in angry words and injured tones that really rather surprised me because she was usually more understanding. She actually accused me of being ashamed of them!"

Class Differences

Parental age differences also tend to be associated with differences in career status. The fifty-five-year-old parent of a fifteen-year-old may be a corporate executive, tenured professor, or senior law partner, for example, whereas the forty-year-old parents of that fifteen-year-old's classmates may be middle-level managers, junior faculty, or the new partners in the firm. The social gatherings of the fifty-five-year-olds will undoubtedly be different from those of the forty-year-olds, and it is unlikely that their social paths will cross.

To the extent that parental age and size of bank account are related, children of older parents may live in bigger houses, have nicer (or at least more expensive) toys, and go to private schools, while most neighborhood kids attend the local public school. These accoutrements of social class can also make a child feel set apart from his or her peers.

This difference appeared in recollections of going off to school or camp in fancy, "dress-up" clothes, while the rest of the kids wore jeans and T-shirts. It was also reflected in memories of summer vacations in Europe or being given cars on their sixteenth birthdays, when most of their friends were off on driving-and-camping vacations with their families or angling to borrow their mothers' or fathers' cars for high-school dates.

Class differences also can exaggerate or minimize differences in physical appearance among people of different ages. Because socioeconomic distinctions are generally reflected in sartorial differences, children of older parents may well be aware that their mothers and fathers dress better than (or, as they may see it, differently from) other parents. A fifty-year-old mother of a twelve-year-old girl may dress more stylishly and conservatively, with more expensive jewelry, than her classmate's mother who is thirty-five. And the distinction between one mother in a tailored suit or designer dress and another in jeans is unlikely to be lost on an all-too-fashion-conscious teenager.

Different But Better

But was perceiving their parents or themselves as different always traumatic or unpleasant?

The differences in life-styles between older and younger parents—and the implications for their children—often go beyond whether or not a father played catch in the backyard with his son or how a mother dressed. With less-active parents, family conversations and discussions may be more important, and more passive—but hardly less rewarding—pastimes may figure more prominently in their lives. Older parents may be less apt to coach the Little League team, but instead they may take their children to the ball park, not to mention the theater or concert hall.

"They didn't play ball, but they rewarded cultural interests more and reinforced more-adult behavior in their children," said a New York woman whose father was forty-three and mother was thirty-seven when she was born.

Another latecomer who also felt different recalled an epiphany in her life that made her embarrassment turn into pride. "I remember my acute embarrassment as a teenager because my mother was so old—sixty when I was fourteen! It wasn't until a friend's Sweet Sixteen party, when all my friends told me how lucky I was because my mother was so liberal, so understanding, so free with her time, and so warmhearted, that I realized what a snot I had been. From that time on, I saw her as she really was. Gray hair in a bun, no makeup, housedresses and all—she was one dynamite lady!"

6
A Different Adult World

For years the normative American family, as portrayed by social scientists, popular culture, and even political and religious leaders has generally included two parents, about twenty-five to thirty years older than their children, and several children relatively close in age. The "typical" extended family has been seen as including at least two or three living grandparents, a half dozen aunts and uncles, a larger brood of cousins, nieces, and nephews, and perhaps a great-grandparent or two.

But for children of older parents, the picture looks quite different. Not only are the parents thirty-five to forty years (or more) older than their children, but the constellation of siblings and other relatives is almost certain to be different. They are likely to have either more or fewer brothers and sisters than the "normal" family. And because of the greater age difference between generations, grandparents are less likely to be living, aunts and uncles are probably older, and great-grandparents are a virtual impossibility.

Missing Grandparents

While many later-born children are uncomfortable having their parents mistaken for grandparents, they are often sadly aware that—unlike most friends and classmates—they do not have any real grandparents who are living.

"I know people who've had long relationships with their grandparents, but the idea of having a grandparent is so strange to me," a Los Angeles man reflected. "Both my grandfathers died long before I was born, and my grandmothers were very old by the time I came to realize who they were. One I remember as being sort of senile, and the other was really neat—very intelligent and interesting—but she died when I was ten."

In many cases, the grandparents of latecomers were born seventy, eighty, or more years before they were born. Because of this larger-than-usual age difference, all too often their grandparents had died before they were born or died when they were very young. Eighty-two percent of those responding to the questionnaire believed that they had fewer living grandparents than other children did. And of course grandparents were even more rare for children who were born when their parents over forty.

By contrast, "most people are in their 40's or 50's when they become grandparents," according to Andrew J. Cherlin and Frank F. Furstenberg, Jr., authors of *The New American Grandparent*.[1] The fact that three-generation families are very much the norm in late-twentieth-century America can be seen from another demographic vantage point: Nine out of ten fifteen-year-olds in the United States have at least two living grandparents.

But for latecomers, feelings of deep regret about not knowing their grandparents and envy of those who had close relationships with grandmothers and grandfathers were almost universal. As a New York woman put it: "Everyone else had grandparents, and I didn't. I missed the stories, the being cared for, the closeness, the extended family, the history, the sense of roots and connectedness."

"Around Christmastime, particularly, other kids would be getting presents from their grandparents, and they'd come to visit," said a New Jersey man whose last grandparent died when he was five. "We didn't have that. I felt cheated, like I was missing out on something that everybody else had access to."

Gina, a thirty-two-year-old from Holland, Pennsylvania, also recalled: "Kids in high school would complain about their grandparents. I once said, 'You don't know what you have; I don't have any grandparents.' "

Latecomers whose grandparents' lives briefly overlapped with their own had only sketchy memories: They remembered their grandparents' deaths or had vague or caricatured early-childhood recollections of very old grandmothers or grandfathers.

"Since my grandparents were quite elderly by the time I

came along, I lost them early, by age seven," wrote a Washington, D.C., woman. "Their dying, which was a prolonged and painful process, cast a shadow over my childhood."

"My father's mother was the only grandparent I ever knew, and we only visited her occasionally before she died," a Wisconsin woman commented. "She was very old and sat in a La-Z-Boy, with a glass of wine and a Bible. It was like a Bergman film. She scared me."

In lieu of real grandparents, some children of older parents said that they became close to an older person or couple who played the role of surrogate grandparents. Others said that they would call their friends' grandparents "grandma" or "grandpa."

Gina remembered fashioning several elderly women in her life into substitute grandmothers. "My older brother's mother-in-law—who was more the age of the typical grandmother—was one. And there was also a great-aunt who lived two doors down. We'd visit her and buy her church calendars for Christmas, and she would give us little things."

The few studies of relationships between grandparents and grandchildren have found that, while most grandparents do not play a major role in rearing their grandchildren, they "have the potential for significantly influencing the developing child," according to psychologists Barbara Tinsley and Ross Parke.[2]

"Grandparents [may not be] prominent or visible actors in our family system, but they are important backstage figures," as Cherlin and Furstenberg have said. Those grandmothers and grandfathers who are close to their grandchildren play a variety of roles in their lives, ranging from teacher, caretaker, and role model to negotiator between parent and child and provider of a symbolic connection between the past and the future.

Without grandparents, children generally have less sense of their ancestry and their own future as old people, according to Arthur Kornhaber and Kenneth L. Woodward, authors of *Grandparents/Grandchildren: The Vital Connection.*[3] They also tend to be more alienated from the elderly and more likely to subscribe to negative stereotypes about aging.

Always a Two-Generation Family?

"Children's children are the crown of old men," says the Bible (Proverbs 17:6). Yet, throughout their lives, children of older parents may be consigned to living in two-generation families. Because their own parents are likely to die earlier in their lives, their experience of not having living grandparents may well be passed on to their own children.

Even if their parents live to see their children's children, they probably will not share as much of each other's lives as do people in families with shorter generations. The cycle of the two-generation family may only be broken late in life, when these children of older parents themselves become grandparents—provided, of course, that both they and their children have children relatively early in life.

Many whose parents died before they had children spoke not only of their loss but of their children's loss. As one twenty-five-year-old man said, "When my father died, I thought, 'If I ever have children, they will never know their grandfather.' "

"I think our children were shortchanged by having only one viable grandparent (my mother, now ninety), as both grandfathers were deceased and the other grandmother had Alzheimer's," wrote Sabrina, whose husband was also a child of older parents.

Older Aunts, Uncles, and Cousins

Grandparents aren't the only relatives who are more likely to be missing from the extended-family portraits of children of older parents. Their parents' sisters and brothers generally will be older than the "typical" aunts and uncles. For instance, an older brother of a woman who put off childbearing until she was forty could become the sixty-five-year-old uncle of a second-grader.

That same eight-year-old may also have forty-year-old, married cousins—the same age as the parents of that child's friends. And the child's second cousins—its cousins' children—may also be seven or eight. This may not only be confusing and alienating, but it also means that such children of older parents will lose many of their relatives considerably earlier than their contemporaries will.

Many latecomers echoed the recollections of a woman who said: "I was quite distant from my cousins, most of whom were a generation older than I was."

"Holidays have always been depressing," declared another

woman. "It was just the three of us, because there were no grand-parents, aunts, or uncles—they were all dead or living far away. And there were no other children."

Friends' Parents and Parents' Friends

"My friends' parents were never my parents' friends."

This common refrain identifies another difference between the social worlds of later-born children and the social worlds of their peers. Because of the tendency toward age stratification in American society, parents' friends and colleagues are probably about the same age as the parents. Following this social logic, the younger parents of these children's peers undoubtedly also have friends closer to their own age.

Eighty-eight percent of those answering the questionnaire said that few or none of their peers' parents were even roughly the same age as their own. This perception was even more pronounced for children whose mothers were in their forties or whose fathers were in their fifties when they were born.

"I would sometimes meet mothers of my friends who seemed more like peers than parents, like they were of the same generation, and I would think that was wonderful," recalled Thalia, a bank executive. "My parents, however, were definitely of the adult world. I thought they were more impressive, but I felt that these younger parents were sort of more fun. I also thought in high school that if I had a younger, gorgeous, more trendy mother, I'd be more popular. I felt some connection between having older parents and not being in the mainstream."

A man born to forty-year-old parents, who said that he rarely thought about their ages, nevertheless recounted an anecdote that brought the age difference between his parents and his friends' parents into sharp yet amusing relief. "I never gave my parents' ages a second thought until the sixth grade, when I was talking with the mother of one of my best friends," he said. "She told me it was her birthday and asked me to guess her age. So I guessed the age of my mother, which was fifty-something. She was insulted because she was thirty-one. I couldn't understand what she was so upset about, but later I thought, maybe it's not so common that parents are older."

Families often live in areas or neighborhoods where most of their neighbors are similar in age and socioeconomic profile.

When this is the case, neighbors of older parents are likely to have much older sons and daughters—unless, of course, those neighbors also had children in their late thirties or forties.

Latecomers frequently remembered being the youngest in informal neighborhood social groupings. They would be left on the sidelines, observing, as the older children played or talked. This pattern also held true when whole families got together. While forty-five-year-old parents were socializing, the eight-year-old sons and daughters of older parents weren't likely to be hitting it off with the eighteen-year-old children of parents who had had their children earlier in life.

"There were many Sunday visits with neighbors when my sister and I played alone because the neighbors' children were gone or too old to play with," recalled a man who grew up on a Midwestern farm. "The question we always asked was, 'Are there children to play with?'"

∞

Parents aren't the only adult influences on a child, so it is important to consider how grandparents, other relatives, and other adults shape a child's personality, behavior, and understanding of the world. These are the supporting actors in the drama of human development. The roles they play—as adult models, sources of emotional support, links to the past, and friends—can be significant in a child's life.

Since this cast of characters generally looks different for latecomers, the nature and extent of their influence is likely to be different. If children have grandparents for only a few years of their lives, their grandparents will undoubtedly be more marginal than is true for people who grow to adulthood with living grandmothers and grandfathers. Similarly, a child's cousin who is fifteen years older is not the same sort of generational "peer" as a cousin of roughly the same age. And the world of adults will look profoundly different to a ten-year-old when "adult" is equated with fifty-year-olds rather than with people in their mid-thirties.

III

By Chance or Choice

7
Family Constellations
Varieties of Experience

Children of older parents are not a single, monolithic group. They are born later in their parents' lives for many different reasons.

There are the latecomers in large families in which children are born over a period of many years. In these families the last-born may be the finale in a more-or-less continuous succession of births or may be the "baby" born many years after the other children. Either may be quite unexpected and perhaps unwelcome—a poor beginning role for any child. On the other hand, the child who arrives after a long gap may be much wanted, fulfilling some special need of the parents. For example, this baby may represent the last try for a child of a desired gender, a "replacement" for a sibling who has died, or an attempt by parents to reaffirm their youth.

These different trajectories, just within large families, can play an important role in defining an individual's experiences and relationships with parents, siblings, and the world.

In contrast to the large family constellations are the family contexts of other children of older parents who are the products of delayed childbearing. With no preceding siblings, they may be the result of a relatively late marriage or remarriage. These children may have been precisely planned or scheduled into their parents' lives or the successful culmination of long, failed efforts to conceive a child. They are likely to be very much wanted, and their chances of being only children are great.

These varied entrances into the family—as last-borns or onlies—place children in birth-order positions that have long interested social scientists. Ever since the influential psychoanalyst Alfred Adler proclaimed in the early twentieth century that "position in the family leaves an indelible stamp upon [a person's] style of life," researchers have investigated and speculated about the effects of birth order on child development, personality, and achievement. Adler argued that different positions in the birth order shape different environments for child development and, thus, profoundly influence how children cope with other people and the world.[1]

Recent writings also recognize the different circumstances within and outside the family that appear to be associated with an individual's position as the oldest, middle, youngest, or only child. However, the findings on birth order have been neither overwhelming nor consistent, and many social scientists have attacked the idea that birth order alone makes any difference in a child's personality or behavior. Because the simple fact of a particular birth-order position masks such factors as a child's wantedness and gender or a family's values and economic well-being, conclusions must be regarded with caution.

Nonetheless, some psychologists and observers have been drawn to make sweeping generalizations about the effects of birth order.[2] For example, Lucille K. Forer and Henry Still, authors of *The Birth Order Factor*, assert that last-born children in large families are particularly likely to be outgoing, playful, and charming—attributes the authors interpret as reactions to their lowly position in the sibling order. They tend to be teased (and their opinions discounted) by their siblings, and their parents tend either to be less patient with them or to "baby" them. Consequently these youngest children may feel a strong desire to get attention, show off, or charm the world into taking them seriously or recognizing their importance.[3] Other studies have found that last-borns are more frequently chosen as playmates than onlies or firstborns.[4]

One recent, provocative study suggested that last-borns more often challenge accepted orthodoxy. In the study, Frank Sulloway, a historian of science, asserted that last-borns are more likely to be scientific innovators and political or social reformers, whereas firstborns—whom he said are more accepting of parental authority and identify with parental values—have a greater tendency to defend the status quo.[5]

Although only and last-born children tend to be different in many ways, neither has a younger sibling to look up to them as a role model or mentor. In contrast to Sulloway's hypothesis some researchers have also concluded that onlies and last-borns are more likely to be dependent and impulsive, and susceptible to such problems as alcoholism, because their upbringing tends to be more permissive and they are less able to internalize control.[6]

In addition, because last-borns often suspect or learn that they were unplanned, "change-of-life," babies, they may "[bend] over backwards in a lifelong effort to avoid further displeasing or inconveniencing anyone," according to Bradford Wilson and George Edington, authors of First Child, Second Child.[7]

Another study, by University of Michigan psychologist Robert Zajonc, found that last-borns do less well on standardized achievement tests like the Scholastic Aptitude Test. He cautioned, though, that the spacing between children and family size may have more of an effect than birth order. Other research has suggested that that the bigger the family and the shorter the intervals between children, the greater the chances of deleterious effects on last-borns.[8]

In fact, the importance of spacing has been addressed in studies of the self-esteem of middle-born children, a group that has been largely neglected. A study by psychologist Jeannie Kidwell found that middle-borns have poorer self-esteem and believe that their parents love them less than their older and younger siblings.[9]

Similarly, many facts and fictions surround only and first-born children. As they become increasingly prominent types of children of older parents, studies and hypotheses relating to their birth-order position also warrant examination.

Firstborn and only children have received special attention ever since the nineteenth-century British scientist Sir Francis Galton concluded that they accounted for a disproportionate number of eminent scientists. More recent studies have found them to be overrepresented among such groups as graduate and professional students and those listed in Who's Who in America.[10]

Adler asserted that onlies feel more privileged because they are the focus of their parents' attention. Later psychologists have said that onlies and firstborns are more loved, protected, intellectually influenced, and disciplined than other children.[11] Because parental expectations are greater, some scholars assert, firstborns are often high achievers, who are conscientious and driven but also tense and jealous.

At the turn of the twentieth century, American psychologist G. Stanley Hall cast another light on only children, saying that "being an only child is a disease in itself." And in 1972 a Gallup poll found that most Americans believed only children to be disadvantaged.[12] The popular stereotype of the only child is that he or she is self-centered, "spoiled," attention seeking, temperamental, and lonely, yet also more successful in life. These perceptions are major reasons that most parents cite for wanting at least two children.

The notion of the emotionally disadvantaged only child has rarely been supported by research, although studies have found that onlies do tend to be more independent and self-reliant and less likely to share or participate in group activities, according to psychologist Toni Falbo, editor of *The Single-Child Family*.[13] They typically have fewer friends, join fewer organizations, and visit relatives less often, but have more interaction with their parents and get along better with adults than other children. In a review of more than two hundred studies, Falbo reported that only children are likely to be more intelligent in childhood, show more autonomy and psychological maturity by late adolescence, and have more prestigious, high-paying occupations in adulthood.

Studies have also indicated that onlies tend to receive more education and are disproportionately represented among high achievers, compared with children from large families. For example, Judith Blake, a professor of population at UCLA, found that an only child is likely to get three more years of schooling than is a child from a family of six—although a family's financial resources per child are probably as important as the degree of parents' emotional investment.[14]

During the baby-boom years between about 1946 and 1964, the percentage of only-child families in the United States stood at around 15 percent.[15] However, the simultaneous trends toward smaller families and later parenting have led some experts to predict that that figure may rise to 30 percent in the 1990s, comparable to the proportion at the end of the 1930s.

Undoubtedly the impact of birth order varies, but it is clear that the patterns of childhood and adulthood for children of older parents are influenced by their different family constellations and birth-order positions. The ways in which these contexts may uniquely affect "tail-end" last-borns, "accidental" children, and delayed only or first-born children are explored in the next chapters.

8

The Baby of the Family

"Mother always referred to me as 'my baby,' and unfortunately I believed her. Growing up in a houseful of adults, I felt like either an eternal child or a complete outsider."

Large families may offer warmth, camaraderie, and security for all the children, but they may also present problems that bear down hardest on the youngest, last-born child, as this woman, who was the last of five children, suggested.

These "tail-end" children often have parents who really are considerably older than most, as well as a houseful of siblings who are five, ten, or fifteen years older than they are. "Older parents" who are forty-five when their fifth child is born are also generally at quite a different stage in life and have a different socioeconomic profile from thirty-five-year-old "older parents" having their first child. In the past, as we have seen, the vast majority of children of older parents have been the third, fourth, or later-born offspring of couples who began their childbearing in their twenties and continued for ten or twenty years.

Such veteran parents were often remembered as having little emotional and physical energy to devote to their last child. Although they were frequently seen as having more experience raising children, they were sometimes perceived as worn out by two decades of child rearing and, as a result, less attentive to the needs and wants of their youngest child. Some last-borns were pampered as the "baby" of the family, while others were treated as "mistakes," with benign neglect or worse. Privacy was also at a premium for these late children, who often wound up being lost among a large tribe of older siblings.

"My parents had been parenting for twenty years when I

came along, and I feel I missed out on their best years," said Betty, a fifth-born child of older parents. "They had lost interest in the events of my life. If it had been the first time around, maybe it would have been more appealing to them. I always felt I was imposing when I asked them to attend an event that I was involved in. And I always felt a general lack of interest, which caused me to exclude them from the important parts of my growing-up years."

Last-born children in large families were particularly likely to recall their mothers and fathers as perpetually tired, distant, or physically and emotionally uninvolved. They felt that their parents "weren't very interested in doing things" with them or didn't take their problems as children seriously and "had given up on" them by their teenage years.

"Detached parenting" was the phrase used by one man who was a last-born child. Others said that they envied those with younger parents, who had a seemingly greater inclination to help, teach, or play with their children. They spoke of various ways in which their parents seemed uninvolved in their lives.

"My brother and I tended to be loners, since what we wanted to do—to go on picnics and outings—wasn't what they wanted," said Evelyn, from Massachusetts, who remembered her parents as impatient and tired. "They preferred quiet times at a time when we needed out."

"Being the last-born of seven children, I got little attention," added Martha, whose mother was thirty-six and father was forty-six when she was born. "As I grew older, it got worse. My older brothers and sisters were having kids of their own and would call on mom and dad for assistance. My mother especially helped my older sisters raise their kids, and my dad helped my brothers with their problems. So, they became less concerned with me and what I wanted. They were definitely tired of raising their own kids."

It is certainly impossible to predict whether an older couple's prior experience at child rearing will make them better, more doting parents or tired and less involved. Sometimes parents became very emotionally invested in their last child, lavishing that child with greater attention than they had given their earlier children. In fact, some last-born children in large families said that their older siblings resented them because their parents gave them preferential treatment.

"I had an easier time than my older brothers and sisters, because my parents didn't have the energy to be as repressive with me," said Arlene, whose mother and father were forty-six and fifty-two when she was born.

And one last-born said that her two much-older brothers gave her "the best perspective on being the child of older parents." "They never felt particularly loved or cherished and were not close with our parents. On the other hand, when I was born, I was doted on and obviously adored. My memories of my father are vivid; had he lived, I would have been spoiled outrageously. My brothers and I had totally different upbringings, and a great deal of my stability and strength today comes from . . . my mother's investment of time and more time!"

On the other hand, parents may have been quite involved, but not in a way that pleased their children. For example, a woman who was the last-born child of a father who was fifty-five and a forty-four-year-old mother speculated as to why her parents seemed more strict. "I think because they had already raised four other children," she said, "they knew all the things that could go wrong."

Veteran Parents

Many last-borns in large families had a profound appreciation of their mothers and fathers as "more experienced" because of their long résumés as parents. These older mothers and fathers had learned the ropes of parenting with their first children. They often seemed more comfortable and relaxed about being parents and were more understanding of their children. For them, being parents was less of an ad hoc proposition or a skill to be gleaned from a child-rearing manual.

"Older parents are veterans," said Ron, a New Jersey lawyer. "They've been through it, and they've seen a lot more. My growing up was easier than some other kids', in part because my parents had been through so much more."

Although *veteran* clearly carries different meanings for different children of older parents, a seventeen-year-old girl from Wheeling, West Virginia, reflected: "They had a better outlook on parenting because they'd had five other children before I was born. My father says that with their first child, they were overprotective, but with me, they used a longer rope."

"A Forest of Knees"

In most large and long-developing families, siblings play a decisive role in the lives of last-born children. And, as can be said of most things in life, the picture is decidedly mixed.

Some of these latecomers described many benefits of having older siblings. They were role models, playmates, confidants, or substitute parents who took them to the park, provided counsel for the trials and tribulations of childhood and adolescent life, and stood in for their parents at graduations and other important occasions. Much-older siblings also served as a bridge between two distantly separated generations.

One woman recalled that her sister took her in when her parents kicked her out of the house because they did not like her fiancé. The sister, who was thirteen years older, advised her to go ahead with her wedding, helped her prepare for it, and ultimately reconciled her with their parents.

Indeed, many tail-end children saw their big brothers and sisters as substitute or supplementary parents, for better or worse. The world, too, often mistook these older siblings for the last-born's parents. And when mothers and fathers delegated parenting tasks to their oldest children, these older siblings were often all too happy to assume the role.

Many last-borns said that their older sisters, especially, liked to play mother. Younger siblings became living props—much better than dolls—in the familiar girls' game of playing house. Sometimes, this game among siblings might be played, in subtle ways, for an entire lifetime.

"I had three mothers and two fathers," said a young woman whose parents were in their forties and whose siblings were between nine and thirteen when she was born. "My brother raised me and took me places and did things my parents wouldn't do. And my sisters told me what to do. One sister still thinks she's my mother."

"My sister who was thirteen years older played the role of mother to me," said Pam, whose three sisters were all in their teens when she was born. "She took over and didn't like giving it up. She said to me, 'Call me mother, and call mother grandma.' She liked taking care of me and dressing me. And when she married, her husband became like a surrogate father."

And a woman from Baltimore reflected: "When you have

three mothers as a teenager, you tend to become passive and let them do your thinking for you. Since my mom abdicated her responsibility as a parent when I was a teen, I was forced to become self-reliant, but I fell prey to my two older sisters' ministrations. . . . So much of what they did or said benefited them, made them feel better, and served to make me feel less capable."

Many last-borns recalled that their older brothers and sisters were good to them only when convenient. When it didn't serve their purposes to play the kindly big brother or the make-believe mother, they often took advantage of their "little" sister or brother.

"My siblings were a forest of knees until I was old enough to be sent on errands and become the family 'gofer,' " remembered Alexandra, the last-born of six children.

This was also the experience of a Pennsylvania woman who noted that her "five older siblings never lacked for someone to send on errands," although "they later claimed to have 'spoiled' me. The good side was that older sisters would take me out for the evening when they were dateless, and older brothers would provide outings to the park and the beach," she added. But "I was constantly in the doghouse because I was often found guilty of 'borrowing' things from my sisters. Since one was six years older and the other was twelve years older, I was fair game!"

Strong sibling rivalry was another common theme among many late-born children in large families. Much-older siblings sometimes made it exceedingly clear that their little brothers or sisters were unwelcome intruders in the family. These last-borns were resented because they seemed to usurp parental attention or disrupt what had been a stable family configuration.

"My sister, who was twenty years older than I was, never liked me," said Bess, a Midwestern homemaker. "I think it really bothered her that parents that age would have sex and have a baby. She was kind of perturbed when I came along. And I guess I was my parents' favorite."

"The jealousy of my older sister, who called me 'the spoiled brat,' caused me great anxiety and pain," remarked a Brookline, Massachusetts, woman who was the last-born of six children. "Whenever my parents left home, I was tormented and hit because 'everything' came to me easily and I wasn't punished as she had been."

Cindy, a thirty-seven-year-old from Pennsylvania, recalled the never-ending resentment of her half brother, who was fifteen years older. "I got things that he never did. He used to say that I was spoiled, because, when I was growing up, my parents were both working and, if they wanted to go out and buy me a tape recorder or a television, they'd buy it. But when he grew up, my parents couldn't afford those kinds of things."

In other instances, last-borns may hardly have known their siblings, who were so much older that they had left home by the time their baby brother or sister was in grade school. The yawning age gap between siblings made these last-borns feel like outsiders in their own families.

Older siblings were going on high-school dates when these tail-end children were infants, graduating from college when they were learning to read, or getting married when they were being confirmed or bar mitzvahed. Several last-borns who grew up during the 1940s, for example, mentioned that they met their older brothers for the first time when they returned from serving in World War II.

In fact, the biggest generation gap for many tail-end children was not between them and their parents, but between siblings nominally of the same generation. As a New Jersey woman—whose oldest brother was thirty-one and whose mother was nearly sixty-two when she turned sixteen—mused, "I'm not sure which embarrassed me more, his age or my mother's."

Many siblings were not only out of the house and, in a sense, out of the family when their last-born brother or sister was still a toddler, but often they had already started their own families. A number of tail-end children recalled going to their brothers' or sisters' weddings when they were no more than six or seven years old. Others noted that they had nieces and nephews who were at least their age. And one woman in her late thirties mentioned that she already had great-nieces and -nephews, while another said that her great-niece and daughter were just a month apart in age.

"I had two much-older sisters—one who eloped when I was one year old and the other who got married when I was six," said Dorothy, a Pennsylvania school administrator. "I was never close to my older sister till I grew up. It was almost as if she didn't exist. And I remember when the other sister got married, I was clutching at her wedding gown and saying, 'Who's going to take care of me?' So I was raised essentially as an only child."

These differences in age between a last-born and the other siblings often meant that the late arrival was brought up much like an only child, with all the attendant benefits and drawbacks.

"My sister and brother were eighteen and seventeen, so, in a sense, I had the best of all worlds," wrote a middle-aged New Yorker. "I was a child with siblings, yet alone with my parents while my siblings were in college or married."

But the peculiar tricks that such large families play on the "normal" expectations of a life course continue well beyond childhood, as the reflections of a middle-aged Pennsylvania woman suggest. She noted wistfully, "My brothers are now in their eighties and in declining health and vigor, and again I have a new perspective on my parents and how their ages when I was born continue to affect my life."

∞

More than for any other children of older parents, generations are blurred and confused for lastcomers. Where do they fit, and how do they view the rest of their family?

Their parents are almost old enough to be grandparents. Their siblings are nearly old enough to be parents and may well act like parents. And nephews and nieces are their peers.

They may feel like their parents' afterthoughts, whose "real" families were inaugurated a decade or more before they arrived. Brothers and sisters certainly don't seem like generational compatriots. They are either all but strangers, living lives apart from the family, or big people whose raison d'être seems to be to boss their little sibling around.

Of course, much-older siblings can add richness to a child's experience, and the wide range of ages in a family may be at least as likely to diminish as to increase the overall salience of age. If a last-born sees and learns from family members of varying ages, the relative significance of parents being older than the norm may be less.

In short, a key to what makes a last-born's experience distinctive among latecomers is the way in which this generational confusion or blurring is played out in terms of family dynamics and interpreted by a child. If parents are uninvolved and seem tired of raising a family, and brothers and sisters are distant or domineering, the last-born is likely to suffer. But the outlook will be quite different if parents' long experience with child rearing translates into better parenting and siblings are warm and available as mentors, friends, and intermediaries between parents and their last child.

9

"Accidents"

"I am sure we were all surprises," wrote a woman from Rapid City, South Dakota. "My mother told me that I definitely was not a planned baby. But my father was adamant that none of us was ever to be referred to as an 'accident' or 'mistake.' "

A more bitter experience was reported by a woman from Pennsylvania. "My mother told people I was her *mazinta*, she wrote. "For years I thought it meant 'youngest,' but it means 'grandchild' in Yiddish.[1] I was hurt. Mom also regaled me with stories about how she tried to 'get rid of' me. She got some pills from our physician cousin. 'They made me feel so sick I decided to have you,' Mom said. I could have done without that story. She also mentioned jumping off chairs on the 'get rid of' project."

Not uncommonly, these "accidents" were the last of a line of children, with a gap of years separating them from their next older siblings. They often had the experiences of other tail-end offspring, but in addition, these last-borns were often all too aware that their parents had been unhappy or surprised to find themselves with a new baby in their late thirties or forties. These latecomers noted with annoyance and sadness that their births were unplanned. Whether their parents made a point of telling them that they were "accidents" or they learned later that they had been unwanted, this knowledge usually hurt.

Children of older parents not only may be initially unwanted, but—as we have seen—older couples who have already had a number of children over many years may have wearied of child rearing, be less engaged with family life, and find additional children burdensome. From the perspective of their children, this was often a formula for parental resentment and neglect.

As one woman said, "I had to try to fit into the way things were."

Even among the unplanned, however, these feelings were not universal. On the contrary, many said that they were delightful surprises for parents who especially loved and cherished them.

But if children are made to feel that they are accidents or burdens, these impressions can leave long-lasting emotional scars. How and when they learn that they were unplanned and unwanted can also decisively affect their perceptions of themselves and their parents.

"I heard the term *middle-aged carelessness*," said Lois, a social worker from North Carolina. "My mother called me a 'surprise,' and it made me question whether or not I was wanted, and if I was a burden to her."

"Ever since I can remember, my parents always referred to me as an accident or surprise, although not in a negative way," said a man from St. Charles, Illinois. "But they would also call me the 'baby,' a description which did irritate me increasingly as I grew older."

About 33 percent of those who answered the questionnaire characterized their birth as "an accident." Forty-nine percent said they were "a planned baby," and 17 percent were not sure whether they were planned or accidental. The proportion who said they were "accidents" was noticeably higher among last-born children than only children. And "accidents" increased with maternal age: Of those whose mothers were 40 or older when they were born, 43 percent said that their birth was accidental, compared with just 28 percent of children of thirty-five- to thirty-nine-year-old mothers.

"My mother said she was embarrassed to be pregnant at her age," one woman recalled. "She said she wore her winter coat during her whole pregnancy."

Another woman remembered, with bitterness, that she learned that "my mother was very upset when she became pregnant with me at thirty-eight." "My father always told me she was afraid that her child would be mentally retarded because of her age."

"I always felt I was an appendage," added Dorothy, a Pennsylvania school administrator. "I remember on picnics, my mother saying, 'I wish I didn't have to drag her along.' More than once she said that I was her accident. She thought she was finished with her childbearing years, and here I was. She resented me to the point that she pushed me off to my sister, who was fifteen years older—but my sister was only around for five years until she got married, and then I was an orphan.''

These children felt like intruders in their parents' or families' lives. Their mothers and fathers had pleasant, well-defined lives, which regrettably all had to change when their unexpected child arrived—or at least such was the picture the parents conveyed. Children born into such families saw themselves as having disrupted their parents' or siblings' life-styles or invaded their privacy.

"My mother went for the ideal of getting married, having kids, and having a good suburban life-style," said David, whose mother was in her mid-forties when he was born, more than a decade after her two other children. His parents had been successful, he said, and this dream of a happy life in the suburbs might have come true if he hadn't been born to complicate their lives and his father hadn't died when David was four. "My mother made me feel it all would have happened for her if I hadn't been born and my father hadn't died," he said.

This sort of perceived parental resentment of their children's intrusion into their lives continued, in some cases, long after childhood.

"My mother complained that my father couldn't relax and enjoy his retirement with two kids in college," recalled Ruth, from Poughkeepsie, New York. "I felt guilty even though I worked all through college."

Because of this sense of being unwanted, many later-born children consciously or unconsciously sought out substitute mothers or fathers. Sometimes these "substitutes" were much-older siblings, cousins, or other relatives. In other cases, they were a friend's parents, a teacher, or a Little League coach.

The knowledge or suspicion that they were unplanned also gave rise to fantasies that their mothers and fathers were not their real parents and that, somewhere, they had parents who were younger. Some mused that they might have been born to young, unmarried relatives and that their parents took them in to bury a skeleton in the extended-family closet and give them a normal family. Others still remembered vivid dreams about imaginary parents who were young-looking and energetic.

"Is it more common for children of older parents to believe that their parents weren't really their parents?" one woman wondered. "When I was a child, I thought that one of my unmarried cousins or possibly my older brother had forced my parents to adopt me to keep me in the family."

Children were also made to feel that they were mistimed or not wanted when their parents expressed guilt and worried loudly about the effects of their ages. These midlife parents felt that their accidental children were hurt psychologically and socially by their own relatively advanced ages. (Although there may be tactful ways and appropriate times to express such concerns to a child, in most cases conveying these worries will hardly be helpful.)

"My mother has pondered and sometimes worried about how her age affected my sister and me," said a woman from Salt Lake City. Her ongoing concern with the issue, she said, was reflected by periodic letters including clippings of articles about older parents. Another woman added: "My mother always says she wishes she were younger, and that she shouldn't have had me so late. But that's really very insulting."

Certainly many children not dubbed "accidents" are not specifically planned babies either. Yet their parents welcome them into the family and care for them as much as they would for a planned and wanted baby.

Indeed, the crucial difference is not so much between being an "accidental" or "planned" baby as between being unwanted or wanted. There can be many reasons for not wanting a child, but age and social attitudes about the "correct" timing of childbearing clearly play a major role in convincing parents of the desirability of having children at different ages. In 1965—before the birth-control pill, sterilization, and other forms of contraception were widely used and later childbearing became more socially acceptable—one-third of all births to married women thirty-five or older in America were unwanted.[2] Undoubtedly most of these were last children in large families. And, as we have seen, the survey of children of older parents indicated that the percentage of those who saw themselves as "accidents" increased sharply with the mother's age.

Thus, the pejorative label *accident* was generally a function of timing and parental perceptions of the appropriateness of having children at a given age. But of more consequence than parental or societal notions of improbable or unacceptable timing are its implications for a child.

Here, the comments of later-borns offered clues. Although not often talked about or even fully conscious, feeling that one was an "accident" frequently meant low self-esteem, shame, bitterness, and sadness.

10

Long-Awaited Children

Onlies and Firstborns

"**I** was my parents' only child, so they adored me and took every opportunity to make that clear," remembered a woman from Brooklyn. "So my childhood was idyllic."

If a latecomer is a first or only child, the parents' years of intentional waiting or trying to conceive probably will make their son or daughter feel especially wanted. These long-wished-for children may be doted upon, and their parents may invest considerable psychological energy in their upbringing in the form of teaching, play, affection, and encouragement. Among those surveyed, only children more often said that their parents were very involved with and helpful to them during childhood and adolescence. Boys in particular felt wanted, perhaps because their arrival finally ensured that the family name would be carried on.

But the most striking difference between onlies and last-borns in the survey—and one that speaks volumes—was that an overwhelming majority of only children saw themselves as having been "planned" babies, while a plurality of the last-borns believed that their births were accidental.[1]

It appears that the "typical" advantages and disadvantages of being an only child are magnified if parents are older. The tendency for parents of onlies to emotionally and materially pamper their sons and daughters does seem to be exaggerated if the parents are older, since they may be better off financially and their children may have been long awaited.

Only children of older parents—in the past and even more so in the present—are likely to be the offspring of professional mothers and fathers who put career development and advancement ahead of starting a family in their twenties and early thirties. Thus these later-born onlies often have parents who are doctors, lawyers, academics, or other professionals—while many of their classmates' younger parents may be in less-high-powered or -high-status occupations.

As might be expected, only children in the survey more often benefited in monetary terms during childhood than last-borns did. Three-fifths of the onlies said that their parents' financial status had a positive effect on them, compared with half of the last-borns.

Older parents with one or two children may well take their parental roles especially seriously, planning the minutiae of their children's lives and expecting great things of them. All along, from the spelling bees and piano recitals of childhood to the college admissions and professional sweepstakes of youth and early adulthood, these later-born children are likely to feel prodded by their parents to achieve and succeed.

"Maybe because my mother was older, she looked to the future more and thought about what she wanted for her children," suggested Gina, a thirty-two-year-old pharmacist from suburban Philadelphia.

A young woman named Jill recalled: "My parents were able to devote many hours to me, playing and teaching. I was reading the alphabet at age two, and read books by three. My mother never worked after I was born. I don't know if that's primarily because she was of an era when women just didn't work if they didn't have to, or because she had no desire to. All I know is that she greatly enjoyed being there for me when I came home from school."

During her childhood she participated in regional and national spelling bees, and her mother spent hours each day for months testing her on words. "Perhaps a younger mother would not have had the patience for that," she mused. "Almost certainly a younger mother with another child or children wouldn't have had the luxury of a choice. Those experiences were wonderful for me."

If later-born children are more intellectually stimulated and expected to know more about the world and how things work, it may make them particularly savvy about life at a young age.

It also may make them more precocious than their peers, as some latecomers speculated. Certainly, in childhood many are exposed to varied cultural experiences and mature adults. A number of respondents suggested, perhaps a bit self-servingly, that later-born only children tend to be intellectually gifted and high achievers. And several went out of their way to mention that they were members of Mensa, the society for people with high IQs.

Such social and intellectual precocity was noted by a number of depression-era children. Their parents were often ambitious and imparted many of their ambitions to their children.

"I have always wondered about 'us' as age cohorts," wrote a woman from Montana who grew up during the 1930s. "Our parents were generally older, educated through their own bootstrap efforts, with dreams of glory, prosperity, contentment, and success for their cherished, special children."

A woman from Indiana who was an only child gave a somewhat different twist to her parents' emotional largesse. Her older parents provided her with special classes and took her on many exotic vacations not only because they were financially well off, she argued, but also because they had the overindulgent attitude toward children stereotypically associated with grandparents.

These families of onlies tended to be more tightly bonded units than families with many children, which were characterized by a greater variety of ties among siblings and between each child and the parents. Onlies in the survey more often reported doing things together with their parents than did last-borns—who of course had the option of doing things with siblings.

Another measure of greater parent-child involvement in these small families is the extent to which children are a part of their parents' lives outside the family. In the survey it was found that onlies were much more likely than last-borns to be acquainted with their mothers' and fathers' friends and included in their parents' social circles.[2]

Onlies also said that they had more friends and playmates who were latecomers than last-borns did. Nearly one in five had a fair number of friends whose parents were about the same age as theirs, compared with only one-tenth of the last-borns.

The lives of only children of older parents, however, were not uniformly happier than those of later-born children in large families. They experienced a more pronounced generational divide than last-borns did, perhaps because they had no siblings to help bridge the gap. Lacking siblings, they also did not have anyone else in the family to talk to about strains or difficulties with their parents. Furthermore, these onlies felt more set apart from their peers than only children whose parents were younger.[3]

"There were a few other classmates and friends whose parents were also older," recalled an only child from Illinois. "But I remember thinking it didn't count for them because they all had several grown and sometimes married brothers and sisters, which meant their parents started earlier."

Whereas firstborns of young parents can legitimately expect that other siblings may arrive, firstborn children of older parents are probably destined to be only children. And they are likely to know that, with them, their families have been completed.

Later-born onlies frequently blamed their parents' advanced age for their not having any siblings. If they were born when their mother was around forty, they reasoned—or were told—that it was impossible for their parents to have another child. As a woman from Hunlock Creek, Pennsylvania, said, "The one heartbreak of my childhood related to my parents' ages was the fact that I could not have a sister or sisters."

It is interesting that adult children's concerns about their parents' aging took somewhat different forms depending on their birth-order status. While last-borns more frequently expressed fears about their parents' dying, onlies were more worried about caring for aging parents and were decidedly more negative about the prospect of having the sole responsibility of providing such care.

In some respects, what is learned from the lives of only children of older parents suggests what the experiences of present and future generations of latecomers are likely to be. Since later-born children will increasingly be members of small families, they may have more-involved, adoring parents but may still feel lonely because of their small families and worried about having to care singlehandedly for aging parents.

IV

Childhood Themes

11

Problems and Privilege

Two Case Histories—Tom and Charles

Family lives and dynamics, of course, are never simple. Strains and strengths shape an individual's experience not only during childhood but long beyond, and children of older parents are no exception. The latecomers surveyed were decidedly mixed in their remembrances and current feelings about their relationships with their parents. Like most people, their life histories were a blend of problems and privilege. But recurrent themes emerged that made the course of their lives different from those of people with younger mothers and fathers.

Indeed, the feeling of being different often continues from childhood into adulthood, although the most salient issues change as individuals grow older. A twelve-year-old may feel especially embarrassed that his or her parents look older or have more "outdated" ideas than do others. A twenty-two-year-old may feel the difference more in terms of seeing a father or mother retire while friends' parents are at the height of their careers. And a thirty-five-year-old may feel set off from peers because he or she is cast in the role of caring for an aging parent, or has lost a parent, while friends' parents are still healthy and active. Even as they grow older, children of older parents continue to be followed by a sense of being different from others their age. When later-born children turn fifty, their parents—if they are still alive—will have moved into the ranks of the "very old," while their peers' parents may be active retirees.

The mixture of problems, privilege, and conflicts in childhood and adulthood are suggested in the stories of Tom and Charles.

Tom

"I was a happy accident."

Tom's parents had married in their mid-twenties and had tried to have children for thirteen years before finally conceiving when his mother was thirty-eight and his father was forty-two. "There was an auto accident about eleven months before I was born, and my mom was hurt the worst," he said. "My cousin, a biologist, came up with the half-serious thought that something happened biologically to Mom, and I was the result of the accident."

Naturally his parents were overjoyed at his birth, and their happiness colored Tom's entire childhood during the 1950s in Monterey, California. "People would always comment how much joy I brought to my parents," he said. "And I always felt there was an incredible amount of unconditional love.

"I was aware that my parents were older—to a lesser degree when I was young than during my teenage years," he continued. "But I felt I was keeping them young. My parents were circulating with my peers' parents. They didn't have the values of older people, and they were just as contemporary as my age-mates' parents.

"We went on vacations every year—to Disneyland and Canada, and to this spot in the mountains that my parents and their friends went. We would go swimming and crawdad fishing." Tom's father didn't play football or tennis with him, but that was not for lack of energy. Rather, he worked long hours as a car salesman. And, in any case, the two of them would often go to Giants baseball games at Candlestick Park in San Francisco.

His parents put little pressure on him to do things the way they wanted, Tom said, and they gave him comparatively free rein as a teenager. "I think they gave me more independence than other parents gave their kids. I might go out to a party till 2 A.M., and even if, deep down, they were in a near panic, I think they had confidence that I was OK.

"My parents always communicated to me in an adult fashion," he remembered. "My mother and I would drive to the ocean, and she'd talk to me very confidentially, like a friend. I realized, by my late teens, that I related very well with older people and that I was as close with some of my friends' parents as I was with my friends."

Many of Tom's friends during his high-school years were older, but that didn't prevent him from developing "a big network of kids that I could always rely on to be with and do things with." If anything, he said, "being raised as an only child with older parents may have made me develop the social skills to reach out and meet more people."

His only regret about always being around older people, he said, is that "there's a child in there who never got an opportunity to be a child. Even today, I think I'm pretty serious, and I have to work at having fun."

Tom married at twenty-four, and his daughter was born when he was thirty. Now, at thirty-seven, he admits that he does think about the "age issue" when he and his wife consider having another child. "I don't always feel the energy I felt when I was younger, but many people who are older than I am are having a ball with their babies. It's a mistake to say they shouldn't have had them. When I consider my level of maturity in my early twenties, having children when you're young is the real mistake."

His parents were both in good health throughout Tom's childhood and young adulthood. In his mid-thirties, however, his mother had a series of operations to correct a chronic hip problem. "The attempts to repair her hip were unsuccessful and left her with a great deal of pain," he said. "During that three-year period in her seventies, I saw her age considerably."

His mother died just a few months before Tom was interviewed, and, because his father had been so dependent on her, he moved into a retirement home. "He's had a series of strokes since his early seventies, and he comments that he forgets things and isn't as clear as he once was," Tom said. "But he still has a lot of friends, and, even at age seventy-nine, he goes out to work three days a week."

Tom acknowledges, "In recent years, I think a lot more about their being older when I was born, and how that's affected me. When I see some of my peers take vacations with their parents, who aren't sixty yet, I miss that and think about how nice that might have been.

"But then I think that both my parents were settled in their lives and were comfortable with who they were and what they were doing. Older parents, on the whole, are more patient and willing to spend time with their children. Younger parents I've seen have a shorter fuse. They're more inclined to punish their children than to sit down and talk with them. They're also more concerned with survival issues of paying the bills and establishing themselves in careers. Older parents are more established and don't project those kinds of life stresses onto their children.

"I know I felt very comfortable and quite loved."

Charles

"When I was young, my dad's age was a great novelty," Charles recalled. "He was real proud that he'd had a kid at his age. It was like some sort of badge, and it made me think I was special too."

Charles, a twenty-six-year-old theology student at a leading Protestant seminary, was born on a farm in eastern Tennessee when his father was nearly fifty-nine and his mother was forty. Like many children of much-older fathers and so-called blended families, he was not the product of a first marriage. His father had been married twice before, had had two children (when he was twenty-five and thirty-five years old), been widowed and divorced, and had two grandchildren by the time he married for a third time at age fifty-five. Charles's mother was a schoolteacher, who married for the first time when she was thirty-six. She and her husband had their first child together, a daughter, a year later, and Charles was born three years after that.

By the time Charles was six, however, the distinction of having a father at retirement age had already "worn pretty thin," he recalled.

When he saw his cousins, the children of his mother's younger brother, playing catch and roughhousing with their parents, he became jealous that his parents lacked the vigor and stamina to play like that with him.

"I missed out going camping or swimming," he said. "We grew up on a lake, but we never had a boat. My father didn't want to get out and do things. My best friend and his dad were really good friends. They went hunting and camping together, and I was envious of that too. I resigned myself to the fact that that wasn't going to happen with my father. But that would bring on feelings of blaming him for being so much older."

Charles also knew that his home life was different from that of other families in which the parents were younger. "At night, we watched Lawrence Welk on TV, because that's what my parents had grown up with," he remembered. "And my mother had gotten the *Reader's Digest* collection of big-band-era music. So I knew Tommy Dorsey and Glenn Miller before I ever heard of the Beatles. My friends felt it was a little weird, or else they thought I was being punished for something."

Most people who came to the house were older, and Charles had few friends his own age while he was growing up. "I didn't feel comfortable with people my age," he said. "I always felt more at ease with much older people." At church he became friendly with several elderly members of the congregation and thus acquired a host of "pseudograndparents." Later, when he was in college, he felt perfectly at ease talking with the president or the dean, he said, "but I was absolutely terrified of going to the game room to talk to people my own age."

Charles felt like a "little adult" from an early age. He remembered having more serious, "adult" attitudes than other children, and his mother and father would encourage him to read or watch educational television. He often referred to people his own age as "dumb kids," and he saw himself as a sort of a "goody two-shoes." At camp one summer, he recalled feeling different from the other children because he was the only one who didn't wear jeans. Even though he became rebellious as a teenager, he always maintained the facade of being the well-behaved "little adult" when he was around grown-ups.

The subject of his parents' ages often came up in conversations with his sister. "I remember she once read an article that said if you had children after thirty-five, you ran a fifty-fifty chance of having Mongoloid kids, or else the children would be very talented," Charles remembered. Only later did he learn that this was not true. "So, depending on what mood we were in, we would joke that one of us was the Mongoloid and the other was really talented."

When Charles got to high school, the age differences between his parents and other children's parents became especially noticeable in terms of his mother's and father's attitudes and behavior. "They were much more restrictive about when I could go out or who I could go out with," he said. "Even my mother's standards were more those of the 1950s than the 1960s or 1970s, when we were growing up."

The stories that his father told—of the hardships of the

depression, when his store went out of business—were of an era that seemed to Charles like something out of his history classes. Nonetheless, he was spellbound by his father's tales of the 1920s and 1930s. Charles dreamed of living in that long-ago time, but the stories reinforced his awareness that his father's life experiences were very different from those of his schoolmates' parents.

Charles forged a close relationship with his mother, who tried to compensate for his father's unwillingness or inability to be actively involved with his son and daughter. She would take him to band concerts and play with him. And Charles appointed himself his mother's defender when his father became jealous, imagining that his much-younger wife was flirting with various men in the community.

"I asked my mother why they had kids at their age," he recalled, "and she just said that they had wanted to. But I felt that she deserved something better than this old man.

"The fact that there was a nearly sixty-year age difference between my father and me really worked against my forming a close relationship with him," Charles said. "It created a lot of problems. He wasn't a confidant or a role model."

Like other latecomers, Charles also felt set off from children of younger parents because he had to confront the physical facts of his parents' aging while he was still quite young. People often mistook his parents for his grandparents, which was usually quite embarrassing.

Three of Charles's actual grandparents, however, had died before he was born, and the fourth, his mother's mother, died when he was five. He recalled feeling cheated, especially at Christmastime. Other children would be getting presents from their grandparents, and "we didn't have that." I felt like I was missing out on something that everybody else had."

His mother's hair was gray for as long as Charles could remember, but his father always looked twenty years younger than his age until he reached his mid-seventies. At that time, when Kevin was in the eighth grade, his father began to develop Alzheimer's disease.

"By the time I was a junior in high school, the Alzheimer's was really apparent," he recalled, but neither he nor his sister or mother really understood what was happening at first. "I blamed him, and it gave me an excuse to alienate myself from him. I would tell him that he was too old to have had kids."

Because of his mental deterioration, his father once backed the tractor into and over a fence, and Charles and his mother had to forbid his father from using it again. "One time, my best friend was over," he remembered, "and my father asked him to help him zip his pants. That was a major embarrassment!"

Charles remembered talking with his half sister, who was thirty-four years older than he was and whom he thought of as sort of an aunt, about his father's Alzheimer's. "She said to me, 'You're having to deal with issues that most people don't have to until their mid-thirties or later.'

"I was in my teens, and my parents were aging. There were all the role reversals—having to worry about my father and reprimand him. It was very confusing. And I had to deal with the prospect of a parent dying when that was the farthest thing from most of my friends' minds.

"I remember talking with a guy at the local truck dealership who was in his thirties, who said that his dad was in his sixties and that he was seeing his parents' health deteriorate. When I told him my dad was in his late seventies, it pointed out to me again that I was going through things that most people did much later. But I hadn't developed the coping skills, even though I had been a little adult for a long time."

One summer, he and his father had a big fight just as Charles was leaving for a summer theater apprenticeship. "I was about to drive away, and my father came down the walkway and said, 'I love you.' This was what I'd been waiting to hear for eighteen years, and it really blew me away. I had a hundred miles to drive, and I was bawling my eyes out all the way." The incident made Charles somewhat closer to his father, yet his father's Alzheimer's disease had already progressed to the point that it was difficult to interact with him.

Around that time Charles started drinking heavily. He had blackouts—much like the ones his father was having because of his Alzheimer's. His mother could not understand what was happening when his father faded out of consciousness, but Charles would say to her: "He's really not aware what he's doing. He's not doing it to be mean.

"Here I was taking up for him because I had a shared experience," Charles said, "but I wasn't ready to tell my mother why I knew about doing things and not being consciously aware of them."

When Charles was twenty-two, his father died at age eighty-one. Charles's drinking had become such a serious problem by then that he was arrested for drunk driving and jailed for forty-five days. "My father died just before that summer," he remembered. "There were an awful lot of unresolved issues, but I had a lot of time to think about things. I had the shock of realizing that I really did have strong feelings for him, and I really did feel a sense of loss."

Charles entered a recovery program for alcoholics, which helped him develop many of the coping skills and interpersonal skills he had never developed when he was a teenage "little adult." He graduated from college and went into public relations but then realized that he wanted to enter the ministry.

"I felt I'd had a calling when I was about thirteen," he said, "but for more than eight years I would do anything I could to show that God was wrong, even though I'd present this serious, well-behaved image to adults. Coming to grips with my alcoholism and my feelings about my father made me take another look, and I realized I accepted God."

Charles has been in the seminary for two years and hopes to become a pastoral counselor. He goes home to Tennessee to visit his mother several times a year and has become much closer to her. But he has also become aware that she is "elderly," while his friends' mothers are comparatively young.

He regrets that he did not know his father as a young man and that, in the twenty-two years of life they shared, their relationship was so strained. He has come to believe that his parents truly did love him and that he did benefit from their emphasis on education.

Charles does not want to have children soon, because he has never really felt comfortable with young people. Yet he also doesn't want to wait fifteen years or more and duplicate his own experience with his children.

But it's the little, everyday things that stand out and remind him that his life has been different because his parents were older. For example, he says, he is always a little saddened when he sees people his age out doing things with parents who are only in their late forties or fifties.

12

Parents of Another Era

One of the most obvious facts about grown-ups to a child is that they have forgotten what it is like to be a child.
—*Randall Jarrell*

"My parents were relics of an earlier age, compared to my friends' parents," said Lauren, from Washington, D.C. "They seemed like Victorians to me, whereas my friends' mothers and fathers were 'young' and 'modern.' I read *The Way of All Flesh* as if it were a contemporary novel, identifying strongly with its protagonist. At a time when younger parents harkened back to the Second World War, mine were still reminiscing about the depression. In many ways, they were still living in it, even in the prosperous 1960s. It had been the crucial, formative experience of their lives. They passed on to me a defensive hoarding ethic—rather than an expansive consuming one. It's been a mixed blessing."

∞

Because more time has passed since their own childhood or adolescence, is it harder for older parents to remember what it was like to be a child or teenager? Are older parents more out of touch with current trends in fashion and popular culture, and more conservative in their values? Does the wide age gap make later-born children feel that they were born after the best years in their parents' lives had passed? Does their situation demonstrate, as Shakespeare said, that "crabbed age and youth cannot live together"? Or can the reality or perception that their parents belong to another era have beneficial effects on children of older parents?

Many latecomers agreed with a New York man who said, "The greatest problem of having older parents was the 'generation gap,' since my parents' mentality was more similar to that of my peers' grandparents."

Generation gaps are hardly restricted to later-born children, but many of those interviewed or surveyed vehemently asserted that they felt a more pronounced gap in understanding between them and their mothers and fathers than that separating parents and children who were closer in age. They remembered their parents' mind-set as "ancient" or "antiquated" and referred to their parents' values, tastes, and life-styles as particularly old-fashioned.

This perception of a greater generation gap was substantiated by the survey of urban college students whose parents varied in age. Among those born to parents under thirty-five, less than one-third were bothered by a generation gap during adolescence, compared with nearly three out of five of those born when their parents were at least thirty-five.

Even among latecomers, the effects of the distance of years between generations were varied. Some described their parents as more calm and tolerant, while others insisted that their mothers and fathers had more staid life-styles, and were "more conservative" and "set in their ways" than their friends' younger parents. These older parents were stricter, less tolerant, and spontaneous and more "old-fashioned" when it came to such things as dating, overnight trips, rock and roll, and "hip" styles of clothing.

"It was pretty obvious that she was older than other mothers, because the music you'd hear around the house and the phrases she used seemed outdated," said a man whose mother was forty when he was born in 1947. "She'd refer to 'twenty-three skidoo' when the other kids listened to Elvis Presley records their parents brought home."

Indeed, most parents of children growing up in the 1950s were influenced by Elvis and Eisenhower, "I Love Lucy," and *The Man in the Gray Flannel Suit*. While older parents of that era also lived through these cultural milestones, the memories and influences of their formative years were also likely to include Franklin Roosevelt and Pearl Harbor, Cole Porter, and movies like *Citizen Kane* and *Casablanca*.

When the outlooks of older parents were rooted in very different historical eras, the psychological divide often made it feel like a "double generation gap." If parents lived through a significant period that left a deep imprint on their thinking, such as the depression, World War II, or the 1960s counterculture, the chasm between parent and child seemed greater than if more cultural and political continuities existed between generations.

"While my friends' mothers were telling stories of the 1930s to their daughters," wrote Joyce, who was born in 1936, shortly before her mother's forty-sixth birthday, "my mother was relating tales of her large family during the turn of the century and early 1900s. The result was that sometimes I felt we skipped a whole generation in my home—a logical feeling since everyone constantly mistook my mother for my grandmother anyway."

A Cold Family Climate

"Older parents probably have more psychological barriers to expressing their feelings," said a northern California marriage counselor who was a child of older parents. "They're more likely to be tightly defended, which may make them less sensitive to their child's needs and vulnerabilities. My parents' tendency was to invalidate my feelings, because I think they were more defended against remembering their own childhood feelings. If a child's feelings aren't seen or heard by their parents, there will be bruises on the heart."

Later-born children often lamented that their parents were emotionally distant, serious, and formal. There may have been considerable love and warmth at one level, but at another, many remembered a relative lack of humor and physical affection compared with the norm in other families.

"My mother was never 'Mom,'" recalled Mary, from Virginia, whose parents were forty when she was born. "She was always 'Mother.' Other parents seemed to joke with their kids more. Although she wasn't devoid of a sense of humor, there was no horsing around. She was very dignified, and I'd never be embarrassed by things she did—unlike other mothers—but she was never a pal."

Spontaneity, too, frequently seemed to be missing. There might have been planned evenings at the theater or summertime trips. But many later-born children felt that they had fewer spurof-the-moment, fun outings with their parents—going to a movie on a Saturday afternoon or for an ice-cream cone on a summer night.

"We took a lot of vacations at Christmas and in the summers," said Mindy, from Milwaukee. "But my parents seldom took me to a movie or played with me in the yard like other parents did. I always thought it would be neat if my parents went dancing. Other parents seemed more festive and to like to party."

"It would have been nice to have had a little more humor in my childhood," recalled Carla, an only child who grew up in New York. "Once in awhile we'd go to the zoo or circus, and we had a ritual on Saturday of going to a late-afternoon movie and dinner. But it would have been more balanced if I could have had more of these more-frivolous types of outings."

Children of older parents often contrasted the more reserved emotional ambiance of their own families with the informality of their friends'.

"I remember walking into a friend's house, and there was a full-fledged water fight going on," said Dean, whose mother was forty when he was born. "My friend's mother, who was in her late twenties, would be shooting away with her water pistol. I could never imagine my mother doing that. She felt it wasn't parental dignity or something. There was a formality in my house. If friends came by to drop in, it was sort of tenuous if they didn't call ahead."

On this score, many later-born children had memories similar to those of a woman from Springfield, Massachusetts. She said, "Everything was overanticipated, overplanned, and anything but spontaneous."

Old-Fashioned and Dated Values

"When you grow up with older parents, you think older automatically," said a forty-year-old Midwestern woman. "You have the values of an older generation. I grew up during the Vietnam War era, but I couldn't identify with using pot or other drugs. My values are those of people in their fifties. I feel more of a generation gap with people my own age than with my parents."

Certainly parents' values and tastes are often transmitted

to their children. But this frequently creates a dilemma for children of older parents: Rejecting their parents' tastes and values is likely to cause or exacerbate family tensions. Accepting and internalizing them may foster a sense of being out of sync with their contemporaries.

One respondent, who is a therapist, noted, for example, that many older parents of the late 1980s were "still convinced that the Rolling Stones play the only 'real' rock and roll, and that Prince is some kind of 'pervert.' They hate MTV. They need to make some big changes in attitude to deal with young children. Even the 'with-it' generation can become ossified in its attitudes."

Older parents also were seen as taking a more conservative approach to child rearing and being more restrictive about what their children may and may not do. If parents' ideas are more set, there will be less room for negotiation. Thus their children's behavior will inevitably be defined in more black-or-white terms: Either they are especially obedient "little adults" or particularly defiant. In either case, if this attitude is taken to extremes, the child ultimately loses.

Parental values, expressed in the form of rules and restrictions, were accentuated markers of the generational difference. For example, some remembered that wearing jeans or makeup was taboo or recalled that they were not permitted to go to slumber parties or junior-high dances, while "all the other kids" could go.

"I was brought up like someone born in the 1930s rather than the late 1940s or 1950s," said Christy, who was born in 1946. "My mother didn't work, and she seemed very old-fashioned. There was a subliminal strictness: 'I don't think you're old enough to spend the night with friends or go out on dates.' Or, 'Don't do this, you might get hurt.' "

"My father didn't want to accept things that had changed since his time, like people living together before marriage," added Joan, from New York. "But as much as I argued with him, I didn't rebel that much. I didn't get involved with men who weren't of our religious background, and I didn't live with anyone before I got married. I internalized his values, and that did set me apart from my friends a bit."

But Edith, whose parents were about forty when she was born, recalled the generation gap as fueling her rebellion. "My brother and I were never allowed to talk back or argue," she said. "We were raised as Orthodox Jews. We kept kosher and observed the Sabbath. There were a lot of restrictions and rules, which we both rebelled against. When I was thirteen, I refused to go to the Jewish high school, and we both started eating non-kosher."

∞

Not only were these older parents typed as more socially conservative in their outlooks and behavior, but their children saw them as less inclined to take risks and more realistic than younger parents about the ways of the world. These qualities were believed to rub off, making their children a bit less idealistic and somewhat more cautious and conservative. This cautiousness may have beneficial, protective effects, but it also may limit children's ideas of what is possible to attain or desirable to strive for.

"Having older, more economically stable parents was a detriment," argued a thirty-seven-year-old from Minneapolis. "It discouraged me from trying harder for 'success' and made it harder to be innovative."

"I once had kicked around the idea of going into modeling," recalled Sally, a young keypunch operator from Levittown, Pennsylvania. "But my mother said, 'You should be satisfied with what you are and not try to reach for the stars.' It was an old-fashioned type of idea. Most mothers who are younger probably would have said, 'Go for it.'"

Such ideas and values, labeled "dated" by the children, led some to make a very conscious and strenuous effort to be more "modern" and "with it." Maureen, from Portland, Oregon, for example, wrote that she "devoured women's and girls' magazines, trying to learn the correct and normal way to conduct my life."

But whether or not their parents' values were shaped by a more "old-fashioned" cultural Zeitgeist, many latecomers did feel that their mothers and fathers were distinctly out of step with the times. The term *Victorian* was frequently used pejoratively by children of older parents—regardless of whether they were now in their seventies and their parents had lived during the reign of the venerable, straitlaced British queen or they were in their thirties and their parents presumably had grown up during the relatively freewheeling 1920s. In any case their parents' ideas seemed to have been formed by one era, whereas their friends' parents came of age during a very different time.

Political and cultural values, which are conditioned by both the historical and family contexts in which one lives, are an illustration of this. Later-born children, naturally, are politically socialized, at least in part, by the perspectives and terms of debate of an earlier time, when the values of their parents' cohort were formed.

Many latecomers born during the postwar baby boom specifically noted the long-term effect of the depression on their mothers' and fathers' lives and values. This experience—which the younger parents of their friends did not live through—left a mark on many of these older parents. This, in turn, often set the tone of parenting and colored the lives of their sons and daughters.

"I was a child of the 1940s, but my mother's ideas were shaped by the depression," a New York man reminisced. "The economy and population were going up, though she would insist they were going down again. I was embarrassed by her ideas and resented that she wasn't closer to my age and I couldn't share my thoughts with her. My ideas were mid-twentieth-century ideas and hers were early-twentieth-century ones."

Other later-born children of this generation spoke of their parents' strong beliefs in the goals of Franklin Roosevelt's New Deal, while their peers' parents—born ten or fifteen years later— were likely to have had their political values molded by the more conservative and conformist culture of the Eisenhower era. Likewise, forty-year-old, first-time parents of the late 1980s or early 1990s, who were youths during the 1960s, might convey more liberal social and political values to their children than twenty-five-year-old parents who came of age during the Reagan-Bush years.

"My friends tended to be more conservative, Republican types—like the government is always right—but less willing to go along with social programs," recalled Gina, the young woman from Holland, Pennsylvania. "My father was always very liberal—almost a socialist—economically but not socially. And my mother was a diehard New Dealer."

The sense that older parents have more dated values raises interesting questions about how the length of generations may affect political beliefs and social change. Are children of older parents more conformist, assuming that they accept their parents' values, or more rebellious, because they feel their parents represent an oppressive old regime? Of course, other factors come into play, but it is nonetheless tantalizing to speculate how parents' ages may influence the degree to which children are conformist or rebellious, conservative or liberal.

The Gap in Adolescence

The generation gap typically became worst during adolescence, especially as sexual issues arose. It may be difficult enough for teenagers to try to relate to parents a generation apart from them, but children of older parents often said that their parents were not one but two generations removed.

They complained that their parents did not talk with them about the "facts of life" and were less able than others to accept the changes in social mores that came with the sexual revolution of the 1960s and 1970s. Their parents' more "old-fashioned" values might mean that they were not allowed to date until well into high school or that they were expressly told not to go out with people of other religious or ethnic backgrounds.

"I couldn't go out driving with boys, and my mother tried to spearhead a rule with my friends' mothers that we couldn't go in cars with guys," recalled Lisa, a New York executive whose parents were forty-one when she was born. "My mother was very conservative about sex. She was saying things that might have been appropriate ten or fifteen years earlier. I had a slumber party one night, and she threatened to have a gun if guys came over."

"There were things that a young lady just didn't do," added Marta, a Pennsylvania nurse. "My father, who was about seventy when I was thirteen, said it was horrendous for a woman to put on nail polish or makeup. And if there were boys playing ball in front of our house, I wasn't even allowed on the front porch to watch them."

And a woman from Virginia recalled: "Other parents let us play spin the bottle, but my mother would have died! She wasn't very modern in her thinking. I remember when I had been going steady with a guy, she said, 'You haven't let him kiss you?' "

The coincidence of a mother reaching menopause and a

daughter entering puberty could also accentuate the generational divide. One woman recalled, "When I first got my period, my mother stopped having hers."

But because the gap in communication and understanding was so wide, it allowed some latecomers to "get away with" more than children of "hipper," younger parents.

"Older parents are more gullible," said a woman from Wisconsin. "I used to be able to hide things behind their backs, like smoking cigarettes and doing drugs."

Yet others found it harder to rebel against their parents because they were older. Whether it was because their mothers and fathers were more mature, tolerant, and experienced as parents or seemingly more fragile and grandparentlike, a surprising number of children of older parents said that they never experienced—or acted out—the usual Sturm und Drang of adolescence, with its attendant parent-child conflicts. It was not uncommon for them to recall trying to rein in emotions so as not to upset their apparently-more-vulnerable older parents.

"The strongest effect" of having a mother who was forty-six and a father who was fifty-one when she was born, wrote Jeanette, "was to keep me from getting angry at them openly in normal teenage fashion." She did not want to upset them because she constantly worried that they might die, she said; thus, "I kept everything inside."

Some degree of psychological distance between parent and child, of course, is crucial for an adolescent trying to discover and assert his or her independent identity. A very young parent may be less able than an older parent to provide that emotional space. For example, a young father may try too hard to act like his son's best friend, or a mother may try to dress like her teenage daughter or inadvertently flirt with her daughter's boyfriend.

Conversely, a greater age difference is more likely to provide needed distance and spell less competition between parent and child during adolescence, as a woman from Austin, Texas, suggested: "As a teenager, I had no problems competing with a mother facing the first fading of youth."

"I remember friends with very young parents," added a twenty-eight-year-old from Cambridge, Massachusetts. "The girls always felt they competed with their mothers in terms of appearance."

"You Should Have Known Us When We Were Younger"

"My parents were married a good twenty years before they had me," recalled the daughter of two musicians. "They had great fun before I was born. When they were young violinists, they went on bus tours with various orchestras. And they went on tours with ballet companies in South America. But my mother said that her fun and her life ended when I was born.

"I never really saw my parents in their prime, when they were happy," she added wistfully. "I only saw their lives in decline."

These feelings were shared by others who felt not only acutely aware of the span of years separating them from their parents but also that much of their mothers' and fathers' lives had been lived before they were born. The "good old days" in their parents' lives seemed long past, and the present—however tranquil and secure—was almost like a coda to the years of excitement and challenge that they would never really know or understand as children of younger parents might.

"I have always felt like the odd man out, an afterthought, like all the important family history, and the fun stuff, happened before my birth," wrote Roslyn, from Ithaca, New York, whose parents were forty-five and forty-six when she was born and had already had five children. "So many of the important events in my mother's life happened sixty, fifty, forty years ago."

Edith, a corporate manager, recalled that it wasn't until she was thirteen that she learned that her mother had been married before, had owned a business, and had lost her first husband in a plane crash. "I was shocked," she said. "It made me realize there was a whole life I didn't know that she had had before me."

The Biggest Gap: Much-Older Fathers

A thirty-five-year age difference between parent and child is one thing, but when the divide grows to a half century or more, a child can hardly help feeling that his or her parent is of another era. Biology and culture conspire to make such circumstances exceedingly rare.

Nonetheless, whereas menopause imposes an upper limit on women's childbearing years, men can become fathers at virtually any time. Certainly there have always been men who were twenty, thirty, forty, even fifty years older than their wives, and the ranks of celebrated or well-known men who became fathers after sixty have included such disparate figures as Pablo Picasso and Senator Strom Thurmond; authors Kurt Vonnegut, Jr., Leon Uris, and Budd Schulberg; and cartoonist Jules Feiffer. Of the hundreds of children of older parents surveyed, 15 percent were born when their fathers were fifty or older.

"May-December" unions have rarely been looked upon favorably, however, and continue to make many people uncomfortable. "It touches upon one of the profound unsettled issues of biological difference between men and women," said Dr. Donald A. Bloch, director of New York's Ackerman Institute of Family Therapy. "It tests the issues of envy and distress in both directions. Women live to be widows, but men are reproductive into their 60's and 70's and more."[1]

And a television talk-show host addressing a group of men who became fathers between the ages of forty-two and sixty wondered rhetorically if a "double standard" exists. "Is it OK for men to have kids at sixty, but not for women at forty?" she asked.

Much-older fathers still remain comparatively rare in the United States. Only 19,026 American babies born in 1987, or 0.6 percent of those whose fathers' ages were known, had fathers over fifty. Of these fathers, 11,945 were between fifty and fifty-four, and 7,081 were fifty-five or older.[2]

When the questionnaire responses of children of much-older fathers were compared with those of people who were born when their fathers were thirty-five to forty-nine years old, some striking differences emerged. Surprisingly, those born when their fathers were fifty or older consistently had more positive recollections. These feelings were particularly strong concerning their fathers' impact on their personalities, maturity, and social skills.

Children of fifty-plus fathers much more often said that their fathers were helpful to them and that their relationships were closer during childhood and adolescence than did children of the younger fathers. A greater proportion also saw their fathers as role models and denied that there was a generation gap.

Consistent with these differences were their evaluations of the positive effects their fathers had on their personalities. Forty-six percent of children of fifty-or-older fathers recalled their fathers' influence as positive, and just 31 percent said the effect was negative. By contrast, 34 percent of those whose fathers were thirty-five to forty-nine years old cited their fathers' positive influence during adolescence, whereas 36 percent expressed negative feelings.

A Connecticut woman whose father was fifty-two when she was born recalled her intense pride in him. "He was so dignified," she said. As the president of the PTA and a church elder, he was "looked up to by everyone."

These more-positive feelings of children of much older fathers even carried over into perceptions of their fathers' appearance. Thirty-two percent recalled their fathers' appearance in positive terms, compared with only 17 percent of the children of thirty-five-to-forty-nine-year-old fathers.

At first the reasons for these feelings seem hard to fathom. Yet much-older fathers are clearly a very unusual breed. Since they are almost all men who have married considerably younger women, one may assume that most of them are highly successful or charismatic. Indeed, as many children of such fathers reported, and the examples of famous older fathers illustrate, many of these men *are* "stars" of one sort or another. Whether their success is in business, politics, or entertainment, they seem to have impressed their children as well as the world. In both society and family, their individual personalities appear far more important than age.

Nevertheless, children of fifty-plus fathers did feel that their fathers' age set them off from their peers, and the age difference between parents often stood out in their minds. As a Minneapolis woman whose father was thirteen years older than his wife said, "I always felt like I was living with a mother and a grandfather."

"The wide gap between my mom and dad made me realize a lot of problems between them," added a young woman from Hong Kong, whose father was sixty and mother was thirty-five when she was born. "I decided I'd never marry someone much older than I am."

A significant age gap between parents is inevitable if a father is over fifty when a child is born, but not all much-older fathers are part of May-December unions. In some of these families, in which the parents have already had many children, the marital relationship might be better described as July-October. These much-older fathers are becoming less common today, as couples tend to have fewer children, yet a sizable minority of those interviewed did come from such a background.

Bernice's father, who was fifty-five when she was born, was a farmer in eastern South Dakota, and she was the last of five children. But her memories were of a charismatic father who seemed to defy the expected course of aging. "My father was never an old person," she said. "He made his own food and drove his car and went on vacations. He never was decrepit or wrinkled. He was in good health until he died, after an accident, at eighty-three."

Interestingly, children of much-older fathers also expressed more positive feelings about their mothers. This appeared in their evaluations of their mothers' energy and health, as well as feelings of closeness and recollections of sharing experiences with their mothers. Even those born when their mothers were in their forties were generally more upbeat about their mothers than were children of thirty-five- to thirty-nine-year-old women.

All too frequently, however, these last-born children of much-older fathers had less-than-happy experiences. In fact, they often scarcely knew their fathers.

Pam, a Florida woman who was born when her father was fifty-one, had three siblings eleven to fifteen years older. Her father died when she was seven, and her only cryptic memories were of a man with "old-fashioned values, who was a strict disciplinarian."

The specter of death early in a child's life is an inevitable concomitant of becoming a father after fifty. Albert, a student in Boston, was adopted when his father—a successful investor and art collector—was sixty-seven. Barely six years later, his father died, and because his mother remained a distant figure he spent his childhood and adolescence being ministered to by three governesses.

The positive picture of much-older fathers certainly all but vanishes by the time their children reach adulthood. When asked about their feelings as young adults concerning their fathers, 53 percent of those born to fifty-plus fathers responded negatively, compared with only 33 percent of those who had younger fathers.

These oldest fathers clearly age, ail, and die sooner in their sons' and daughters' lives than the 99-plus percent of American fathers who have children before turning fifty. Emotional scars and practical difficulties associated with fathers' medical problems were much more often reported by children of much-older fathers. Even in childhood they more frequently recalled fears that their fathers would die.

Thus much-older fathers are a sort of exaggerated version of older parents in general. Their children are frequently the recipients of a bounty of love and attention during childhood. The benefits of their maturity and the force of their personalities appear to leave a strong, positive impression on their children. But age catches up with them, leaving their children worried about their health and, all too often, fatherless early in life.

Tales of Long Ago

Despite the very real difficulties associated with generational divides of forty or fifty years, older parents *can* provide a link with an earlier time in history. Some children saw their mothers and fathers almost as living historical sources who provided them with a greater sense of connectedness with the past. These parents told rich and vivid tales of long-ago events and people—the stuff of history books.

"I would hear fascinating stories from my parents that I knew other kids weren't hearing from their parents," recalled a Washington, D.C., woman born in the late 1950s. Whereas her friends' fathers may have been old enough to be enlisted men in World War II, she said, "My father was a psychiatrist at the Nuremberg trials, and my mother was in naval intelligence and told stories about breaking a Nazi spy ring. They also talked a lot about the depression, so I got a real sense of history in the twentieth century, which I didn't get from anybody else's parents. But in terms of what was going on in the 1960s and 1970s, my parents really separated themselves from that."

"Age seemed nothing to me, except perhaps for my father's being born in the last century and his going to Hull House in Chicago when Jane Addams was still alive," added a middle-aged woman named Holly. "I remember when he told me about it. I was in grade school, and Jane Addams was already long entrenched as a historical figure."

But older parents like these were apparently more than just storytellers with good stories to tell. They were often admiringly recalled as colorful figures—people whose lives had been richer, more interesting, and perhaps more offbeat than those of other, seemingly-more-prosaic mothers and fathers.

"My parents were slightly eccentric and much livelier than other kids' parents," reminisced a Brooklyn woman, with a touch of humor, "so they seemed younger, except for those World War I songs my father sang to me and their memories of the Roaring Twenties."

Some firsthand family memories went even farther back. One respondent noted that his grandfather had remembered a torchlight parade the night Lincoln was shot. And Maureen, a forty-five-year-old from Portland, Oregon, recalled stories of her grandfather, who had served in the Civil War. She said that she liked to tell these tales to her "historically minded friends, who think I've gotten mixed up about it. It's hard for them, with their youthful parents, to understand that youthful little me would be having a one hundredth birthday party for my father next year if he hadn't died at eighty-three!"

No Generation Gap

Although they may have felt a generation gap, many later-born children also felt strongly that, at least in part because of their ages, their parents had had a good effect in shaping their values. Overwhelming majorities said that their parents influenced their beliefs positively. For example, 63 percent said that the values transmitted to them were good, whereas only 8 percent rejected their parents' values.

Moreover, even if they felt distant from their parents during childhood, adolescence, or young adulthood, many said that there was anything but a gap as they moved into their mid-twenties and thirties. They spoke of being especially close to their parents by this time, and said that they were able to relate well with them as adults and as friends. In many instances, relationships with their mothers and fathers, in fact, had become better than those of their friends with younger parents.

"There was a generation gap a mile wide between my mother and me," wrote Rebecca, a forty-three-year-old from Berkeley, California. "During the sixties, many of my friends with considerably younger parents felt as estranged as I did, and to this day are not particularly close to their parents." Rebecca, however, said that she became quite close to her mother after the turmoil of the 1960s had subsided.

Many also said that there was no greater generation gap in their families and that their experiences were no different from those of other teenagers. Some asserted that they had helped keep their parents young in spirit. And others argued that they experienced less of a "gap" than that which divided younger, less-patient, and less-reflective parents from their children.

"My parents were very concerned that they not be perceived as old fogeys who were behind the times," said a woman who was born when her father was fifty and mother was forty-one.

"My friends adore my parents and find them quite hip," added June, whose parents were well into their forties when she was born. "They often comment that they wish their own parents were as 'with it.' "

And one woman from Connecticut proudly enclosed with her letter an old local newspaper clipping reporting her third-grade open house. It spoke of "a sweet little girl and her dad . . . a handsomely dressed businessman [who] seemed enchanted with the world of 'little people,' and particularly that of his daughter. . . . The silver-grayness of his hair seemed to shine, as did his eyes. The 'generation gap' seemed to have sprung a leak! This father and daughter, though separated by many years, proved once more that love, mutual trust and understanding can and do tighten the string on the generation gap."

13

Children of Privilege

The old pearl-oyster produces a pearl.

—*Chinese proverb*

"I thought having older parents was wonderful," said Bonnie, a nurse from Philadelphia. "Parents in their twenties are growing up with their kids. My parents were more grown-up and had more time to share their lives. People who are older are also more financially set. I think I was closer to my parents because they were more patient and gave me more encouragement than other kids got. They instilled a sense of responsibility, love, and hope. That ghost of fear—that skeleton in the closet of old age, that fear of death—was there, but there wasn't a loss of love."

In a number of ways, the offspring of older parents are children of emotional and economic privilege. Many feel very intensely about the benefits deriving from their parents' maturity and position in life, compared with children of younger parents.

Emotionally Stable and Mature Parents

"Our parents had done with the lion's share of their nonsense before we came along," said Beth, from Los Angeles. "Imagine being four and trying to nurse your parents through adolescence!" she joked.

While younger parents may be more concerned about their own identities, job promotions, family finances, and mortgages, children of older parents are likely to take center stage in their mothers' and fathers' lives. With the psychological searching and initial career struggles of their twenties and early thirties behind them, these parents may be able to focus more on their children, putting their sons' and daughters' needs first.

"My parents were very satisfied with their role as parents and were willing and ready to be parents," said Amanda, from Beaver Dam, Wisconsin. "They didn't need anything else to make their lives satisfying. Older parents are more settled and ready to give to their kids."

"I suspect that my parents' self-security and maturity had something to do with the security I felt while growing up," added a woman from Delmar, New York, whose parents were forty-six and forty-seven when she was born.

Erik Erikson, the psychologist who developed an influential theory of developmental stages in the life cycle, asserted that people in their twenties and early thirties are concerned with working out issues of intimacy and balancing their needs for autonomy and togetherness. However, after thirty-five, he believed, people's concerns tend to focus on the next generation.

"The older you get, the less you think about your own future, so you probably get more involved with the future of your kids," speculated a New York man whose parents were in their mid-forties when he was born.

Indeed, older parents may have a better-defined sense of self and be more secure in their self-image. As one respondent put it, "I was never in competition with my parents' ambitions and desires." By contrast, parents in their early twenties are often growing up with their children and have yet to work through issues of who they are and where they are going in life—concerns that may weigh mightily on their relationships with their children.

"People who have reached a plateau in their lives and aren't striving for great glory have more time to love their children," suggested Beverly, a young musician. "Because my parents were grown-up and settled, they had the time to love me, which meant a lot to me."

With maturity generally comes knowledge about life and the world. Thus older parents have a greater fund of experiences to draw from to teach their children.

"They were more sophisticated about the world, maybe because they had a whole lifetime of experience before they had a kid," said Charles, an only child of much-older parents. "They had more history as adults."

Calm, Patient, and Tolerant Parents

Many social scientists and family therapists, as well as older parents themselves, say that fathers and mothers in their thirties and forties are usually on a more-even emotional keel than parents in their twenties. They may be more understanding of their children and get less upset about minor problems, experts say. These qualities of patience and tolerance and relaxed attitudes presumably result in better parent-child relationships.

"Older mothers tend to be calmer, and thus have more relaxed relationships with their children," said Jerome Kagan, professor of developmental psychology at Harvard. Such parents are more "attentive and more rational. They lose their tempers less easily and take their children's problems more seriously." If mothers are more relaxed, he concluded, "one would expect less conflict and anxiety in the child."[1]

The National Survey of Children, a privately funded longitudinal study of more than seventeen hundred households conducted between 1976 and 1988, also found that older mothers—defined as twenty-eight and older—less often reported behavior problems in their children and felt more in control of their environment and future than younger mothers did. They also less frequently said that they felt tense, sad, and worn out. In addition, the children of these older mothers were considerably less likely to say that they misbehaved than children whose mothers were younger.[2]

These findings are supported by a child-rearing study by Grazyna Kochanska at the National Institute of Mental Health (NIMH). She observed that interactions between mothers and their five- to six-year-old children, involving attempts to influence each other, differed depending on the age of the mother.[3]

Mothers who were at least thirty-five when their children were born frequently tended to be more considerate of their children and attempted to influence them more indirectly than younger mothers did. Older mothers were also more receptive to their children's requests and wishes. Younger mothers were more negative toward their children, who, in turn, were more defiant than the children of older parents.

The contrasts continue into other areas of parenting. Younger parents often have unrealistic expectations of what babies can do and have less knowledge of milestones of early child development, such as when infants are able to sit up, walk, or talk. To take an extreme case, researchers have found that children of very young parents are much more likely to be verbally and physically abused than are the offspring of older parents.

The memories of many later-born children are consistent with the speculations and findings of experts. "Older parents aren't so serious about silly things," said a woman whose parents were nearly forty when she was born. "Young parents can get so upset about things that are so meaningless. The years bring a greater wisdom."

A Pennsylvania woman also recalled that her older parents "seemed more easygoing and mellow, and not so off the wall about every little thing. "They weren't as uptight as other parents when we did something wrong or didn't do well in school," she added. "My mother still worried about us and wanted us to wear our mittens and hat and all that motherly kind of stuff. But there wasn't as much pressure. If I was all upset about not doing well on a test, she would just say, 'Do the best you can.' "

Many echoed her sentiments, saying that their mothers and fathers were "wiser than most." As one man reflected: "I'm sure a good deal more thought went into my upbringing than would have been the case if my parents had been twenty-five years old."

More Stable Families

"I always felt very secure as a teenager, because my parents were very stable in their relationship and work," said Maryann, from New York. "It was wonderful to have *real* parents rather than parents who acted like friends."

Older parents, whose marriages and careers are likely to be more stable, give their children a more secure and harmonious family environment than they could have offered a decade or more earlier. Because older mothers and fathers often have married later or been married longer than younger parents, the chances are good that they will bring their children into a stronger family relationship. The likelihood of divorce for couples in their late thirties or forties is significantly lower than it is for those in their twenties.

As Elizabeth, from San Diego, said: "My parents were mature, responsible, cautious people—the type to marry and start a family only after they felt that they were as ready as they could be. It seems only natural that their children might turn out differently from those of parents whose marriages and/or life situations weren't as stable."

But the best perspective on the relative merits and demerits of younger versus older parents was offered by a woman from West Airy, Pennsylvania: "It would be ideal to have the wisdom of a forty-year-old and the body of a twenty-year-old for a parent."

Parents' Professional and Economic Security

Later-born children often noted appreciatively that their parents were well established in careers and had the resources to provide material things that younger parents often could not give their children. This was true not only of couples with just one or two children but even of those with larger families. Because of their stage in life, older parents may not only be better off financially but also have more social prestige—making their children especially likely to admire them.

"My father, already long set in his career as a dentist, was able to spend a great deal of time with me, and my mother gave me her undivided attention," said a twenty-three-year-old New Yorker whose parents were forty-three and forty-nine when she was born.

Many successful professional parents may be wedded to their careers, leaving little time for their children, but another consequence of greater professional and financial security is greater flexibility in work schedules. This, in turn, may allow parents to spend more time or more "quality time" with their young children.

Older fathers—especially today, when parental sex roles have become less rigidly defined—may be likely to devote more time and attention to their children than do fathers in their early twenties. One study found that three times as many older fathers had regular responsibility for the care of a preschool child as did younger fathers.[4]

Time, in fact, may be the most precious commodity that older parents can give to their children. But even if they are busy and at the peak of their careers, at least they have the resources to provide nannies, baby-sitters, nursery schools, or other kinds of child care.

In families with one or at most two children, the picture of material privilege is particularly evident. These parents can often afford not only the best medical and child care but also more toys, outings, and trips. It would follow that the children of these financially more secure older parents are less likely to live in crowded apartments or houses. The chances of their having to share bedrooms with siblings are low, affording them more space and privacy than their younger-parented peers.

Nearly five out of six survey respondents who expressed an opinion said that they benefited during childhood from their parents' financial well-being. Perhaps because they were born during a boom era of American history, respondents who were under thirty were most emphatic about the impact that their parents' financial status had on them as they were growing up. Fifty-five percent felt that they had profited from having older, more economically secure mothers and fathers. Only 2 percent said that they had not.

These conclusions are consistent with data from the National Survey of Children, which include comparisons of children of parents over twenty-eight with the offspring of parents who were under twenty-one when their children were born. Half the "older" parents in this large-scale study said that their children took special classes or lessons in music or athletics, whereas the proportion among younger parents was about one-fourth.[5]

The economic advantages for these later-born children continue as they grow older. Their parents tend to be better able to send them to private schools; pay for piano, dance, or swimming lessons; take them on overseas vacations; buy them cars and expose them to more varied and culturally enriching experiences like concerts and plays. And if older parents are more likely to expect their children to go to college, they also seem to be in a better position to support their children's education.

Proud Parents and Wanted Children

"I was the apple of my parents' eyes," said a young woman from New Jersey. "Because of that I feel I developed a strong self-esteem and maturity unmatched among my peers."

Firstborn children of older parents, as we have seen, are frequently lavished with love, attention, and many of the advantages that money can buy. But other later-born children can also be especially wanted and are very much the focus of their parents' attention. For example, couples who successfully conceive a third or fourth child after their doctors tell them it would be dangerous to have any more will undoubtedly treat that child as all the more special.

Indeed, many later-born children recalled that their parents had devoted much time and attention to them during their childhood. Parental expectations were often high, but the payoff in terms of achievement generally seemed well worth the pressure.

"My parents took their parental role very seriously," said a woman from Madison, New Jersey, "and I felt great responsibility to achieve and please them."

Half of those surveyed had positive recollections of their mothers being very available and involved in helping them during childhood, whereas only one-fifth did not. And by a clear but somewhat smaller plurality (40 to 26 percent), respondents expressed positive childhood recollections of doing things with their parents.

The National Survey of Children corroborated many of these findings and impressions. The children of older mothers in its sample had higher average vocabulary scores and were more likely to be judged by both teachers and mothers as above-average students. Two-thirds of the older parents also expected that their children would finish college or go on to graduate or professional school, compared to only one-third of the parents who had their first child before age twenty-one. And one of the few studies of the effects of parents' age on their children found "positive relationships between maternal age and children's intellectual development" and even suggested that children of older mothers were likelier to have higher IQ scores.[6]

Midlife parents also may delight in their children for keeping them young. Having a child at forty may not only rejuvenate a person but confer a certain distinction analogous to being a still-successful athlete at forty in a sport filled with twenty-five-year-olds. Several later-born children remembered their parents' pride—not only in them but in the very fact of having borne children at a relatively advanced age. One man, for example, recalled his father, who was in his late fifties when his son was born, treating him as almost a badge of virility to be shown off to people in his hometown.

Too Doted On?

Does such parental largesse—emotionally and financially—however, carry the risk of "spoiling" or "overparenting" a child? Midlife parents may have more intense relationships with their children, lavishing them with love and attention. But does this mean that they are overly permissive? Or do they worry about their children's well-being and become overly protective? Or are they both?

Older parents, especially those who have small families, often unintentionally make their children feel too important in their lives. As a result their children may feel it necessary to create emotional distance between them and their parents.

"I always knew how important I was to them, that I completed their marriage," recalled Lisa, an adopted only child of older parents. "But it was burdensome."

Greater parental attention, while intellectually stimulating, can also be stifling, some child-development specialists warn.[7] Whereas some older mothers and fathers who have already had children may be more mellow and accepting of their later children, many first-time older parents may feel driven to produce "perfect" children. They may follow their children's every act, dote on them, and set unrealistically high expectations for them. And by treating their children as very special, parents also may make them feel somewhat odd, outsiders among their peers.

Perhaps because older mothers have waited so long to have children, frequently having endured miscarriages and fertility treatments, they may view motherhood with exaggerated reverence. And professional women who have had to be aggressive overachievers to succeed may transfer their desires for success and excellence to their children.

"Older parents may be more perfectionistic and care more about doing a perfect job," said Harvard pediatrician T. Berry Brazelton. "But there's a danger that the child may be a little bit overwhelmed and not allowed enough autonomy, which is part of growing up." Overindulgent parents, he added, may "hover" and expect too much of their children.[8]

Many later-born children recalled their parents as fearful

and overprotective. These mothers and fathers did not allow their children to do things that other children were permitted to do or let them discover the world on their own.

"I was an overprotected child," one woman said. "My parents were always afraid that something would happen to me. I couldn't go roller-skating until I was ten or eleven, and I wasn't allowed to go to summer camp."

∞

But, as a woman from Venice, California, concluded: "There are many ways in which being the child of older parents is an enriching experience, perhaps giving you added maturity and sensitivity. I did very well in school, as I had been trained in reading and other 'quiet' activities by my older parents, who weren't up to wild physical games and chases. I developed self-confidence from being taken seriously by adults I admired."

"Privilege," of course, does not exist in isolation in an individual's upbringing. Strong pros and cons in parent-child experiences often evolve together. For example, a generation gap, a sense of being different, material well-being, and devoted parents are not an unlikely combination. There are many themes and variations on being a child of older parents; which will be dominant depends not only on the parents and family circumstances but also on the child's perceptions.

14

Growing Up Fast?

"There's an old saying: 'Old people have old babies,'" recalled a New York man whose parents were in their mid-forties when he was born. "A friend once called me an old fogey. Ever since I was young, I was old. I had old attitudes and a sedate look about me. I was always the one who could buy the liquor, because I acted older. As a young actor I always played old men. I think I grew up old."

Many adult children of older parents declared that they "grew up fast" and that, during childhood, they felt older than their years. They were "cheated out of childhood" and felt that they were treated like adults and given more responsibility than their friends with younger parents.

Through the pattern of their lives and interests, older fathers and mothers contributed to their children's accelerated maturity. These parents often communicated with their sons and daughters in more "adult" ways, and their children frequently had greater exposure to more mature adults—people at least their parents' age. Older, more settled parents, it seemed, were involved in more "serious" and "mature" pastimes, like reading or listening to classical music, and these interests were frequently passed on to their children. Higher parental expectations and increased responsibilities because of parents' illnesses or deaths were among the reasons given by latecomers for their premature maturity. The perception of entering an adult world at an early age was also widely viewed as affecting interpersonal relationships with both peers and older people.

Premature Maturity

Over and over, children of older parents said that their mothers' and fathers' ages and maturity affected their own maturity. They remembered themselves as more grown-up than other children, and as youngsters they often felt like "little adults." But this premature maturity took a wide variety of forms.

"Growing up surrounded by older people pushed me to act in ways they defined as 'mature' and to express myself in ways that would please them," wrote a woman from Washington, D.C.

Andrea, from Hayward, California, also felt that she "probably became adult too fast." "I was cheated out of my childhood. Because I was surrounded by older people, older people were my models. When I was fourteen, on the telephone, I know I sounded like an adult. I felt more mature than my peers, but it wasn't necessarily good for me. Since kids are basically conformists, I didn't like feeling different."

Many latecomers said that they saw the world from a more mature perspective than their peers did because they tended to be around grown-ups more and frequently found themselves in more formal, adult social situations. They described themselves as emotionally and intellectually more comfortable with adults and more awkward in the company of people their own ages.

The family environment itself—from parents' behavior and tastes to their social circles and economic status—often suggested greater maturity than did the family circumstances of children with younger parents. Even children who were ostensibly of the same generation—siblings and cousins, neighbors' children and the children of their parents' friends—were usually older. This exposure to older children, they speculated, contributed further to their maturity and made them more open to people beyond their immediate age cohort.

Parental expectations about what a child could or should do at different ages could also be very high. If children were given the message that they should always do better, "more advanced" work in school or other competitive settings, it is likely that they would feel psychologically "more advanced." A fifth-grader driven to perform at an eighth-grade level might be no more emotionally mature than other fifth-graders but would inevitably feel in some ways "beyond" his or her peers.

A college student from Amherst, Massachusetts, remembered a specific set of pressures. Her parents pushed her to start reading early. "They got tired of speaking in monosyllables," she said. "People told me that, as a child, I was a good conversationalist. I think my social skills with adults were overdeveloped."

One woman who became a bank executive expressed what many of these "driven" later-born children felt: "I got the message that I was intended to go on to something of merit."

Maturity was accelerated in yet another way. Older parents may be more protective, but they may also hurry their children toward adulthood by treating them as particularly responsible, self-reliant, and grown-up. They may have expected their poised little eight-year-old to accompany them, in jacket and tie, to a cocktail party of business associates, or they may have been more likely than younger parents to let their children take plane trips or go on other outings on their own at an early age.

"They encouraged us to be more independent, directly and indirectly, and allowed me to do things that other parents didn't," said Sally, who grew up in Philadelphia. "For example, I wanted to visit my relatives on Long Island when I was eleven. It was pretty unheard of to take the train alone to New York at that age. I insisted, and my mother said it was OK. I later learned that she had talked to the conductor before. But there was a trust there. We were never given curfews. We were told to use our own good judgment."

And a Massachusetts woman summarized these feelings: "If our family was different in any way from my friends', it was in the degree of responsible self-sufficiency that we were taught."

"My parents always reasoned with me, and they treated things a little more seriously than other parents did," added Martha, an only child who grew up in Brooklyn. "They always tried to foster my being sensitive to other people's needs, and that I should be polite and grateful."

Maturity was foisted on some last-born children, who felt that their mothers and fathers were relatively uninvolved in their upbringing. In such cases they were forced to make their own way in the world from an early age. Other tail-end children said that they became "older" faster because they were exposed not only to older adults but also to siblings ten or fifteen years older.

As a Virginia woman recalled, "My mother left me more on my own than other parents did. She played no role in encouraging me to become involved in high-school organizations or helping me with my college decision. She didn't object or approve. Her attitude was, 'It's your business.'' I might have wanted her to be more involved, but I was more self-reliant, and it did make me grow up faster.''

And for some children of older parents, early maturity came as a result of family responsibilities they had to shoulder early in life, when their mothers or fathers became seriously ill or died.

"I had to assume an adult role when I was seven or eight, by having to take care of my mother,'' said a woman who was adopted when her mother was fifty. When she was a child, her mother had already become ill. "When she fell, which she frequently did, I'd have to take care of her, and I'd call my father to have him come home from work. I was becoming a parent to my mother, and it made me a confidante to my father.''

Indeed, older parents occasionally—and perhaps inappropriately—were said to treat their children more as confidants than as sons or daughters. As a thirty-two-year-old Los Angeles filmmaker recalled: "They confided in me as a child about their economic and physical situation, in ways that were really none of my business. They treated me more as a peer than their child, and I had more of an adult understanding of their personal situation. In hindsight, it strikes me as bizarre.''

But maturity also took a toll, particularly in adolescence. One consequence of seeming older than their years—in values and behavior, interests and experiences—was that latecomers often felt different and isolated. They saw themselves, or were seen by peers, as "old fogeys.'' They may have been stars of the debating team or officers of the student council, yet they were far removed from the "in'' crowd. As one man said, "My identity in high school was that of a mature person. I always did well and had leadership positions. I didn't smoke or drink or hang out. People characterized me as very responsible, but also probably as old and dull.''

Such perceptions even continued well into adulthood. "The main thing that bothered me about having older parents was that everybody thought I was older,'' said a middle-aged woman named Hope. "When people learned that my mother was in her eighties, they thought I must be in my fifties, when I was actually in my forties.''

Being cast into maturity early in life carried with it another emotional double edge. "Little adults" they may have been, but many were also the perpetually pampered children or the serious, adultlike youngsters yearning to be just a child. They learned how to handle the adult world as children, but their exposure to the childhood world of play and freedom from responsibility were limited. Never entirely children when they were young, they often described themselves as having a childlike side as adults. Thus, in certain ways, the price of their maturity as children turned out to be a sort of immaturity when they were older.

"Sometimes I think that people with older parents tend to be more grown-up," said a Milwaukee woman. "But at other times, when they don't get their way—maybe because they're more spoiled—they fall back to acting like children who don't get their way."

Charles, an only child of much older parents, who grew up in Philadelphia, also tried to explain this seemingly paradoxical but common emotional state of affairs. "I think I had a greater maturity prematurely because I was around older people and was instilled with older values. But I also think I had a greater immaturity for my age as a result of being in a cocoon, of not having to develop in a lot of ways."

A Lifetime of Relationships

Many later-born children drew a connection between their growing up too fast and the kinds of interpersonal relationships with which they were most comfortable. They not only felt more at ease with people older than themselves but sometimes felt alienated from people their own age. Compared with their peers, they said that they had more older friends. Several women suggested that they had married, or always been attracted to, considerably older men because their fathers were much older.

"There were a lot of older people around when I was growing up, so I related more with my parents' peers than my own," said an only child of two much-older professional parents. "Even now, I relate a lot better with older people. I have a greater understanding of how they feel and their viewpoints. It's an understanding I don't see my peers having as well."

Later-born children also frequently claimed to have greater empathy and compassion for the elderly than their peers did. They attributed their presumed empathy to being more conscious of aging in their parents, and having had more contact with elderly grandparents and other relatives at earlier stages in their lives.

"I never ran away from old people or had a fear of them, like so many children have," said the daughter of a forty-year-old mother. "Society tends to downplay old people, but because I knew my parents were older, I could never do that."

"I think I'm less 'agist' than many other people," ventured a twenty-seven-year-old Midwestern woman. "I don't have stereotyped views of people based on their ages."

∞

Although having older parents and relatives often made people more sympathetic and better able to relate to older people, sometimes the effect was quite the opposite.

Connie, a forty-two-year-old therapist in Rhode Island, was offered a job in gerontology and turned it down because "my parents and all my relatives are in their upper seventies or eighties and have health problems. I felt I'd had enough of older people."

The flip side of feeling more comfortable with their elders was that many did not feel particularly comfortable around children. Some spoke disdainfully of "childish" behavior, even by children, or said that they always thought that children were "silly." Because of such feelings, several opted to remain childless.

"I always got along much better with older people, and I never could relate to little kids," said a forty-year-old single woman from Wisconsin. "I really don't know how to talk to them. I never felt I would be a very good mother, so I just didn't have children."

"Kids bored me when I was a child," said another woman, whose siblings were from eleven to twenty years old when she was born. "I didn't go for that play stuff. I spent more time with adults. I was fascinated listening to adults and watching them. I think I respect and can understood older people better than most, because my parents were older. And I've always enjoyed going to nursing homes and visiting with older people."

∞

But how did these "little adults" relate to their peers? While many later-born children felt less socially adept in relationships with people their own age and found it difficult to form close ties, others plunged into friendships and romantic relationships to fill an emotional void resulting from their parents being distant and uninvolved, or having died early in their lives.

"Since I grew up with adults, I didn't get along well with my peers," recalled a woman from Baton Rouge, Louisiana. "They picked on me physically and emotionally. I had no idea what it was like to dish it back and fight for myself. So I would sometimes follow the grass patterns at recess to amuse myself. I was always the last picked to be on someone's team. Those things didn't do much for my self-esteem. But my mother's attention and abundance of love gave me a very strong sense of self. This security helped me withstand the cruel teasing."

The specific circumstances that fostered or necessitated growing up fast also had an effect on relationships. As a Madison, Wisconsin, woman suggested: "If you have to deal with the death of a parent when you're young, it can create a kind of maturity and lead you to seek other kinds of security or stability earlier— through a relationship, spiritual things, or making a lot of money. It was part of the reason why I married young. I longed for a close relationship. I wasn't so consciously looking for a husband as for a close relationship."

Occasionally the lingering effects of childhood losses contributed to a pronounced fear of losing others who were close. A woman whose father died after a protracted illness when she was fourteen spoke of years of pain that colored all her relationships. "I was constantly afraid that people would go away forever, that relationships were transient. In my romantic relationships, it was very important that people didn't go away from me."

Conversely, others suggested that children of older parents might be better able to handle interpersonal commitments and have more faith in the institution of marriage because their parents were likely to have had long, stable marriages.

Whereas some women sought relationships with "high-energy, powerful" men, as one said, perhaps to compensate for their fathers' lack of energy, others said that having an older father made them more likely to be attracted to older men. As a woman from the Philippines commented, "I was very fond of my father, and thus felt comfortable with older men. I twice married men considerably older than myself. I wasn't looking for a father, as the cliché would have it, but simply liked spending time with men I respected and could learn from."

A final twist concerning relationships was the observation that children of older parents choose other children of older parents as friends. Some speculated that this common denominator in their backgrounds made them more compatible.

"If I were to really think hard about it, I suspect I might discover that many of the children, and later, teenagers who were my friends had something in their personalities that attracted me that indirectly stemmed from their having older parents." This woman was not alone in noting, too, that her husband was a child of older parents and that this factor strengthened the bond between them.

∞

Whether or not parents' ages affect personality in clearly defined ways that shape interpersonal relationships, it appears that having older parents frequently scripts the maturational process. The repeatedly noted effect of feeling older than their years and of having a more serious childhood, however, clearly did define a different kind of life experience and affect how later-born children related to people of different ages. This fast track to adulthood often meant missing out on some of the playfulness of childhood, facing high parental expectations, and becoming self-reliant earlier in life. This, in turn, led many to feel less in tune with their peers and greater kindred with people older than themselves.

15

Facing Mortality

Late children, says the Spanish proverb, are early orphans.
— *Benjamin Franklin, Letter to John Alleyn*

Perhaps the biggest—yet least easily articulated—issue for children of older parents is the sometimes barely-conscious yet gnawing fear that they will lose their parents much earlier in life than other children. They often feel aware of their parents' mortality to a much greater extent than do children whose parents are ten to twenty years younger. In young adulthood such fears may lead to the grim conclusion that they will probably live more of their lives without their mothers and fathers.

"I was always afraid of my parents' dying, and I read obituaries almost daily to see what ages people were at death," recalled a woman from Richmond, Virginia, whose parents were forty-two and fifty-two when she was born. "Those I found that were older than my parents gave me a victory. Those that were younger frightened me."

Psychologists say that it is common for children to have fears or nightmares about their parents dying, yet for children of older parents, the fears are frequently vividly remembered and have long-lasting effects. Many of those who were interviewed or surveyed spoke of recurrent or unremitting fears that their parents would die. Such fears were simply but movingly expressed by the eleven-year-old girl from Washington State who wrote: "My dad is going to die before everyone else's dad dies."

When death actually strikes a parent of a later-born child, it also may reinforce a feeling of being cheated by fate. "When my mother died when I was twenty-eight, it hit home that she was older," said a woman whose mother was forty-two when she was born. "I remember my brother, who is thirteen years

120

older, saying to me, 'How many guys are lucky enough to have their mother live till they're in their forties?' And I started crying and said, 'Yeah, isn't that great. She isn't going to be there when I'm forty.''

If parents die earlier in one's life, "it also brings our own mortality closer at a much younger age," added a woman from Rhode Island. "On the one hand, we say, 'We have more than half our lives to go.' And on the other hand, we say, 'We're next.' "

Whereas only one-fourth of the questionnaire respondents described concerns during adolescence about their parents' health, in adulthood, this proportion jumped to more than 50 percent. And when asked about specific interests or concerns relating to their parents' ages, more people (22 percent) mentioned that they feared or had experienced their parents' physical decline or death than any other issue. Such concerns were most pronounced among people in their twenties; 36 percent of the youngest respondents indicated that this was a principal consequence of being a child of older parents.

This issue was even more on the minds of children of much-older parents. Twenty-six percent of those born to women forty or older mentioned such concerns, compared with 17 percent of children of thirty-five- to thirty-nine-year-old mothers, and 29 percent of children of over-fifty fathers cited them, compared with 21 percent of the survey respondents born when their fathers were thirty-five to forty-nine.

A Childhood of Fears

Even for those who had never really thought of their mothers and fathers as older, illness can suddenly make children all too aware of their parents' mortality, and make them feel as if they too have aged. Fears that a parent may die obviously may be triggered or greatly exacerbated by serious or chronic illnesses. The details of parents' heart attacks, bouts with tuberculosis, or diagnoses of cancer were remembered with chilling precision by many children. Fears and prayers sparked by illness loomed large in many memories.

"My father had a heart attack when I was eight and had heart trouble for seventeen years, until he died," recalled Eleanor, a psychologist from New Jersey. "His illnesses overshadowed my childhood. I always worried that he might die at any minute. From a very young age, I was taking care of him, and I felt that I couldn't upset him because I was very fearful about his health."

Some children of older parents recalled being terrified even by relatively minor ailments. They would listen attentively yet with trepidation each time their mothers or fathers coughed too long or were out of breath. Some would watch, with the eyes of a spy, to be sure that a sleeping parent's stomach was moving up and down.

Many whose parents were perfectly healthy still felt that their mothers and fathers were more fragile and more likely to die. One woman, for example, wrote, "I was often afraid that I could anger them to the point of a heart attack."

Parents also can fuel children's fears not only by actual medical problems but by morbid comments about their age, health, and mortality. Several children of older parents recalled their mothers or fathers saying that they didn't think they would survive to raise their children to adulthood. One woman said that she was "constantly worried" that her mother would not survive long because her mother told her "I needed to be strong in case she died."

"My mother told me several times when I was an adult that she never expected to live long enough to see me graduate from high school," wrote another woman, who added, with a droll sense of humor: "This reflected more her concern for her health than for my scholastic abilities."

Early Loss and Young Survivors

Children of older parents obviously do face a greater statistical risk during their childhood or adolescence of having one or both parents die. That was especially true in the past, when life expectancies were decades shorter than they are in the late twentieth century. The combined effects of later childbearing and shorter life expectancies are illustrated in the biographies of many famous children of older parents.

Marya Nikolayevna Volkonskaya, the thirty-eight-year-old mother of Leo Tolstoy, died when her son was two, and Susannah Wedgwood Darwin, who was forty-four when her son Charles was born, died when he was eight. Both children were said to have been haunted by the memories of their dying mothers.

Augustine Washington, a thirty-seven-year-old when his son George was born, died eleven years later, leaving the future "father of America" to grow up with a half-brother fourteen years his senior. Similarly, Wilbur and Orville Wright, whose mother was thirty-six and forty when they were born, were consumed by the tragedy of their mother's slow death during their teens.

Although today most later-born children in their twenties and thirties have living mothers and fathers, significant numbers do experience the early death of a parent. As a New Jersey woman, whose father died when she was eight, said: "It's an unfortunately common happening for children like us."

Many explicitly said that because their mothers and fathers were older when they were born, they had fewer years in which their parents were alive than others did.

These children had to deal with powerful and complex feelings of grief and helplessness, which are difficult at any age. In addition, bereavement in childhood often is linked to adolescent and adult emotional distress. The immediate and short-term effects of loss can include feelings of betrayal, anger, and vulnerability and can result in difficulty making emotional attachments as well as insomnia and hyperactivity. The death of a parent "strikes a blow to the child's developing sense of trust and self-esteem, causing feelings of powerlessness and shame," according to family therapist Claudia Jewett.[1] It may also disrupt "the sense that events are predictable and meaningful."

If a parent dies during a young child's time of so-called magical thinking, the child may blame him- or herself. He or she may painfully wonder, What did I do to be punished like this? And many children who have lost a parent remain neurotically bound to the dead parent, their emotional lives filled with dreams and fantasies of what might have been. Regrets were frequently expressed that they were never really able to get to know or become close to a parent who died when they were young.

As many respondents suggested, a bereaved child is likely to feel jealous or bitter toward peers whose parents are alive and healthy. Their friends may feel uncomfortable with them or, at best, they may simply be unable to comprehend the pain or grief.

"I was robbed by them dying so young," said a Fort Lauderdale, Florida, woman whose mother died when she was eleven.

"Everyone has parents but me! I resent it. It took me years to learn not to blame them."

And Maryann, whose seventy-three-year-old father died when she was sixteen, said: "I was the first one to lose a parent within our extended family and among my friends. I felt very cheated, that this shouldn't happen to someone my age. My aunt and uncle, who had been married much longer than my parents, didn't really realize how devastated I was or how lonely the house was."

Many later-born children spoke sadly of feeling especially alone and alienated from their peers because their parents and so many of their relatives had died comparatively early in their lives.

"One of our big social events was going to funerals," recalled Arlene, a therapist in a northeastern city. "My brother died when I was four; my father died when I was twelve, and my aunts and uncles all died in my childhood. It certainly made me feel different from other kids."

A child whose parent dies is also faced with the pain and confusion of the other parent's bereavement. The surviving parent may be so caught up with personal grief that children inadvertently get shunted to the periphery. On the other hand, the mother or father who is living may cast the child, consciously or unconsciously, into many of the roles of the deceased spouse. The children may have to prepare meals, take care of siblings, become their parent's confidant, or go to work to help support the family.

∞

"Perhaps the greatest problem I experienced was my father's inability during my adolescence to relate to what I was going through because he was still grieving for the loss of my mother," said Lisa, from Venice, California, whose mother died when she was fourteen. "He was trying to be both father and mother to a normally difficult adolescent—and it must have been tough for him."

A man from Riverdale, New York, felt that his father's death when he was fifteen made it harder for him to be close to his mother. "I found it difficult to share my feelings and thoughts with her because I figured they would upset her," he wrote, adding that he believed the gap between him and his mother widened after his father died.

In some cases children may be drawn closer to their surviving parent, but that can lead to further difficulties. "It threw the natural balance of the family unit off, and all the energy of love flowed between just me and my mother," recalled Tracey, whose father died when she was seven, after her two older siblings had already grown up and moved out of the house. "I resented my mother's constant interference and scrutiny. I felt the need to be alone a lot more than other kids, just so that I could breathe."

The surviving parent also may be resented for outliving the other. "I was real mad at my father for a long time," said a New York photographer who was sixteen when her mother died of cancer. "I blamed him at some level for her death because I was very close to my mother."

Long-lived Parents

Premature death, of course, can strike anyone, as can the blessing of longevity. A young parent can die at twenty-five in an auto accident, just as an older parent can live to be a hundred or more. Such alternately cruel and kind quirks of fate are illustrated by examples from history and were also pointed out by several latecomers whose mothers or fathers survived well into their children's fifties or sixties.

Alexander Graham Bell's mother, Eliza Grace Symonds, who was thirty-eight when he was born, lived well into old age—long enough to see her already famous son achieve world renown as the inventor of the telephone. Maria Aleksandrovna Blank also lived nearly half a century after giving birth to her later-born son; but this devoted, long-suffering mother died a year before the Bolshevik Revolution brought her son—under the nom de guerre of Vladimir Ilyitch Lenin—to power at the head of the newly formed Soviet Union.

More-striking examples were offered by several of those interviewed or surveyed. Linda, a forty-two-year-old from North Carolina, for instance, said that her eighty-year-old mother was in excellent health and still working more than full-time. And a fifty-eight-year-old woman from Indiana reported that her mother, past ninety-six, continued to tend to a business.

"There Was a Lot of Death . . ."

Even if their parents live well into old age, children of older parents are still more likely to find their lives tinged by death. Because their grandparents as well as aunts and uncles are inevitably older than the norm, later-born children may well lose other relatives comparatively early in their lives. These grim odds were confirmed by many who recalled childhoods filled with funerals and wakes. They grimly ticked off all the deaths they had experienced and said that they expected to lose most of their remaining older relatives by their late thirties.

"There was a lot of death while I was growing up," said one Midwestern woman. "During grade school it seemed like someone in my mother's family died every year."

"The losses came in regular cycles," added a twenty-nine-year-old New Yorker. "First my great-grandmother, then my grandfather when I was nine. Then my father, when I was fourteen. Now I'm dealing with being the conservator of an aunt who is dying in a nursing home and another aunt in remission for breast cancer. My uncle has skin cancer, and my one remaining grandmother is ninety and in a nursing home. And my mother is in remission from Hodgkin's lymphoma. I'm dealing with the possibility of five very close family members dying in the next ten years."

A somewhat older woman from Southern California reflected on the pervasiveness of death in her early life and the effects of losing most of her extended family: "My relatives of my parents' generation were lost to me while I was still quite young. Now I am in my forties and have few relatives left alive. Early experiences with death and loss have deepened me and perhaps made me more sensitive to other people's pain, but these were difficult experiences for a young person to go through."

∞

Everyone inevitably confronts the death of parents and others close to them. However, in modern times that usually happens in adulthood, when one is presumably better equipped to cope with loss. But what are the effects of facing mortality and being conscious of death as a child or teenager, as happens all too often for latecomers? Undoubtedly a child's blissful sense of timelessness and immortality is prematurely destroyed, and he or she will feel angry, guilty, vulnerable, and alone in the world. Does the personal reality of death in the family bring philosophical issues to the surface? Are feelings of vulnerability generalized?

∞

It certainly would not be surprising if such children were more pensive, morbid, and morose. It also follows that people whose childhoods were marked by loss would have lives more colored by sadness. But does that translate into a higher incidence of long-term depression? From latecomers' recollections, it seems that there is a heightened sensitivity to the fragility of life and the specter of death, yet darker questions about lasting effects on mood and mental health remain to be explored.

V

The Child as Adult

16
Family Lives, Family Responsibilities
Two Case Histories—Jack and Kathryn

The combinations and interactions of many issues described in preceding chapters can be seen in the following stories of Jack and Kathryn. They especially illustrate how the effects and perceived importance of parents' ages and family circumstances evolve over the years. (Being a later-born child can have one set of meanings in childhood and a completely different emotional impact later in life.) They also bring into focus the inescapable reality that children of older parents often must confront their parents' needs for care and mortality earlier in life than most people. Even if their fathers and mothers do not die when they are relatively young, fears about their parents' deaths and practical caregiving responsibilities often make them feel that their youth is cut short.

Jack

Jack—a chemist living in a large Midwestern city—was born when his father was forty-two and his mother was forty-one. His two sisters were twelve and eight when he was born, and the reason he was born, he said, was that his father just wouldn't give up on the idea of having a son. Consequently, Jack always thought of himself as a tail-end child.

For him, however, the impact of his parents' relatively advanced ages was not principally that they had less energy or more conservative, old-fashioned values. Instead, the major effects of having older parents resulted from what he considered his peculiar family constellation.

131

Jack believes his parents had wearied of parenting by the time he came along. "I felt like they had done everything before I was born," he said. "I was jealous that other kids would come back from summer vacations. My parents had taken trips with my sisters, but all their money was going for their mortgage, so they didn't do things like that when I was growing up."

When his sisters were children, their grandparents were still alive, but all the grandparents had died before Jack was born. Indeed, his experience of family life was different not only *from* his sisters' but *because* of his sisters. They both married when they were teenagers, leaving Jack a de facto "only child" by the time he was ten.

"Instead of growing up with my sisters, I was growing up with their children—my nieces and nephews," he said. "I was an uncle by the time I was in third or fourth grade. I was kind of proud at first, but the pride wore off real fast.

"I had grandchildren competing with me for my parents' attention. And I had a lot of bad experiences growing up with my nephews. It really soured my outlook on children." (Years later, he noted, it took a lot of convincing by his wife for him to agree to have children.)

Because Jack's father worked night shifts at a local factory and his mother didn't drive, his mother also became dependent on him after his sisters left home. "For many years, I became my mother's husband, doing errands for her," he said. "It became a sore point between my mother and me when I moved out of the house. All of a sudden she realized she was going to lose this, and she became resentful of my having a life of my own."

He recalled that, with his older parents, older sisters, and other older relatives, he was always around adults as a child. "I think I had an older view of things for my age. My wife always laughs when she tells the story of our first date. Her mother had told her that I was too old for her. Two dates later she learned that she was actually older than I was. They thought I was in my forties, when I was really under twenty-five."

Just as he had played the part of uncle at ten, his mother's confidant and chauffeur at sixteen, and the middle-aged suitor at twenty-four, Jack found himself faced with caring for an aging parent in his early thirties.

"My mother had always been in excellent health, so I was

really surprised when I got the phone call at midnight that Mom [was] dead," he recalled. His sisters, who had always received a lot more assistance from their parents than he had, were totally unable to deal with their mother's death or their father's needs, he said. "My middle sister tried to commit suicide after my mother died. And my other sister, who is divorced and living with someone, was off on a camping trip with this guy, and when Mom died, we couldn't get hold of them. When she was told, she was a total wreck for weeks, and she's barely ever visited my dad."

Just before Jack's mother died, his father became quite ill. He had a history of cardiovascular problems going back to the days when Jack was a teenager. But now—when Jack was thirty-two, shortly after his own son was born—his father was diagnosed as having cancer of the colon.

He was successfully operated on but subsequently became very dependent on his son, since his daughters seemed to lack the ability or interest to help him.

"Since my mother died, I've been over to my father's house almost every day," Jack said. "My sisters just won't do it.

"It makes me feel very tired. I won't say 'used,' but that's what it is. I really don't have a chance to live my own life and do what I want to do. I went to a seminar on aging parents. Everyone was between their late forties and sixties. I was the only one in their early thirties."

Kathryn

"My parents never gave me a straight answer about how old they were," recalled Kathryn, a thirty-four-year-old nurse who grew up in Pennsylvania. It wasn't until her teens that she even learned that her mother had been married before and that both she and her sister had been born when their parents were in their late thirties.

Her father, an army man, was "happy, loving, and very gentle," she said. "He went to work and came home and watched TV and never said too much. My mother was generally pretty easygoing, but she really ran the house. She managed the money, and she'd be the one to yell if my sister or I did anything wrong.

"As a child, I always kept to myself, so I didn't really have a lot of experience with other people's families," she continued. "I didn't think about [mine] being older or that [my parents] were different from other parents until I was a teenager."

But in junior high school she started comparing herself to her classmates, and began to realize that her family experience was quite different from that of her peers.

"I remember meeting another girl's parents and saying to her, 'Gee, your parents are awfully young. My mom's fifty-something.' And she said, 'My mom's thirty-five. Wow, your parents are old!'"

Suddenly Kathryn began to feel that her family wasn't "normal." This, in turn, made her acutely aware of other ways in which her life seemed different because her parents were older.

"My friends had grandparents and I didn't," she recalled. Two of her grandparents had died before she was born, and the other two died by the time she was seven. "I never really knew them. I missed the experiences that other kids had, of going to Grandma's and Grandpa's."

Her parents weren't as strict as other parents, she said, but her father seemed much more protective. "He never wanted us to iron or do housework, and he didn't want us to play hard— I guess, because he was afraid we would get hurt. I think they figured that, since they couldn't have any more children, they had to be careful with us."

Kathryn's mother and father also were very careful about money. Although they didn't talk much about their youth, they had grown up during the depression, and it clearly influenced their values. Even though most families in their neighborhood were also struggling financially, none seemed as "security conscious" as hers, she said. "My mother would say how she only had two dresses and one cloth doll when she was a child, and that she had to go out at an early age to do housework. It made her always very tight with money."

Kathryn's parents both liked to sing, and they encouraged her to participate in high-school choirs, she said, "but they didn't do a lot of things with us. They were kind of tired. While other kids' parents would take them someplace, to a show or to New York, we rarely even went to a movie. And some kids would go out and play tennis with their parents, but I couldn't do that."

If it had just been a matter of not playing tennis, Kathryn

wouldn't really have cared so much, she said. But the physical differences between her parents and her friends' parents became clear in much more significant ways.

"My mother was going through menopause during my teen-age years," she said. "Then my father got hit with renal failure in his early fifties. He was on kidney dialysis for three years. He fell one day and had hematoma, and he died soon after. I felt cheated that he died so young, and I resented all my friends, whose parents were alive."

Because her father had come from a large family, Kathryn had many aunts and uncles while she was growing up. But when he died, "they stopped coming around," she said. "They didn't want to see my mother. And because they were older, they all died when I was in my twenties."

She also regretted that she had been too young to ask her father much about himself or his past. "So when he died, a lot of my ancestry and different things about family history kind of got lost," she said.

Just before her father became ill, her sister had gotten pregnant, at age fifteen. She "rejected her child," leaving Kathryn and her mother to take care of the baby. "My mother's focus was on the baby, so I was kind of left alone," Kathryn said. "I had to go out and find the world, and I had to mature on my own."

The combination of her father's illness and death and her being essentially alone—without the support of her mother, sister, or relatives—did take its toll. "I got involved in a cult," she said, "but I discovered it wasn't any good for me, so then I joined this new-age religious group.

"When my father died, I was a novice in a religious order in Boston," she recalled. "At first I said to my mother, 'I have to finish my training; I can't come home.' But I felt very guilty that I was leaving her alone, especially since she had my niece, who was having behavior problems. I loved living in Boston, but I decided to come home."

Kathryn has lived with her mother and niece for much of the last decade. She became closer to her mother but resented spending most of her twenties helping to raise her sister's child. Her niece also became pregnant as a teenager, so now that baby also lives with them. And recently her mother developed myasthenia gravis, a potentially crippling autoimmune disease.

"It's not fair," she said. "I'm probably going to have an invalid on my hands in a few years. My sister has a husband and three children, so I'm going to be the one with the responsibilities for my mother. Most people my age are getting their lives together. They have families and houses. And even if they're single, they've probably built up savings."

"I have none of that. I've had to help my niece, and now my mother, and I'm trying to get through school. Will caring for my mother at home hinder me from having the career I want? And here I am, unmarried; I'm going to be alone. If I can just get through school and get some stability and money before anything happens to my mother.

"My friends all say: Get out; you have your own life to live. But I can't."

As she finished talking, Kathryn opened an old photo album. There were many pictures of her as a child with her parents and aunts and uncles. But then the family chronicle ended abruptly. "I don't remember taking pictures when I was older," she said. "By the time they were in their fifties, we didn't do things. Then my sister got pregnant and my father got sick. Although I didn't think about my parents' ages when I was a child, I'm sure now that my life would have been a lot different if they had been younger."

17

Youth Foreshortened

In spite of my great love for my parents, I regret having to
be caught in the world of the old before my time. Their
age accelerated my maturity and still does. I had too little
time to be playful. And, too early, I became the parent of
my parents.

These feelings, recorded by a woman from
Westport, Ontario, were common among children of older parents. All too often, the fears of childhood and adolescence turn
into very concrete problems in young adulthood. Whereas conventional wisdom about stages in the life cycle suggests that
an individual's twenties and thirties are a time to "find oneself,"
have fun, pursue career goals, and establish homes and families,
later-born children frequently have other items thrust onto their
agendas.

Indeed, their agendas often resemble those of people ten
or fifteen years older. Many daughters and sons of older parents
must assume the role of caring for elderly, ailing parents at a
time when their friends are devoting their energies to jobs, relationships, travel, and their spouses and children. It is most common for people to provide emotional and physical assistance
to aging parents during their forties and fifties, yet later-born
children may be barely out of college when their parents are
nearing retirement or in declining health. As more age-appropriate concerns get shunted aside, later-borns often feel as if youth
has been lost or foreshortened.

"I am amazed when my friends speak of their parents, who
are still for the most part young, vital, and independent," wrote
a thirty-two-year-old from Idaho who takes care of her mother.

"None of my peers has elderly parents whose health is fail-
ing, who are dying by inches," added a forty-year-old woman

whose parents are in their eighties. "What people normally experience in their fifties and sixties, I've been experiencing since my early thirties."

And a Massachusetts man bitterly reflected: "My father died when I was twenty-eight, and my mother is now in a nursing home with Alzheimer's disease at the age of seventy-five, while my friends' parents are enjoying their grandchildren."

Such experiences, of losing a parent or seeing a parent's health deteriorate while peers' parents were in good health, were mentioned over and over. As one woman summed up: "I feel off sync with everyone, and I miss the fact that my parents and I didn't have an adulthood together."

This is certainly quite different from children of younger parents, whose families are more likely to be intact and who may be building adult friendships with their mothers and fathers during their twenties and thirties, inviting them to parties or going on trips with them.

Those whose parents died when they were children or teenagers invariably felt that their circumstances afforded them little time for self-discovery—much less fun—during their twenties. Youth, for them, was not foreshortened; it was all but nonexistent.

"Other people, I think, are less aware that time really flies," said a thirty-year-old only child whose parents both died after protracted illnesses during her twenties. "I'm a lot more conscious of time and how it seems shorter. I think more about the long term and where I'm headed in a broad way, and what I want to accomplish by a certain age."

Because of this sense that their young adulthood has been, or may be, cut short, many latecomers feel they must try to squeeze in as many experiences as possible with their mothers and fathers. Both children and parents often experience a poignant yet generally unspoken awareness that, for them, time is limited or passing more quickly.

These children know that they will have less time with their parents than most people. Since the risk of losing a parent in early adulthood is naturally greater for children of older parents, there may be fewer years in which their lives will overlap, compared to parents and children who are closer in age. Thus children may feel wistful about not knowing their fathers and mothers in their prime, and both children and parents may develop a keen sense of time and its passage.

One young woman from Brooklyn, whose parents were forty-six and fifty-one when she was born, said that she would not take jobs in other parts of the country because she did not want to be far from her mother and father. Her simply stated reason: "I feel I may not have much time with them."

And many children of older parents would agree with a Los Angeles woman in her mid-twenties, who said, "I think I'll miss my parents when they're gone more than my peers will their parents, just because I expect I'll lose mine when I'm much younger."

This anticipation of early loss may make them feel an "urgency to get to know [their parents] more closely," as a West Virginia woman wrote. Unlike her peers in their early thirties, she felt a strong need to know what her parents' "childhoods were like, how they met, what their struggles were . . . before they are dead or senile."

One silver lining in this scenario, suggested by a forty-three-year-old woman whose mother is now eighty-four, is that a later-born child may begin to develop a mature, adult friendship with his or her parents sooner than people whose parents are younger and who have the luxury of time. If parents are older and "start getting sick or frail," she said, "there's an awful lot that binds you to them, whether you love it or hate it. It happened for me much younger than my friends, and, in a strange way, I think it's a benefit of having older parents. I love the rich, rich relationship I have with my mother."

∞

The pressure to accelerate their own life clock can have many other effects on children of older parents. They may feel a need to marry and have children earlier than they might have wished, so that their parents will have grandchildren or their children may avoid the problems they faced.

They may drive themselves to accomplish things at work and in life at an unrealistic, breakneck pace, so that their parents will have been able to see their successes and achievements. Not achieving these goals by their accelerated deadlines—or taking "time off"—may lead to feelings of guilt.

Later-born children also may feel selfish if they don't settle down, start working, and have a family before their parents retire. The idea of being supported by parents while going to graduate school or until making a late start on a career may foster much more guilt and unease in a twenty-eight-year-old child of seventy-year-old parents than in a twenty-eight-year-old whose parents are in their fifties.

A twenty-nine-year-old woman from New Jersey said that she moved up her wedding date because her seventy-one-year-old mother was suddenly diagnosed as having a brain tumor. "She aged overnight and has deteriorated greatly. My fiancé and I decided to set our wedding date after three of our four parents were in the hospital in the same year. We had not planned to get married as soon as we did."

A young woman from Louisiana who was expecting her first child lamented that—compared with other young mothers—she probably would not get as much help with the baby from her own widowed mother, who was nearly seventy and "physically unable to 'keep up.'" "Now that I'm having my first child, I wish my mother could be more supportive of me physically and emotionally," she said. "She has already told me she can't keep the baby because she won't be able to lift it. She will be of some support emotionally, but I will always have to worry about how it's affecting her. . . . When my time and energies are drained by the baby, she'll probably be depressed [and] feel neglected."

But even without being faced with the health crises or emotional difficulties of aging parents, later-born children still may feel that they must start their families sooner than they would like.

"My mother is saying, 'You got to have kids, I'm getting so old,'" said Claire, a twenty-seven-year-old from Rhinelander, Wisconsin. "It puts a lot of pressure on me."

Given the salience of aging in their lives, children of older parents may even start thinking about their own retirement and old age decades before they turn sixty-five or seventy. As children they were "little adults," and as young adults they face the life-cycle tasks of middle age. For them the future always seems to come too quickly.

∞

Their parents were "behind schedule," in society's eyes, so perhaps there is an odd sort of poetic justice that these later-born children will spend their lives "ahead of schedule."

18
Caregiving

"Just at the stage that one is needing to use one's energies and psyche to build a career, to marry and have children, a child of older parents suddenly may be absorbed with caring for aging parents," said Dr. Robert N. Butler, Brookdale Professor of Geriatrics and Adult Development at New York's Mount Sinai School of Medicine.[1]

For many latecomers, parents' needs for extensive care made them feel that they had moved into middle age before their time. Their caregiving ranged from the emotionally and physically grueling experience of round-the-clock care for a bedridden parent to helping with routine housework and doing occasional errands for a mother or father still in more-or-less good health. In either case, however, such caregiving can have quite different practical and psychological implications for a thirty-year-old than a fifty-year-old.

June, a thirty-year-old from Washington, D.C., spent her twenties watching her parents die. During her grade-school years, she enjoyed many of the benefits of having two older, established professional parents. Her mother, however, had had an alcohol problem that scarred June's childhood, but it was during her college years that she became aware that her mother's health—and her parents' lives—were rapidly deteriorating.

"When I got home from college, they had completely fallen apart," she said. "My mother's doctors said that she was terminally ill with cirrhosis. It lasted for three years. She should have been in a nursing home, but my father was taking care of her. She was incontinent and would scream for alcohol.

"I was living at home. I was supposed to be developing my own life, but I was caught up in taking care of them. I felt like I wasn't allowed to be your typical twenty-two-year-old.

From the time I was twenty-two until I was twenty-nine, I cared for my parents.

"My mother died when I was twenty-six, and then my father really began to go downhill. He was uremic, and I had to put him in the hospital, and that started a whole slew of events. The doctors told me he had Alzheimer's and had to be put in a nursing home. I wound up taking him to a lot of specialists. None of the relatives were willing to help, so I had to sell the house. First I found a woman to care for him at home, and then I had to find a place to take care of him that was afford-able."

Two years later June's father died, and after seven nightmar-ish years she began law school and started picking up the pieces of her life. "I felt like I was dealing with things that other people do in their forties, like I was doing things backwards. I feel now that I'm trying to make up for lost time, which I can't quite do successfully."

Although June's story may be extreme, the need to provide emotional and, perhaps, medical and financial assistance to par-ents early in life can take a considerable toll, many children of older parents said. The suddenness of the role reversal between parent and child—of who is the caregiver and decision maker and who is cared for—can be a shock for people in their twenties who always looked on their parents as sources of support and security. This may be particularly difficult today, when cultural, financial, and educational factors prolong children's dependency on their parents well past age twenty.

Among those interviewed and surveyed, the very fact of being confronted early in life with the need to care for their mothers or fathers was often seen as the most profound effect of having older parents.

"Younger people just aren't as prepared for caring for aging parents," said Mirca Liberti, a cofounder of Children of Aging Parents, a support group based in Levittown, Pennsylvania. "It's very difficult if you're in your twenties. It's scary, and they often don't know what to do or how to find the resources for their parents."[2]

Human aging is, of course, a subtle process of slow physical, psychological, and social changes. Because of dramatic improve-ments in health care and the introduction of Social Security,

Medicare, and other economic assistance programs in the United States, as well as similar programs in other countries, many of the worst physical and financial problems of old age have been attenuated in much of the Western world in the late twentieth century.

However, with increasing life expectancy, the ranks of the elderly and the "very old," as well as the sheer amount of time most people can expect to spend in old age, have grown significantly. In 1925 only 5.8 million Americans were sixty-five or older; by 1990 the number was estimated at nearly 32 million. The fact that people are now living longer after the onset of chronic illness or disability has been aptly described as "the failure of success" by gerontologist E. M. Gruenberg.[3]

These developments have had profound implications for both public policy and family relationships. Because people are surviving longer, multigenerational families have become far more common than a century ago—despite the cozy myth of the long-lost extended family. Between 1900 and 1976 the number of people who experienced a parent's death by age fifteen dropped from one in four to one in twenty, and the number of middle-aged couples with two or more living parents increased from 10 to 47 percent, according to Elaine Brody, associate director of research at the Philadelphia Geriatric Center.[4] More people than ever before have living parents, grandparents, and great-grandparents. This also means that more adults are confronted with the physical and emotional problems of aging parents over a longer span of time.

The physical assaults of aging take many forms. They can range from vision and hearing problems to diminished stamina and mobility to chronic illnesses and severe disabilities. As one ages, too, memory loss and mental impairment can be very mild or painfully severe. Changes in physical well-being and appearance also take a psychological toll. These assaults to the ego tend to be compounded by the transition to retirement, widowhood, and other social losses resulting from the deaths of friends and relatives. Indeed, such psychological problems as loneliness and depression may well be more common among the elderly than medical afflictions like arthritis or senility.

These physical and psychological blows, in turn, often cause fears of being unable to care for oneself and being abandoned by one's children and society. "Cast me not off in the time of old age; forsake me not when my strength faileth," it was written in the Bible (Psalms 71:9). Sentiments like these are undoubtedly even more common today than when they were expressed some two millennia ago.

It is estimated that anywhere from about 17 to 40 percent of the noninstitutionalized elderly are in need of some form of assistance, according to gerontologist Elaine Brody. Spouses are the most frequent providers of care, but—given the fact that more than eleven million Americans are widowed (four-fifths of them women)—about seven million people in the United States care for an aging parent or relative at any given time.[5] Other estimates are considerably higher. The 1985 Travelers Employee Caregiving Survey, for example, found that at least 20 percent of the workers in one large corporation were helping an elderly relative.[6]

The overwhelming majority of people caring for aging parents are adult daughters. A 1988 study by the American Association of Retired Persons (AARP) found that three out of four caregivers are women. The reason, according to an association official: "Because it is expected of them. As part of our religious and social backgrounds, women cook, clean, and take care of people."[7]

This pronounced sex difference was substantiated by the survey of children of older parents. Caregiving was a major issue for 13 percent of the women, compared with only 3 percent of the men.

∞

The caregiving relationship has been defined as "the existence of some degree of physical, mental, emotional or economic impairment on the part of the older person which limits independence and necessitates ongoing assistance."[8]

Children of aging parents tend to think of the elderly's needs principally in terms of health and personal care, according to Victor G. Cicirelli, author of *Helping Elderly Parents*.[9] Yet the chief concerns of the elderly themselves, he found, were for recreation, transportation, dealing with bureaucracies, physical protection, and psychological and social support. Additional practical needs included cooking, cleaning, and other household maintenance, not to mention moving, financial planning, and preparing a will.

Nonetheless, it is estimated that about 25 percent of all people over eighty-five need help walking, 10 percent require assistance in dressing and going to the bathroom, and 4 percent need to be fed by someone else.[10]

Although most people are faced with caring for aging parents when they themselves are in their forties or fifties, gerontologists have estimated that about 18 percent of caregiving children are over sixty and 12 percent are under forty.[11] These differences, of course, are a function of how long a parent is healthy and active, and of the relative age difference between parents and children. Children who were born when their parents were twenty are not likely to be confronted with the complex of problems associated with aging parents until they are at least fifty or sixty. Conversely, children of forty-year-old parents may have to deal with issues of their parents' aging by the time they are thirty or thirty-five.

The children of older parents who were surveyed were very aware of their mothers' and fathers' health and the issue of caring for their parents. About 51 percent were worried about their parents' physical well-being, and only about 40 percent had not felt the impact of caring for a parent. Some felt, as a thirty-year-old from Hamden, Connecticut, put it: "I only hope I can take as good care of them now that they need it as they took care of me." Yet many agreed with another respondent who said, "I often wish that burden hadn't hit me so soon."

Caregiving was a particular concern among people in their thirties and early forties. When asked to comment on any salient issues having to do with their parents' ages, 16 percent of the thirty-one- to forty-five-year-old respondents brought up problems related to caring for their parents, including practical problems, feelings of sadness, or emotional conflicts. This compared with between 5 and 8 percent of respondents of all other ages.

The amount of help provided by children of elderly parents "increases steeply" with the age of the caregiver, according to Brody. She found that people in their fifties spent, on average, five times as many hours each week helping their parents as did subjects between forty and forty-nine.[12] This undoubtedly reflects the fact that older adult children are likely to have relatively older parents with greater needs. But it also suggests that younger people—regardless of the ages or needs of their parents—may need to spend more time with their own children, have less flexibility with work schedules, and, in general, have less free time for such intensive caregiving.

Geriatric specialists urge children of aging parents to prolong their parents' independent functioning by whatever means are necessary. However, one inevitably may have to face the need for institutional care. About 1.3 million elderly Americans were confined to nursing homes in 1985, according to the National Center for Health Statistics (NCHS). One percent of those sixty-five to seventy-four years old, about 6 percent of those between seventy-five and eighty-four, and 22 percent of those over eighty-five were institutionalized.[13] The issue of whether and when to move a parent into a nursing home is likely to be an extremely difficult one to resolve, often leading to deep feelings of guilt.

∞

At any time of life, parent care can entail considerable ambivalence and stress. "As a grown child of aging parents," wrote Robert R. Cadmus, author of *Caring for Your Aging Parents,* "you will spend more of your waking hours thinking about your parents and their problems than ever before."[14]

A study at the Brookdale Center on Aging at New York's Hunter College found that one-third of those caring for elderly parents reported deterioration of their own health; half developed anxiety or depression; one-fourth performed less effectively on the job, and one-fourth felt that their financial circumstances had worsened.[15] The 1988 AARP study found that one-third of caregivers with jobs lost time from work because of their responsibilities. Many of these said they had to change their working status from full-time to part-time and that benefits like vacation and insurance were consequently reduced. Furthermore, the average caregiver was found to spend about $1,400 a year for such things as travel, telephone calls, medicine, and food for their elderly parent, and 7 percent spent a quarter of their monthly income.[16]

While some caregivers manage well, and many derive feelings of satisfaction and self-respect from knowing that they are fulfilling a responsibility and coping with a challenge, sleeplessness, nervousness, and lowered morale are all-too-common symptoms of strain. Personal-care tasks—such as bathing, dressing, or toileting—tend to be the most emotionally draining, and coping with mental impairment is often the most frightening.

This emotional and physical fatigue is generally exacerbated when a parent lives with a child. Many of these children find that their responsibilities interfere with their privacy, social and recreational activities, and plans for vacations and the future. Not only are the life-styles of adult children disturbed but disposable family income is reduced.

Because these adult children are providing the same types of emotional and practical support that their parents once gave them, many describe this role reversal as psychologically wrenching. Furthermore, caring for an aging parent arouses strong fear and anticipation of the parent's death, and may make one aware of one's possible future dependence on one's own children.

It can also be very painful to see a parent's health and mental faculties gradually deteriorate and to realize that the parent is no longer the pillar of strength that the child remembers. Adult children can become preoccupied with their parents' arthritis or slower gait and be obsessively worried by every complaint their mother or father may make.

"Intellectually one can say, 'I realize my mother is depressed because she has lost her husband and her peers,' but emotionally one may feel, 'I can't stand this depressed person hanging around,' " said Mirca Liberti of the Children of Aging Parents support group. Adult children beset by the problems and needs of elderly parents may throw up their hands and think, " 'Why me? Why did I get stuck? Why doesn't the government provide more?' " she added.

∞

Deep-seated and perhaps long-dormant sibling rivalry can also be reawakened by the need to care for parents. Arguments and tensions may arise among brothers and sisters about what is best and who can best provide it.

Because research has shown that one family member is usually the primary caregiver, the child providing care may resent his or her siblings for eschewing responsibilities, or the other siblings may become jealous of the closer relationship between the caregiving child and the parent.

"Other family members or friends, if involved at all [in

caregiving], play secondary roles, and shared responsibility between two or more members of the informal support system is very much the exception to the rule," according to gerontologist Amy Horowitz, director of research at the Lighthouse, the New York Association for the Blind.[17] In families with several children, differences in their relationships with their parents, as well as the gender and relative geographical proximity and income of the children, tend to be the principal determinants of who provides care.

Only Children as Caregivers

Caregiving can be especially difficult and its effects particularly profound for children without brothers or sisters to share responsibilities.

"Every time there was a crisis with my father, I had to mobilize everything," said a thirty-four-year-old from Little Neck, New York. An only child, she had to place her father in a nursing home because her mother was also in bad health. When her father died, she found herself having to take care of her mother.

Given the coincidence of parental aging and young adulthood for children of older parents, it can be very difficult indeed for a twenty-seven-year-old only child with a seventy-four-year-old mother. This was just the situation that Amanda faced. Now sixty-three years old and recently enrolled in college to begin a new career, she recalled the more than twenty years that she took care of her mother: "My father died suddenly of a heart attack when I was twenty-seven. I wasn't married, but I was about to move out of the house. And my mother wasn't a very independent person. So she became my responsibility and charge, just when I was venturing out in life.

"My mother was very frightened, and—with no brothers or sisters—I was truly alone," she continued. "I was living at home till my late forties, when my mother died at ninety-five. It curtailed my independence a great deal, and it affected my work. She was very upset about being alone, and she would call up my office and make a big commotion. I lost two jobs as a result. On the next job, I spent a lot of time away from her, and she went off the wall. It was a terrible experience; I was advised to commit her, but I vowed never to let her out of my sight. I stopped thinking about my career. I couldn't travel. I didn't move out of the apartment, and that affected my social life. I just sort of closed the door to what I might have done. I couldn't think about myself, and it kept me from developing my talents or realizing my potential. And I never married."

"As an only child, all the responsibility for my mother's care is mine," remarked a forty-two-year-old Albany, New York, woman whose father had died. "I have made great strides in my career in the last five years, but I consider myself very tied down geographically because of my mother, who is getting very senile and unpredictable. I fear that my good fortune careerwise will end when she gets worse. And later, after she passes away, I fear that new opportunities won't be forthcoming, especially because then I'll be competing with much-younger people for jobs."

Davis, a fifty-one-year-old public employee in a small Ohio town, was another only child of older parents whose entire life was affected by caring for his mother. He was four when his father died, and his mother, now ninety-four, recently entered a nursing home. Davis took his first jobs when he was seven to help support his mother, and he lived alone with her for nearly half a century.

"My mother was in good health until 1965, when she lost her sight," he recalled. "I was in my late twenties, so I started taking care of her, and I have ever since. I was tied down a little bit, but I was able to function pretty well up until January of 1987, when she had a series of strokes. Then I had to spend all my time with her, and I lost a lot of work.

"It was pretty hard to move her to the rest home, after living in the same house together for fifty years," he continued. "It triggered a lot of stress. I felt like I was up against a brick wall, not having any brothers or sisters to talk it over with. Now, I get up to see her three or four times a week. But if I don't come, she cries, they tell me."

Davis began seeing a psychotherapist, who prescribed medication for him to cope with his stress.

"Maybe I would have married if my parents had been younger," he reflected. "But I made it my priority to take care of my mother until God called one of us home. I know that she had sacrificed a lot for me."

The Unmarried Caregiver

Berry, a New York artist, had a different but no less painful experience. Her parents, both about forty when she was born, were in good shape until she was thirty-one, when her father suddenly died of a heart attack. "There were two years when my mother was OK," she said, "but then her illness began when she was about seventy-five and I was thirty-three. She was losing her short-term memory and would be driving around and get lost."

Her brother was married, had three children, and was living with his wife's father, while Berry was unmarried at the time. So caregiving responsibilities fell to her. "At first I wanted to deny that I had to give more of myself. It didn't seem right to move her into a home, so I moved her to New York to be near me to find out what was wrong. She lived with me for several months in my one-bedroom apartment, and then I got her a studio apartment in my building.

"It was difficult. I didn't have any privacy, but when I was working, I never knew what she was doing. I was afraid she was doing something embarrassing or hurtful to herself. It was difficult to get away. I had to have a friend stay with her for a week just so I could take a vacation. My friends felt sorry for me because it was limiting and it hindered my social life. Any man I was involved with would feel jealous of the time I'd spend with my mother." Seven years after her father died and three years after her mother came to live with her, Berry's eighty-year-old mother died. Berry was thirty-eight.

"Women in the Middle"

"I am the mother to my mother at the same time that I have my own children to care for."

This predicament, expressed by a forty-year-old woman from Redcliff, Alberta, is typical of those whom gerontologist Elaine Brody has called "women in the middle." Although unmarried daughters are often likely to assume the responsibility of caring for aging parents, in actual numbers, married women account for the largest proportion of caregivers.

These middle-generation women find themselves and their allegiances torn between caring for their own young children and their elderly parents, not to mention the demands of the working world. Brody's study of these overwhelmed women found that almost 84 percent had at least one child living at home and roughly 60 percent worked. Yet 51 percent provided a parent with one or more needed services, and 20 percent had a parent living with them.[18]

Many of the estimated one million American women whose households contained both young children and an elderly parent had significantly poorer mental health and were more likely to report symptoms of depression, restlessness, and feelings of isolation and "missing out" on something, according to Brody. With no free time left, some were forced to quit their jobs to assume the full-time task of caring for both dependent generations.

"I was so naïve, trying to be a wife, a mother and a daughter!" said a woman whose eighty-one-year-old mother lives with her family. "I want to be totally for my husband and my children, but I find I'm a divided person. If my husband says, 'Let's go out to dinner,' I have to think about my mother and fixing dinner for her."

The children of these "women in the middle" sometimes benefit from a close relationship with a live-in grandparent, but they also may resent that their mothers spend less time with them, or they may feel that their home life and social life are disrupted by the presence of their grandparent.

"I'm like the middleman," said a thirty-seven-year-old Pennsylvania woman whose eighty-one-year-old father lives with her family. "I make sure he eats and takes his medicine, and I run him back and forth to doctors and do his insurance forms. I'm more or less a nurse and a mother to him.

"But it's hard having him at the house with a family," she continued. "It's made the marriage rough. My dad will say something about my husband he doesn't like, and my husband will say something about my dad. There's no real privacy. And there are problems with the children as well. Kids aren't going to sit there like dummies and not make noise. But when they do, my dad hollers at them, and that gets on my nerves."

Even when an aging parent does not move in, many middle-aged women feel caught between two generations needing their attention. This crunch may be most oppressive if children are very young and parents are relatively old—a scenario most likely to be played out among daughters of older parents.

These "women in the middle" are typified by Valerie, a thirty-five-year-old living in a suburb of San Francisco. She has a five-year-old child and a seventy-eight-year-old mother who lives alone in a town forty miles away. Her mother does not drive and suffers from glaucoma and arthritis. "I'm the only person under fifty that I know who's having to deal with an old-age parent," she said. "I feel *pulled*. Do I leave my child and husband one day every weekend to spend with Mom?

"Where will she live if she can't live alone?" she worried. "I have a two-bedroom apartment, and so does my brother. We can't afford a house around here. So, just when my job, marriage, and child take all my energy, now I have to factor my mother's old-age infirmities into my equation. I feel a real strong obligation to stay in the Bay Area to be nearby in case anything happens to her. Most people my age don't have to worry about that. They can just move; their parents still have each other and their health."

"Better Dead"

Despite the caregiving difficulties latecomers must generally contend with earlier than most people, very few interviewees and only about 1 percent of the survey respondents noted that at least they won't have to face such problems when they are older because their parents have died.

"My husband's parents are dead and my father is dead," wrote a thirty-five-year-old California woman. "That has its good points, macabre though it sounds. We only have to nurse my mom through the long good-bye." Noting that her seventy-eight-year-old mother is in declining health and is increasingly dependent on her, she added, "If we had four aging parents, my marriage would suffer and so would my kid."

A man whose parents died when he was in his thirties was even more direct: "I had the advantage of not having them around to a later age, as is true of less fortunate people, who are still coping with parents in their sixties."

"When I see the difficulties some of my friends have now, fooling around with hospitals and Medicare, I'm glad I never had any of that to worry about," added a middle-aged Long Island woman whose parents both died when she was in her early thirties. "I did miss having my parents, especially for my children's sake, but if your parents die when you're younger, any money you inherit will be more useful then. You can use it for your kids or to start a business."

Comments like these are admittedly a bit jarring. They all too bluntly recognize that, if one's parents have died, one need not confront the responsibilities and strains of caregiving. Under the guise of being realistic, however, such words come across as crass and uncaring.

Not Something to Think About

Most people having children understandably don't think about their own old age and what their relationships with their children may be at a time that seems to lie in the impossibly distant future. Of course, no one wants to consider the hypothetical maladies one may face thirty, forty or fifty years down the road, or ruminate about one's possible future dependency on one's children.

Nonetheless these issues are as ineluctably real as any in life. Parenting decisions should hardly be made with an eye to old age, yet sheer chronological and actuarial realities remain: If one has children at age forty, one's children are likely to be confronted with the responsibilities and strains of caregiving ten or fifteen years earlier than if one had children at twenty-five or thirty.

"I hope all the people choosing to have kids in their late thirties are really thinking about their future," one professional in the field of aging pointedly declared. "God forbid, if they have a stroke at sixty, what twenty-year-old can, or wants to, take care of them?"[19]

∞

As for the future, it is hard to assess what effect the trend toward increased later-life parenting will have on both younger and older generations in terms of the provision of parent care. Because people are staying healthy longer, today's children of older parents may not be cast in caregiving roles until they reach the same stage of their lives as children of twenty-two-year-old parents two generations ago. Thus the crunch felt by young "women in the middle" may be attenuated somewhat. Furthermore, as the population ages, new institutions and means of caring for the elderly may come into being. But, no matter how one looks at it, later-born children will have aging parents before most of their peers do.

19
Into the Next Generation

"I had my five children before I was thirty," said Helen, of Watertown, New York. "Deliberately!"

Another woman, who obviously had extremely strong feelings, declared: "To this day I actually get angry when I see someone over thirty who is going to have a baby."

The desires and decisions of children of older parents to have their own children early or later in life, or to have children at all, were strongly influenced by childhood experiences with their own parents. Latecomers frequently used their parents' situation to reflect on where they would be in their own lives at important times in their children's lives.

When childhood was a bitter memory, it was more than likely that the "children" making choices about a new generation would accelerate childbearing. Often the reasons expressed reflected the particular deprivations or hurts that had marred their lives.

Choices of postponed childbearing, too, had various origins. Among some of those who did delay, their parents stood out as valued models. The benefits they had as children they expected to replicate with children of their own. The postponers also included people whose lives and careers had propelled them into their late thirties or beyond without children. If they still wanted children, they pointed to the fact that their parents had successfully produced them, and concluded that it could be done.

In most cases the decision was not a neutral topic but one discussed with surprising emotion. Sixty-six percent of the later-born children surveyed—and 85 percent of those who were thirty or younger—said that their parents' ages influenced their feelings about what is the best time for childbearing. Although some said that their parents' example had shown them that it is not only all right but beneficial to be and have older parents, about twice as many believed that it is better—especially for the child— to have children earlier in life. These were the latecomers whose feelings were most intense.

"I Couldn't Have Done That to a Child"

"I would have hated to have children in my forties," said Julia, a bank teller in Ohio, whose parents were forty-five when she was born. "I couldn't have done that to a child."

Like Julia, others were adamant that they did not want to repeat the experience of their own childhood, and they consciously decided to have children well before turning thirty-five. Those who sadly recalled their parents as "old" seemed to bend over backwards to be as unlike their mothers and fathers as possible.

The parent-as-a-negative-role-model was a pervasive theme and a powerful force directing childbearing choices. A common refrain was: "I was determined to be the young father/mother I never had."

Many latecomers emphasized that they wanted to be healthy and active when their children reached adulthood. They hoped to be able to share more of their children's and grandchildren's lives than had been possible for their parents. They also hoped that they would not become a burden when their children were still relatively young. These motives for having children early and avoiding problems in their upbringing were often expressed in the spirit of commitment to good parenting and good relationships with their children.

They believed that, as younger parents, they would be able to get along better with their children than their own parents had with them, and that their children would have more of a chance to know their grandparents.

"If you have children when you're young, there's more time to do things together," said a woman from Philadelphia who had her three children when she was ten years younger than the age at which her mother had had her. "When they're older, you can travel. And when you're older, you're still young enough to be your children's friend."

Marie, who was in her early thirties when her children were born, also compared herself with her parents. "Having grown up in a family with literally elderly parents, with whom I had been afraid to share much, I was concerned that this would happen to my children," she said. "I don't think it has. I feel my girls are good friends of mine, and all of us are enjoying being friends with our adult friends and their children. This was an experience completely missing from my life as a young adult."

She went on to recall an incident when her college-age daughter was ill and she went to pick up medicine for her. "I ran in" to the drug store, she said, and "when I got back to the car, my daughter said to me, 'Mommy, you sure have a young step!' I would never have been inspired to make such a comment to my mother."

On the one hand, the feeling that youth is cut short and the realization that their parents wanted grandchildren propelled some to have children relatively early. Conversely, caregiving responsibilities also affected decisions about whether or when to have children. Many latecomers felt that they had no choice about when to have their own children. They had to put off starting their own families because they were faced with caring for their mothers and fathers during their twenties or thirties, while their peers were marrying and having children.

Others reviewed past hurts in their own lives—feeling distant from their parents, different from their peers, deprived of grandparents, and losing their parents early in life. Their underlying feeling was that they did not want to create another childhood like their own. One respondent whose parents died when he was young put it bluntly: "I decided to have my kids young, so I wouldn't die and leave them."

"I knew I never wanted to have a change-of-life child, so I had my children in my late twenties," said Pam, a family therapist in Florida. Her father and mother were fifty-one and forty-one when she was born, and her father died when she was seven. As a child she was acutely aware of their ages, their appearance, their old-fashioned values, and their lack of involvement in her upbringing. "I thought of my experience as a child in the timing of my children. It was too much for a child to go through."

"My overall take on the experience [of having older parents] was such that I was determined to have my children at a younger age," added Pauline, from Massachusetts. "My mother supported me in this idea; she felt that she and I suffered because of her age."

Some childless women in their thirties knew that they still wanted children but were concerned that they might bring their children into the kind of family that they had disliked or resented when they were growing up. Carmen, a thirty-two-year-old from Oakland, California, who recalled her parents as tired and set in their ways, wrote that her childhood experience "haunts me now that I am married to a man twenty-one years my senior." She worried that, if she and her husband had a child, "the daddy will be fifty-three years older than the kid, and I sometimes wonder if that's OK."

Others felt that their parents conveyed the drawbacks of later childbearing more indirectly. "I viewed the world through their eyes and unconsciously picked up on their implications that 'children are pain, work, and expense'—their own personal feelings as fifty-five-year-old parents toward a ten-year-old child," recalled Theresa, from Orinda, California. "Now that I am sixty years old myself, I can understand why they felt that way, and I forgive them."

When looking toward the next generation, an additional factor that later-born children sometimes must consider is the effect of having parents considerably older than the parents of one's spouse. A miniature generation gap may separate the in-laws, creating its own share of tensions.

One man, whose mother-in-law was twenty years younger than his mother, recalled that this age difference was associated with differences in "child-rearing skills, as well as values and attitudes. It was a constant source of conflict, with the younger grandmother always taking charge, assuming that she knew more." He also regretted that his mother died "without fully knowing her grandchildren and without their knowing her."

In the choices of earlier parenting, there was also a longing for generational continuity. A twenty-eight-year-old Brooklyn woman who was generally positive about her older parents none-theless said that she would not "want to replicate the situation in the next generation. One reason I want to have children in the next five years is to maximize the chance that they will know my parents and my mother-in-law. I never knew any of my grandparents—my mother's mother, the last living one, died one month before I was born."

A surprising number of latecomers indicated that their childhood experiences with their parents completely soured them on the idea of ever having children. Their older, more mature milieu often left them feeling uncomfortable around babies and children.

"There was always the feeling that children were a burden," said one woman who opted to remain childless.

"I wasn't around many infants or children when I was young, and my world was always an adult one," added a married woman who did not want children. "I never really had this great need to reproduce myself. It may have been that I didn't want to go through the whole process of growing up again, which you do as a parent. One time was sufficient."

"Not Such a Bad Idea"

"Having children late wasn't such a bad idea," argued Priscilla, from Brooklyn, who indicated that her parents' ages had a "major effect" on her decision to put off childbearing. "After all, my mother had me when she was forty."

The patterns of their parents' lives offered a model for a substantial number of later-born children who had their own children in their late thirties or beyond. The knowledge that their mothers had trouble-free pregnancies and healthy babies often reassured them. And those who emphasized the benefits in their own lives of having older parents tended to see their mothers and fathers as examples of what makes a good parent.

"I always felt I had plenty of time to make decisions about having a family," said a woman from Palisades, New York, whose mother was forty-two when she was born. "My mother's age definitely made a difference in my view of my available options in life. She also chose a man twelve years younger—another option I felt I was given by her example."

Erica, age forty-four, says she still has not decided not to have children. "Circumstances haven't allowed me to have children so far, but the fact that I'd still consider it at forty-four probably means that having older parents rather skewed the time frame I have. I probably feel I have more time than most women do, that I didn't have to have kids in my twenties."

Some people who decided to postpone childbearing noted that their grandparents and great-grandparents, as well as their parents, had also been over thirty-five when they had their children. "Perhaps this is a family tradition," suggested a Greenwich, Connecticut, woman who came from a long line of older parents. Similarly, Nancy, a forty-two-year-old Canadian journalist, traced her lineage to find that her grandfather was born in 1861, her great-grandfather in 1809, and her great-great-grandfather in 1772. And Jean, now forty-nine and living in Los Angeles, said that her grandfather was born in 1825, when Thomas Jefferson was still alive.

In addition, several of those who had children in their early twenties because of negative feelings about their own older parents now felt that they had made a mistake.

"I had resolved to have my own children as soon as possible," said Rita, whose parents both died when she was in her teens. She proceeded to give birth to three children by the time she was twenty-six. But, comparing herself with her own, older parents, she concluded: "My parents did a much better job raising me because of their maturity. As my oldest daughter once said, 'Ma, I have plenty of friends; I don't need you to be my friend. What I need is a mother who is a *mother*.' My mother was a real *mother*."

Betty was another latecomer who had clearly decided that she did not want to be an older mother. When she was born, her mother was forty-four, so Betty gave birth to her first child at twenty-three. Fifteen years later, she discovered that she was pregnant again. At first, she said, "I wasn't pleased at all! But then I thought, Mom went through this, and it turned out wonderfully."

∞

What is passed on to the next generation is more than the age of parenthood. The effects of an individual's upbringing on personality naturally color what kind of parent he or she will be. To the extent that parental age is a factor that indirectly influences a child and shapes family circumstances—in the many ways we have seen—its ramifications are felt across several generations.

More concretely, the size of generational differences will affect the composition of families: If parents are older, in the next generation grandparents will be older. If siblings are older, in the next generation aunts, uncles, and cousins will be older. In short, timing decisions have a ripple effect on families through several lifetimes.

But the "next generation" is also the product of individual choices and actions shaped in part by family values learned, directly and indirectly, from one's parents. These learned values certainly include ideas about what are "good" and "bad" ages at which to have children.

When children of older parents make deliberate timing decisions about having their children—either in defiance of or in harmony with the past generation—are conscious comparisons with their parents more likely to guide their own parenting? The intense feelings of many latecomers suggest that they are.

20

Evolving Relationships and Changing Perspectives

Children begin by loving their parents; as they grow older, they judge them; sometimes, they forgive them.
— *Oscar Wilde, The Picture of Dorian Gray*

Adult children and their parents see each other through lenses tinted by memories, desires, joys, and fears. Such distortions, shaped by the course and needs of an individual's life history, may make twenty-five- or fifty-year-old sons or daughters see their mothers and fathers as they were ten or forty years before, rather than as they are in the present. The enduring images of "Mom" and "Dad" may be ones seemingly frozen in time, of a smiling playmate tossing a ball on a summer afternoon or a harsh authority figure scolding or screaming about chores not done or curfews not met.

Current realities may be hard to see clearly and may never really take hold. If that once-energetic parent is now beset with arthritis or the stern authority figure is now a sad, frightened widow, the adult child may still see the parent largely in the earlier, more indelibly etched forms. Despite the intractability of such perceptions, individuals and relationships inevitably do change—sometimes profoundly.

In earliest childhood a parent's age is virtually irrelevant, since children tend to see their parents as ageless beings. To a five-year-old, anyone over twenty may seem ancient; to a four-teen-year-old, any adult may seem a hopeless old fogey.

But from the time that children of older parents first become aware of their mother's and father's ages until their parents' deaths, the psychological, social, and practical meanings of their parents' ages may influence their lives in both "permanent" and changing ways.

The significance of parental age, as we have seen, depends on individuals' life experiences as well as a person's current age and situation and the cohort to which he or she belongs. As a New Jersey man put it: "Parents' health and whether one has siblings are the two wild cards of being a child of older parents."

Many later-born children are unaware or unconcerned by their mothers' and fathers' ages early in life. It may only dawn on them that their parents are older than the norm during adolescence, when a generation gap seems to yawn wide, or during young adulthood, when the pressures of caring for an ill or aging parent begin to impinge upon their lives.

"I don't think I became aware that my parents were older till my late teens," said Sally, from Philadelphia. "I always thought they were the same age as everybody else's parents. When I was ten, my mother was fifty, but I saw her as thirty-five. It was almost a shock to realize she was forty years older than I was. When her fifty-fifth birthday came around, my friends said, 'Are you kidding?' "

Indeed, the fact of their parents being older was relevant to some later-born children only at very discrete times in their lives. Having older fathers and mothers could have been psychologically important at one time—whether "good" or "bad"—and trivial or irrelevant at another. This ebb and flow of awareness of parents' ages, and how children interpreted the emotional significance of that awareness, was a recurrent theme. But people had very different opinions and recollections of when and how their parents' ages were important.

"I needed top-quality parents much more when I was five than when I was thirty-five," wrote Libby Colman, co-author of *Having a Baby After 30.* She expressed strong, positive memories of her parents, who died by the time she was in her early thirties.[1]

But a Wisconsin woman, whose mother died when she was

graduating from college, argued: "Parenting doesn't stop when a child is eighteen. It's important to have parents when you're in your twenties, which you may not have if your parents are older."

Not only were there sharp differences about how and when having older parents was important, but many saw the balance of pros and cons change as their lives progressed.

Those who were embarrassed by their parents in childhood and felt two generations removed from them during adolescence frequently said that the effects of being thirty-five or forty years apart in age melted away during adulthood. There was anything but a "gap" as they moved into their twenties and thirties. They spoke of being proud of their parents and especially close to them by this time, able to relate well to them as adults and as friends. Their relationships with their mothers and fathers, they said, had become better than those of many friends with younger parents.

"The embarrassment about their ages that I felt as a child became overwhelmed by other issues, and then vanished by the time I was in college," said one woman who, as a teenager, thought that her mother's age contributed to her feeling set off from her peers. "When I started to work, I became proud of my parents. I realized they were colorful, interesting people, and I quite enjoyed them."

A particularly moving, and happy story of a relationship that dramatically changed over time was that of a Massachusetts-born woman whose parents were forty-one at the time of her birth. When she was a teenager, she recalled, her mother was restrictive and tyrannical, forbidding her to go out with boys.

Then, in her twenties, her father became an invalid, and her mother had to take care of him for twelve years. "Those were very difficult years for her. She would call me, crying, at her wits' end. We'd talk, and she'd feel a little better. It was such a profound feeling of reverse roles, of parenting your parent. One night, we both had the same fear that Daddy was going to die. It was very bonding. It made me really fall in love with her."

When her father died, she continued, "I was afraid my mother wouldn't have much of a life of her own. But she took over the family finances, the maintenance of the car and the house, and, at seventy-six, became a liberated woman. I was very proud of her.

"She lives in Florida now, but I talk to her all the time and visit her a couple of times a year. She recently came to visit for eleven days, and we had a ball. All my friends who met her think she's great. She's eighty-three—a lot older than their parents—but she came out drinking and to parties with us. It's strange. I have this incredible admiration for her—and part of it is because she's an older person. Against all odds, she was a sweetheart in taking care of my father. And when I look back on those teenage fights, those are exactly the things that had to happen. I love this lady."

Some who had blamed their parents' ages for various problems came to feel that other factors also may have played a part in causing or exacerbating particular problems, or that if their parents had been younger, other kinds of difficulties might have arisen. Several spoke of "epiphanies" in their lives that dramatically—and positively—changed the way they viewed their parents. And in some cases the feeling that their parents would not be around so long contributed to a desire to forge closer relationships.

A woman born to parents in their mid-forties recalled writing a college application essay "about how I had been shaped by having parents as old as many peers' grandparents." Eight years later, she felt that only recently had she truly gotten to know her parents. "Now this essay makes me cringe," she said. "I wrote rather mechanically that they did not take me camping or skiing."

"As I grew older, the age difference between my mother and me disappeared," added Nina, from Los Angeles. During her teenage years, she had been adamant that she would have children by her early twenties to avoid the kind of horrible generation gap she experienced between herself and her mother. "I guess as we became comrades in womanhood, I gained enormous respect for couples like my parents who developed and fine-honed their relationship, respective careers and home life before introducing a child into the environment.

"We had a home with a backyard when my friends were living in cramped apartments," she continued. "My sister and I felt much more settled in our lives, being raised by parents established in their jobs and their neighborhood. By contrast, friends' parents were just approaching that stage when they anticipated a major move to a house in the suburbs as a result of their just-peaking careers. This was just the time when the most important thing in the world is being able to stay friends with your best buddy next door 'forever,' and the most horrifying fear is that your parents will 'take you away' to another city and you'll never see your Scout troop again."

∞

As it does for most people, the passage of time dulled old hurts and resentments and led to many positive re-evaluations of parents and the roles that they had played in their children's lives. Sometimes these re-assessments were made in young adulthood on the basis of forming strong new bonds with parents, but in other cases they were bittersweet realizations after their parents had died that the older mother or father by whom they were embarrassed or from whom they felt distant had really been a pretty special person.

Ted, a thirty-six-year-old psychologist from a small town in Maryland, spoke poignantly of how time had changed his view of his father: "When I was a child, my father was distant. This may have had a lot to do with the fact he was forty-six when I was born. I was also his fourth child, and he was probably pretty tired of relating to children. He was of that era that defined women's work as child rearing and taking care of the home, including their husbands, while the father's work was outside the home—bringing home the bacon. So, in this spirit of post–World War II sexism, he probably was doing what he thought he should be doing.

"I remember clearly being embarrassed by him—his age, his baldness, his being overweight—and not wanting to be associated with him. On the other hand, I craved his attention. I was constantly aware of his heart problem and feared he would die on a moment's notice—which he ended up doing when I was seventeen. I remember him not being able to throw a baseball like other fathers and being concerned about not over-exercising. I remember thinking that when he took a nap, he might not wake up. And I remember telling the street-crossing guard that he was over eighty years old, because that's how old he seemed to me, even though he was in his fifties at the time.

"But he engendered very strong, responsible, mature values in me. To this day I wish he were still alive to see my accomplishments, to understand how much he influenced me, despite the distance between us. I think that I created much of that distance. By trying so hard to differentiate myself from him, I chose not to connect with him on the levels that he probably was available to me. For example, he was a voracious reader, and I read only minimally through my teenage years. I was more interested in sports and girls. He loved classical music and jazz, and I only listened to the Beatles. Anyway, I failed to pick up on any of the connecting strings between us."

∞

A brother and sister who, during childhood, had ignored or resented their older father also came to appreciate how he had struggled to take care of them after their mother died.

"It wasn't until my thirties that I realized how my father had sacrificed himself for me," said Marvin, whose mother died when he was twelve. "Five years ago, when he was eighty, he was going to have a cancerous tumor removed. I became much more acutely aware of his feelings." While his father was undecided about whether to have the surgery, he said, "I was adamant that the doctors operate, and I wanted to take responsibility for him."

While Marvin had been all but oblivious to his father during his teens and twenties, his sister, Betty, long resented their father, blaming him for their mother's death. When their father remarried at age seventy, she said, "It took me a long time to accept his new wife. At first I just didn't like her. There was no way she was an equal of my mother. But, in retrospect, I thank God for her existence. She's taken fabulous care of him and has saved his life. She certainly did more than I could or wanted to do. Now we're pretty close."

And even the woman from Pennsylvania whose mother "regaled [her] with stories about how she tried to 'get rid of' " her because she was an unplanned, late child, ultimately felt wanted by her mother. She ended her letter by saying: "Before she died, mother told me I was the child who'd given her the most pleasure of all six kids. . . . Maybe she was glad she [hadn't been able to] 'get rid of' me after all!"

Other later-born children also felt that their parents' ages contributed positively to their having less-stereotyped views of what is "appropriate" at particular ages. This made them feel more flexible about the timing of things in their own lives.

"Knowing my parents were in their late forties when I was in elementary school sort of extended the range of ages that it was acceptable for me to do things," said a New Jersey woman. "Having young children in your forties and working into your seventies didn't seem peculiar to me, because my mother did. I'm in my forties and still consider having children, and I assume I'll work into my seventies."

"I don't have a fear of growing old, because my parents' role-model message to me was that age didn't mean anything," reported another woman. "My friends were traumatized when they turned thirty and forty, but I was never traumatized by age."

∞

On the other hand, some felt that, as they grew older, their relationships with their parents took a turn for the worse. The passage of time made the age difference seem ever more significant. The problems of childhood were magnified, and the generation gap continued to widen.

"As my mother enters her seventies, she grows further away from the issues and pressures that affect my life," said a New Jersey man.

And Mary, the sixth child of forty-year-old parents, recalled that her mother cherished her as a child, but the adoration vanished when she became an adult: "My mother never came when I had any of my three babies. When I got married and moved away, she lost interest. It didn't seem like she cared about my everyday life. Maybe it was burnout. She had all these grandchildren before my children were born."

∞

The differences in how later-born children perceive the meanings and effects of their parents' ages at different times in their lives were clearly reflected in the questionnaire responses of people of different ages. The respondents were divided into groups by their present ages—thirty or younger, thirty-one to forty-five, forty-six to sixty, and sixty-one or older. They were asked to evaluate the ways in which parents' ages affected them in childhood, adolescence, and adulthood. Striking differences emerged both in relation to the present age of the respondents and to their views of different stages in their lives.

The youngest and oldest respondents tended to have the most positive views of their mothers and fathers and the consequences of being born later in their parents' lives. Interestingly, young adults under thirty felt most positive about their parents in the present. Conversely, those over sixty were most positive in their recollections of their mothers and fathers from childhood and adolescence. But they were nearly as upbeat in their early-adult assessments of their parents as were the youngest respondents. Middle-aged respondents were more negative or mixed in their memories and evaluations.

As might be expected, on virtually all affective issues—ranging from how close they felt and how likely they were to do things with their parents to whether they saw their parents as role models—respondents of all ages were significantly more negative in their assessments during adolescence than at any other time. For example, 62 percent felt that a generation gap separated them from their parents during adolescence, whereas in adulthood only 35 percent said they experienced such a gap.

Considering the negative responses during adolescence, it is interesting in terms of emotional development that young respondents—those now in their twenties—tended to have more positive feelings about their parents than did respondents in their thirties, forties and fifties. People in their twenties were much more likely to view their fathers and mothers as positive role models and say that their parents had a good effect on their personality and maturity, for example, than were the middle-aged respondents. These findings were supported by the results of the survey of students at Hunter College in New York City. On almost every question, these students rated their parents in more glowing terms than did those of all ages who were part of the main sample of children of older parents.

Aside from the presumably greater optimism of youth, several factors may account for these relatively upbeat appraisals during young adulthood. After leaving home or graduating from college and beginning to establish themselves in the world, young adults may be forging good new, or renewed, bonds with their mothers and fathers after the strains of adolescence. These relationships may seem all the more positive compared with those they had during their teens. This hypothesis seems to be supported by the fact that, when asked about how they viewed their parents during childhood, adolescence and adulthood, on most issues the under-thirty respondents tended to feel most positive about their mothers and fathers during adulthood. Young adults, of course, are more likely than those who are older to have their parents still alive and healthy.

The age factor seemed to be particularly prominent and problematic for people in middle age. The respondents between thirty-one and sixty tended to have the most negative perceptions of their mothers and fathers and the effects of being children of older parents. It might be argued that these men and women are more disillusioned, grappling with "midlife crises." Or they may have the most realistic perspectives on their lives, unswayed by youthful optimism or the nostalgia of old age. Yet this is also the time of life during which the strains of caring for aging parents are likely to be greatest and the pain of losing one's parents most acutely felt. Furthermore, these are the years when many people are struggling with their own lives and families—perhaps making them reflect more on their parents.

"When you're an adolescent, you don't think very much about who your parents are and what they're about," said Ben, a thirty-two-year-old Los Angeles man who was in his mid-twenties when his father died. "But, lo and behold, you're in your twenties, and they're near retirement, and you start thinking of your parents as very fragile."

As we have seen, thirty-one- to forty-five-year-olds were more concerned than any other age group about providing care for their already aging parents. This issue clearly stood out in their minds, and considerably more respondents in their thirties and early forties harbored negative feelings about caregiving responsibilities than those who were either younger or somewhat older.

"The impact of my parents' ages has become much more apparent to me in recent years," declared a man in his mid-thirties who had cared for his mother until her death and whose eighty-year-old father had recently been institutionalized because of a chronic illness. "I envy my friends whose parents are only in their late fifties. When I see them having fun and going on vacations with their parents, I wish my mother and father hadn't been so old."

By the time later-born children passed their sixty-first birthdays, more positive feelings about their parents once again emerged. Perceptions of parents undoubtedly were colored by time's passage. Any fears, strains, or difficulties experienced during their childhood probably had diminished in importance. The battlegrounds of childhood and youth were long quiet. Painful memories were less raw, and the stresses of seeing their parents age and die had receded into the past. Discontents and might-have-beens had disappeared into the oblivion of personal history, as happier memories rose to the surface.

Their best memories of their mothers and fathers tended to be from childhood. Recollections of parents' appearance, energy, involvement, and health were particularly rosy. People over sixty had decidedly happier memories of their adult relationships with their parents, but they were also most likely to discount parental age as an influence of any kind on their lives.

This perspective among the oldest respondents was well expressed by a woman in her late seventies: "If a person has a happy childhood and a happy adolescence, it is a strong bulwark against further troubles, even tragedies. So, if older parents do give us a happy youth and, hopefully, a good foundation for our own health and education, that is all we can ask, even if we do lose our parents earlier."

∞

As one grows older, not only do the dynamics of parent-child relationships change, but the issues that are most prominent in those relationships also change. Perhaps of equal importance, children's views of their parents—what they see as good or bad, important or unimportant—undergo significant changes as well.

Thus, viewed across the life cycle, later-born children may be thankful for having more experienced, secure, and devoted parents during childhood. Yet in adolescence they may think that their mothers and fathers are "out of touch," and in young adulthood that they are prematurely faced with the burdens of caring for aging parents. And throughout their lives, they may feel out of step with their peers and closer to mortality, tacitly aware that their peers need not fear for their parents quite as much as they do.

VI

Today's Older Parents and Their Children

21

A New Generation of Older Parents

Anyone who has been in a maternity ward recently knows that mothers aren't what they used to be. The number one reason is their age. As the Population Reference Bureau, a private research organization, proclaimed: "Delayed childbearing has indeed become the U.S. fertility phenomenon" of the late twentieth century."[1]

But why are increasing numbers of couples having children in their thirties or forties, and are the circumstances of over-thirty-five parenthood today fundamentally different from what they were in the past? Who is this new generation of older parents? And what do they believe are the immediate and longer-term advantages and disadvantages of later-life parenting for both themselves and their children?

In 1987, in the midst of the late childbearing era, American women thirty-five or older gave birth to 284,140 babies, a 72 percent increase since 1980, according to the NCHS. They accounted for 7.5 percent of births in the United States that year, compared to 4.6 percent just seven years earlier.[2] About 603,000, or 18.5 percent of the births for which the father's age was known, were to men thirty-five or older. However, only about 5 to 6 percent of American babies are born to parents who are both over thirty-five; while it is more common for considerably older men to be married to younger women, a surprising number of thirty-five-or-older mothers have younger husbands.[3] (For additional statistics, see appendixes B and C.)

This much-heralded trend toward later childbearing certainly is indicative of dramatic changes in values and behavior concerning parenting. As we have seen, though later-life parent-

ing is not a new phenomenon, deliberately postponed childbearing on a significant scale is.

"The big increase in births to older women is in first births,"
according to Stephanie Ventura, a demographer with the NCHS
who has studied childbearing patterns among older women.[4]
In fact, the first-birth rate for American women has reached an
all-time high. Even though the median age for first births in
the United States hovered around twenty-four in the late 1980s,
one in six first births were to women in their thirties or older.
In 1987, 19.4 percent of the babies born to women thirty-five
or older were their first, and another 28.5 percent were second
births. By comparison, only 6 percent of children born to over-
thirty-five mothers in 1970 were first births.

It is interesting that the frequency of childbirth among older
women differs somewhat by race. About 7.7 percent of the three
million white babies born in 1987 were to women thirty-five
or older. By comparison, 5.4 percent of the 642,000 black babies
and 5.8 percent of the 44,000 American Indian babies born that
year were to women thirty-five or older, according to the NCHS.
A June 1986 census report on first-birth rates showed that, while
there were 5.7 first births for every 1,000 white women ages
thirty-five to thirty-nine, there were 5.3 per 1,000 among Hispanic
women and only 2.4 per 1,000 among black women of those
ages. Asian and Pacific island women living in America are even
more likely than whites to delay first births.

The reasons for the boom in postponed parenting fall into
three broad categories. First, Americans are getting older, and
the pool of potential parents in their mid-thirties or older is
larger than ever before, thanks to the maturing of the baby-boom
generation. A second factor is that growing numbers of people
are marrying later in life for a variety of cultural and economic
reasons. (Not only are couples putting off marriage, but the increase in divorce has meant that more people are remarrying
and starting families in their thirties or later.) And finally, American families are getting smaller, particularly as the number of
unplanned children has declined.

The Aging of the Baby Boomers

A major part of the numerical increase in later-life childbearing is simply a result of the fact that a larger proportion of the

population of childbearing age is over thirty than a decade or two ago.

This factor will become even more important in the 1990s, according to Martin O'Connell, chief of the fertility statistics branch of the Census Bureau. "In the nineties, the bulk of women of childbearing age will shift toward older women, since so few people were born during the 1970s" in comparison to the 1950s and early 1960s, he said. "Thus the overall median age for child-birth will probably continue to rise."[5]

In the decade from 1985 to 1995, the census estimates that the number of twenty- to twenty-four-year-old women will decline from 10.5 million to 8.4 million, and the twenty-five- to twenty-nine-year-old female population will fall from 11 to 9 million. During the same period, the thirty-five- to thirty-nine-year-old female population is expected to increase from 9 to 11 million.

Cultural Changes and the "Biological Clock"

Most of the increase in postponed childbearing has been related to a widespread and much-noticed tendency toward putting off marriage. In 1960 just one-tenth of twenty-five- to twenty-nine-year-old women had never married; by 1986, 28 percent had never married. For women thirty to thirty-four, the proportion rose from one in fifteen in 1960 to one in seven in 1986. Among women thirty-five to thirty-nine, 8.4 percent had never married, and 5.5 percent of those forty to forty-four had never married, according to the Census Bureau. The increase in divorce, especially among couples in their twenties—many who did not have children—is also increasing the pool of potential older parents.

The rebirth of feminism made it acceptable—if not desirable—for women to pursue their educations, careers, and that amorphously defined ideal of self-realization before (or instead of) marrying and having children. At the same time, the availability of new and effective forms of contraception, and the legalization of abortion in the United States in 1973, made it possible for couples to control their fertility to a degree unprecedented in human history.[6] These developments, together with momentous changes in values about sexuality, have led to conscious decisions by many women (and men) to have fewer children and postpone parenthood until their thirties or later.

Economics has also played a role. In the last two decades, the proportion of women working has gone up from about 45 to 65 percent. This increase, which has affected when people are marrying, has not been entirely by choice. After several decades of rapid growth, American per capita personal income after inflation has stagnated since the early 1970s. According to a Chase Econometrics study, family income for couples ages twenty-five to thirty-four fell from 96 percent of the average American household income in 1965 to 86 percent in 1983.[7] In certain ways the interplay between economics and demography beginning in the 1980s is similar to what happened during the depression. In both periods, earning an adequate income and purchasing a home were difficult, and in both periods, postponed childbearing and childlessness increased significantly.

But as Pamela Daniels and Kathy Weingarten wrote in *Sooner or Later: The Timing of Parenthood in Adult Lives*, "The timing of midlife parenthood may be not so much the outcome of programmatic planning as the culmination of a prolonged process of deferral in which intention and circumstances, desire and delay, are threaded unevenly in and around each other."[8]

Indeed, many new older parents have weathered an anxious period of being single before their first child was born. One of the most talked-about concerns among single women in their late twenties, thirties, and early forties today is the "biological clock," ticking away the remaining years during which they will be able to bear children. As author Gail Sheehy said, "Thirty-five brings the biological boundary into sight."[9] For many women, in fact, the much-dreaded "clock" begins to tick long before they reach age thirty-five.

Studies and magazine articles have described the pressures felt by young women to make their parenting decisions before 35. In addition, "Older mothers-to-be . . . experience additional stress from believing that because of their advanced age, both they and their babies are at 'high risk,' " wrote Phyllis Kernoff Mansfield and Margaret D. Cohn in a review of 104 studies focusing on advanced maternal age. "They worry that they will experience added complications during labor and delivery, and, most of all, they fear that their offspring will somehow be adversely affected by their advanced age. Moreover, they may feel 'out of step.' "[10]

Some of these women—and their male counterparts—have put off marriage and childbearing because they enjoyed single life or could not find a suitable partner. As a reader responding to a 1989 *New York Times* article on delayed parenting wrote in a letter to the editor, "Many mothers in their mid-to-late 30's simply hadn't met their husbands at 27, or perhaps were going through painful divorces. Most women I know who have 'waited' were concerned about having children long before they became wives or mothers, and perhaps would just as soon have been younger, less tired or less pressured by professional obligations during early motherhood. But they didn't want the wrong husband, either."[11]

Others, less concerned about finding Mr. (or Ms.) Right, chose to pursue educations and careers. (Doctors, lawyers, academics, and many performers, for example, have barely started their careers by age thirty.) Many have wanted to be better established in their professions before beginning the juggling act of reconciling careers with parenthood. Other postponers worry about whether they will be good parents or that a child might harm their relationship with their spouse or lover. A few—perhaps not consciously—don't want to relinquish their position as the young, vanguard generation, as "children" themselves. And many in their thirties have tried to have children but have been unable to conceive.

Whatever their reasons for not yet having children, many single women in their thirties feel unfulfilled and incomplete without children. They also feel intense social and personal pressure to have children, thinking it's now or never.

A sort of early "midlife crisis" for women and men in their thirties may lead them to thoughts about their place in the long sweep of human generations. With the dawn of middle age, one may think about one's mortality, and, as Schopenhauer said, one may unconsciously begin to count backward from death rather than forward from birth. Certainly, as Plato suggested, the human desire and love for children may arise from the soul's yearning for immortality.

Many of these conflicting thoughts and sentiments— whether to have or not to have children—are often expressed by childless women and men between their late twenties and early forties.

In Molly McKaughan's book, *The Biological Clock,* one woman said: "I'm coming to believe I will live to regret it if I don't have this important component in my life. At times, I think that having plenty of money and freedom to travel, etc., will be enough for a full life, but at other times it seems as if that will wear thin. . . . Do I want to be old and completely alone with nothing to show for my existence except used plane tickets?"

"My clock ticks loudly sometimes," said another. "I made my decision a long time ago to postpone, and every year it seems to get easier to live with the choice. But the difficult thing is that a lot of my friends who postponed for their careers, as I did for mine, are now starting their families, and I'm attending so many more baby showers. It really makes you take stock of what you are doing with your life."[12]

Millions of childless women and men in their late twenties and thirties are taking stock of their lives and deciding that the time is right to become parents. They have fueled the recent surge in the birthrate among women over thirty. In fact, these young professional parents have been largely responsible for transforming later-life parenting from something that is considered somewhat deviant to something that is thought of as rather chic.

As Nora Ephron, a fashionably late mother who had her first child at thirty-seven, remarked, "Just once in my life I would like to do something that everyone else isn't doing, but that seems not to be my destiny."[13]

Although most of the "new" older parents are married, a small but increasing number of unmarried women thirty-five or older have also joined the ranks of first-time parents. In 1970 only one in twenty children of older parents was born to an unmarried woman; by 1987 that proportion had jumped to one in eight.[14]

"Blended" Families

Divorce and remarriage have provided a relatively new route to becoming a child of older parents. Increasing numbers of men and women who have been married before and have children from earlier marriages are remarrying and choosing to have second families. Thus, the offspring of these new unions may well have older parents with much older stepbrothers and stepsisters. By the late 1980s, at least thirteen hundred new stepfamilies were being formed every day, and 20 percent of American households were "blended" families, the Stepfamily Foundation reported.[15] Given the statistical realities that the modal length of time from first marriage to divorce in America is two to four years (the median is seven years); that remarriages, on average, occur several years after divorce; and that childbearing typically occurs two years after marriage, these second families are not likely to get started until both spouses are at least well into their thirties.

This small-but-growing group of children of older parents was barely represented among those interviewed or surveyed, but one study of blended or "reconstituted" families, by social scientist Lucille Duberman, suggests some of the possible dimensions of their family lives. She found that family stability and "integration" of first and second families were higher among those that included children from the present marriage.[16]

Remarried couples may feel that children from their earlier marriages will profit from a new baby in the household, because it will teach them the responsibilities of child rearing. They may be treated as sort of substitute parents or surrogate aunts or uncles for the new children. But teenagers may have difficulty accepting their new half-siblings and, consequently, feel more alienated from their parents. In other cases, in which the parents' first generation of children is having children, these second-time-around parents may look upon their grandchildren as playmates and companions for their own new offspring.

Children may help cement the new marriage and may benefit from the wisdom of their parents' past experience with child rearing. But it is unclear how this new breed of latecomers—in some ways, like last-borns; in others, like firstborn children—will fare in what is certainly a nontraditional and confusing family constellation.

The Shrinking American Family

Somewhat paradoxically, the third important issue that is relevant to the increase in delayed childbearing is the fact that

American couples are having fewer children. As families have gotten smaller, the average span of childbearing years has grown shorter. In the 1950s, a typical woman might have had four children between her mid-twenties and mid-thirties. Today that same "typical" woman might have just two children. Demographers also predict that the percentage of one-child families in America will double between the 1960s and the late 1990s, from 15 to 30 percent. Because men and women who postpone childbearing tend to have smaller families than younger couples, often stopping after just one child, children of older parents will account for a disproportionate number of only children.

Smaller families have become culturally more desirable as more women work outside the home and the costs of rearing and educating children have skyrocketed. Contraception has made it possible to reduce drastically the numbers of unwanted or mistimed births. Even though most children of older parents are still of higher birth orders, the "tail-end," last-born child in large families is now more unusual than at virtually any other time in history.

The NCHS National Survey of Family Growth has traced the decline in births that were not wanted by the mother "at conception or any future time." In 1965, 33.7 percent of babies born to married thirty-five- to forty-four-year-old women in the five previous years were unwanted. By 1982 that figure had fallen to 15.9 percent. Thus, as the numbers of unwanted, higher-birth-order children of older parents has declined, the ranks of wanted first and second children among older mothers have increased.[17]

Another way of looking at the relationship between declining family size and the increasing tendency to delay parenthood is to examine levels of childlessness and expectations for childbearing among women in their thirties. In 1986, 23.9 percent of women thirty to thirty-four years old and 16.6 percent of those 35 to 39 were childless, according to the Census Bureau.[18] By contrast, in 1976 only 17 percent of women thirty to thirty-four and 10 percent of those in their late thirties had not had children. Even among married women in their early thirties, the frequency of childlessness has shot up since the 1970s.

When the census asked women about the number of children they had and the number they ultimately expected to have, a sharply higher proportion of white women between thirty and thirty-four had not yet given birth to their desired number of children in 1986 than a decade earlier. In 1976, women in this age group had had 93 percent of the children they expected to have; in 1986, that figure dropped to only 80 percent. Another census survey, in 1988, found that 54 percent of childless married women in their early thirties planned to have a baby in the future, up from 34 percent in 1975.[19]

The decline in childlessness from age thirty (31 percent of all women) to age forty-four (12 percent) obviously indicates that many women are having children in their thirties and early forties, yet substantial numbers are likely to remain childless. Studies suggest that roughly one in eight women born in 1946 will never have children, compared with just one in twelve of those born in 1934. The cultural trends toward later marriage and childbearing are indirectly resulting in greater childlessness, yet even these currently high rates are far from being the highest in American history. Of those women who were born in 1910 and came of age during the depression, 22 percent remained childless.[20] On the other hand, two social scientists, Arthur Campbell and David Bloom, have developed mathematical models that suggest that at current rates of childbearing, between 20 and 28 percent of women born in 1955 may never have children.[21]

Married couples also have been waiting longer to have children after getting married. According to Christine Winquist Nord, a demographer with Child Trends, a Washington, D.C., research organization: "The median first-birth interval after marriage for white women 30 and older, and giving birth between 1950 and 1954, was not quite 4 ½ years. For the period 1975–79, the interval had increased to 5 ½ years."[22]

A Snapshot of Older Parents

Given these circumstances for postponed childbearing, who are the older parents of the late twentieth century, and in what ways will their socioeconomic and cultural backgrounds affect their children?

Experts almost uniformly depict today's first-time mothers in their late thirties as having higher educational levels, higher-status jobs, and higher incomes, on average, than do younger mothers.

Paul Glick, the former senior demographer with the Census Bureau, speaks of a "U-shaped relationship between age of childbearing and socioeconomic status." "Those who are having their first or second child after thirty-five are well-educated women, women who have started a career and are in the best circumstances to give a developing child the best chances possible," he said. "But there are also poorer women who keep having children into their forties. And these children are born with a lot more handicaps."[23]

Nicholas Zill, director of Child Trends, agrees. "For the most part, older mothers tend to be a rather select group—more advantaged and better educated," he said. "Although there are still some lower-class women having their fifth or sixth child later, the stereotype of the welfare mother with a lot of children is becoming less common, as the use of birth control and sterilization have increased."[24]

Well-educated, well-to-do couples clearly aren't the only people postponing childbearing. And latecomers who are the last-borns in large families are not only the product of poorer households. However, class differences in parental timing are pronounced.

Among women giving birth in 1987, slightly more than one out of every six babies had mothers who had completed at least four years of college. For infants whose mothers were thirty-five or older, the proportion went up to nearly two out of five.

Older first-time mothers are even more likely to be college graduates. Only a small fraction of first-time mothers under age twenty-five have at least sixteen years of education, but among women thirty-five or older giving birth for the first time, more than half have college degrees.[25]

Similarly, a higher proportion of new, over-thirty mothers are employed. Some 68 percent of women who had their first child after turning thirty remained in the job market in 1987, compared with 54 percent of first-time mothers who were eighteen to twenty-four years old. Older mothers also re-enter the labor force at a faster rate than do younger mothers.[26]

The disproportionate number of upscale older parents is confirmed by reports from maternity wards throughout the country. The California Department of Health Services, for example, reports that 9.9 percent of births in the state were to women thirty-five or older—yet, in the upper-middle-class communities of Marin County and Santa Monica, the percentages jumped to 24.4 and 24.1, respectively; by comparison, in the more blue-collar city of Bakersfield, only 5.7 percent of births were to women in their late thirties or older.[27]

The greater stability of many of today's older parents is also suggested by their relatively low divorce rate. Nearly 40 percent of all divorces occur among couples under thirty, making "the twenties the most likely time to be getting divorced," according to Barbara Foley Wilson of the NCHS. "The divorce rates drop sharply by age."[28] Thus, if a married couple makes it into their thirties and has put off having children—or if a couple does not marry until their thirties—their children are more likely to have an intact family.

Social scientists have also found that older mothers and fathers tend to have higher child-care and other expenditures for their children. And, according to the National Survey of Children, older parents are less likely to move, adding another dimension of stability to their families' lives. This relatively rosy portrait of today's older parents suggests that their children are likely to benefit. Because children's well-being depends so much on their parents' desire and ability to invest in their future, the offspring of delayed childbearers may have an advantage over children of younger childbearers.

The New Older Parents Speak: The Joys of Later Parenthood

These statistics and studies depict the social facts, but what are the emotional facts—and fictions—of the new generation of older parents?

These parents and parents-to-be have been outspoken in recent books, articles, and television appearances. From these declarations, as well as from interviews with today's older mothers and fathers, the designs and desires of this new generation of older parents emerge. They are not as homogeneous as one might anticipate from the headlines, but they do have strong opinions. Some present familiar themes expressed by latecomers; others bring a very different perspective.

Many educated, professional older parents are highly articulate about their reasons for postponing childbearing, and about what they perceive as the mostly beneficial consequences of being older parents. Most people have children when they do simply because they want to, and they do not really consider what their timing decision may mean for their children ten, twenty, or forty years hence. Older parents find it especially easy to cite the reasons why both they and their children benefit from their decision to postpone. Potential drawbacks are almost never mentioned.

Their arguments frequently run something like this:

Older parents are more experienced as people and more secure emotionally, professionally, and financially than they were (or other parents are) in their twenties. Their children are especially wanted. They are generally able to be more involved in their children's lives than younger parents are. And, to top it off, their children make *them* feel "younger."

Indeed, these older mothers and fathers usually wax rhapsodic about how they and their children have benefited, are benefiting, and will benefit from their eminently wise choice to postpone.

"When you're close to forty, you've learned a lot more about life and are probably more mature and stable," said sociologist Iris Kern, who had her second child at forty-two. In a study she did of seventy-five older mothers, most "believed they were better mothers than they would have been or were earlier in their lives."[29]

People coming to parenthood in their mid- to late-thirties have had time to learn about themselves and the world and to sow their proverbial wild oats. They have had years to go on vacations and pamper themselves with clothes and gadgets. "You know what you're missing, and you don't mind missing it" is a common attitude among such older mothers.

"I had 15 years between graduating from college and becoming pregnant," Nora Ephron wrote. "Fifteen years to work at my career and live my life without the responsibilities of motherhood."[30]

The actress, Paula Prentiss, had her first child with her husband Richard Benjamin when she was thirty-six. "You can mess around when you're in your 20's, but in your 30's, you start questioning what you have accomplished," she said. "We decided we wanted children, and we bloomed."[31]

Older parents also say that, because of their age, they feel more sophisticated and self-assured in dealing with doctors, more calm about parenting, and better able to meet the demands of a young child than they would have in their twenties. They also insist, and many experts would agree, that they are less likely to regard minor problems as tragedies and are more aware of the complexities of child rearing than are younger parents. As a *Los Angeles Times* headline proclaimed, these older mothers and fathers believe they have reached "the age of enlightenment in parenthood."[32]

"You're so much more sure of yourself," a thirty-eight-year-old mother told *Newsweek*. "Mothers in their 20's are competing in the park as to how old their children were when they were toilet trained and when they walked. But at my age, you don't give a damn. Everyone walks or talks eventually. No one goes to Harvard still tugging on a bottle."[33]

One successful Broadway actress and director who adopted a child when she was fifty-five, nearly thirty years after her first children were born, added, "I don't really have to prove anything in my career. And I feel more relaxed about parenting since I've done it before."[34]

"I have loved children before, but other things competed for my thoughts—my manuscripts, my standing in the university, my friends, my future," Richard Taylor, a father again at age sixty-seven, wrote in the *New York Times Magazine*. "Now I stand outside the university. Challenges there are all past. I know where I shall always live and what my income will be. My thoughts are entirely free to focus on my wife and baby."[35]

People who marry and have children by their early twenties have little or no time to develop their own adult identities or to explore the potentials for intimacy between husband and wife. On the contrary, older parents say, they not only have gotten to know themselves by the time they have children but they also have been able to build a strong marital relationship.

"You feel more sure about your relationships, especially with your spouse," said a forty-seven-year-old first-time mother in Washington, D.C.

"Older couples who generally have been married longer have the advantage of a deeply established trust of one another," wrote Elisabeth Bing, co-author with Libby Colman of *Having a Baby After 30*, and a mother herself at forty.[36] Such perceptions are reflected in the significantly lower divorce rate for couples in their thirties and forties—compared with those in their twenties.

Many also feel that having children is like discovering a fountain of youth. As former President Jimmy Carter, whose daughter, Amy, was born when he was in his forties, was reported to have said: "She made me feel young again."[37]

Older parents tend to be more advanced in their careers, past many of the years of struggling to carve out a reasonably satisfying, secure, and successful professional niche during their twenties and early thirties. Of course, everyone does not follow the same life trajectory, and new tensions and life pressures do arise in one's thirties, yet many older parents say they feel more relaxed about life and themselves, and less conflict about taking time out for parenting. As a happy forty-three-year-old first-time mother said, "Five or ten years ago, I may have felt a child would have been an interference."

For those midlife mothers and fathers who are further along on a generally ascending earning curve, their worries about making ends meet have been replaced by ones about appropriate investments. As a "yuppie" joke has it, these older parents of today seem to be able to afford their first child and their first Volvo at just about the same time. Employing a sort of family version of "trickle-down" economics, they argue that their children will inevitably benefit by getting a bigger piece of a bigger pie.

∞

Nonetheless, the transition to parenthood is always a rite of passage that involves profound psychological and practical adjustments. For older couples who may have more established routines of work, leisure, and social life, the introduction of a small, crying infant may bring unexpectedly traumatic changes to aspects of their lives ranging from sex and sleep to finances and freedom.

Parenthood also generally brings about significant changes in an individual's self-image. Women who saw themselves as fast-track professionals or men who could never before imagine tolerating more than a few hours with a child seem suddenly to become soft and nurturing, entranced by their children. And some professional women-turned-mothers discover that they are wracked by guilt when they return to work.

One study of the psychological impact of parental age found that older mothers are more likely to feel tension between family relationships and "outside interests" like work than are younger women.[38] Thus, a baby can make a couple closer, but it can also test the strength of a relationship.

"The new baby almost wrecked my marriage," said one older father. "We're much more set in our ways and had a much harder time adjusting to the baby than if we were younger."[39]

Narcissism—at least in the sense of affirming one's symbolic immortality—is always present to some degree in the decision to have children. But there is another dimension of narcissism among some of today's men and women who are intentionally postponing parenthood as long as biologically possible.

Some older parents speak of having a child almost as if it were a new commodity to be added to other requisites of the good life such as a BMW, a country home, an art collection, or a portfolio of blue-chip investments. This feeling was perhaps inadvertently expressed in Terri Schultz's paean to delayed motherhood, *Women Can Wait*. A woman's late thirties, she wrote, are a time "when children are most deeply appreciated, are least threatening, and become, in all ways, a final celebration of oneself."[40]

Such declarations lend support to the have-your-cake-and-eat-it interpretation of postponed parenthood. Is it selfish for a sixty-year-old man—or, for that matter, a forty-year-old man or woman—to have children? For all the joys that a child may bring them, and all the loving attention that child will have early in life, is it fair, in the long run, to the child? Is fatherhood after fifty or even parenthood at forty something of an ego trip, an attempt to recapture youth or deny one's own aging?

"Implicit in their embrace of postponed parenthood is the assumption that the child exists for its parents' pleasure, [and that] its birth therefore should be scheduled for maximum convenience," wrote Merri Rosenberg, a child of older parents. Many who put off childbearing do not "seem to have considered the convenience of the child."[41]

Or that of their own parents. If people delay having children, their mothers and fathers may have less of a chance to enjoy their grandchildren. As *New York Times* humorist Russell Baker quipped, "The years keep rolling past, the hair keeps getting sparser, the vision keeps getting dimmer, and the grandchildren still fail to arrive."[42]

Acknowledging the Problems?

Certainly, few older parents are eager to speak about the disadvantages of later-life parenting, and many prospective mothers in their mid-thirties or older have a sort of knee-jerk reaction to such concerns: "Don't tell women there's something *else* to worry about!"

When pressed, some midlife parents *do* feel a residual social stigma that has caused them, or might cause their children, embarrassment. It is less possible for them to have large families, and less likely that they will have an extended family stretching over several generations. Some even express guilt about their ages, feeling their children will suffer.

"It has taken a tremendous emotional toll on me," said one Long Island woman who had her two children in her late thirties. She added that she felt guilty for not being able to provide her children with the sort of active experiences that she felt children of younger parents usually had. Another older mother noted, with some annoyance, that her children were quite conscious of her graying hair and loudly urged her to color it.

When a forty-six-year-old mother of a young child wrote to Miss Manners, the syndicated advice columnist, asking what to do when people "inevitably ask if I am his grandmother," the columnist suggested the appropriately honest and confusing reply, "No, my mother is."[43]

A few older parents recognize that they might have less physical energy or inclination than younger parents to play games or go on outings with their children. "I don't particularly enjoy, or have the patience for, field trips to the apple orchard crammed in a bus with twenty-five screeching, bouncy children," said a woman from Cambridge, Massachusetts, who had her children in her late thirties. "It doesn't seem like an 'ordeal' to the parents of my children's classmates. Is this a sign of age, or just that I would prefer to be elsewhere?"

But even if their physical vigor is diminished, they have

greater psychological energy and are able to provide their children with greater intellectual and cultural stimulation—or so older parents frequently say. Aside from being better able to take their youngsters on trips or to concerts and plays, some argue that their children will profit intellectually from being exposed to their friends and colleagues who are more mature than those of most younger parents.

A further defense is the argument that people today are "young" longer. Older parents assert that the dividing line between youth and middle age has been pushed back from thirty to forty. They say they are more physically fit and can expect to live longer than could parents even twenty years ago. As sociologist Iris Kern said: "Being 35 or 40 is not old today, whereas it might have been a generation ago."[44] And many women who have put off childbearing for their careers do insist that they will be as active and involved in parenting as they have been in their professions.

Probably the most widely perceived disadvantage of their timing of parenthood is that they find themselves caught between taking care of their children and their aging parents. Unlike twenty-five-year-old couples, whose parents are likely to be working and active, the parents of forty-year-olds are probably in their late sixties or seventies, and may be in declining health. Late-timing parents also may be barraged in their late fifties or early sixties with the simultaneous traumas of their parents becoming ill and dying, their children leaving home, and the winding down of their careers.

Some older parents also acknowledge feeling "out of sync" with their peers. While their children are in grade school, for example, their friends' children are in college. Conversely, most other parents with babies are younger than they are. From play groups to PTAs, couples who have waited to have children are likely to be surrounded by much younger parents. To ward off the attendant discontents, many over-thirty-five mothers have banded together to create same-age support groups whose members are drawn from their own professional circles and neighborhoods.

A few older parents worry about prematurely burdening their children with having to care for them in old age, or that they will not live long enough to get to know their children as adults. They realize their lower probability of surviving to see significant events in their children's lives, such as graduating from college, getting married, and having children: "What really bothers me a lot is that I'm not going to live to see my son really grown-up," said the actress who adopted when she was fifty-five. "I won't really be able to share in his young adulthood."

Another woman, who became a mother at forty, worriedly reflected that she and her husband would be on the verge of retirement when their daughter was in college. She was also saddened by the realization that if their daughter put off marriage and childbearing as long as they had, they might not be alive to see her marry and have children.

One man, whose daughter was born when he was fifty-two and his wife was forty-two, said that he had become "more aware of how many years I have left than how many years I've been." It is certainly doubtful that such thoughts would occur to a twenty-five-year-old father. As a result, he added, "We've gotten much more involved in planning for our retirement than we would have without her—especially in terms of having adequate funds for college and in terms of how we could prepare for our own dependent care without unduly burdening her."

"Death had always seemed to me a hundred years away until my new son was born," Richard Taylor, the sixty-seven-year-old father, wrote. Since his son's birth, he continued, "I began to feel the passing of every precious day," and his thoughts suddenly turned to life insurance, investments for his child's future and composing a will.[45]

But these people seem relatively unusual among today's older parents. Most simply don't think about the long-term future, twenty or thirty years after their children are born. And theirs is but one version of the story.

22

Postponed Parenthood Today

What Children of Older Parents Say

Today's older parents may have many reasons for having children after thirty-five, but what do children of older parents themselves think? Although their vantage point is necessarily one of a generation ago, they can undoubtedly offer insights on what this current trend may mean for the millions of latecomers born in the final years of the twentieth century.

Those who were surveyed for this book were asked about the recent upsurge in later-life parenting: Why are increasing numbers of people having their first child after thirty-five? What are likely to be the effects on the parents? And what are the probable consequences for the children?

In a philosophical mode, one woman said: "I would like to think that people are postponing due to a recognition that parenthood is a big responsibility and necessitates a certain level of psychological stability, but I suspect it's done more for economic reasons." These apparently opposing motives are not so contradictory as they might seem.

Over and over, respondents said that they thought people are taking longer to complete their educations, become established in their careers, and find satisfying and secure relationships. "It takes an average couple much longer now to achieve the same economic security as their parents," suggested a woman from San Mateo, California.

"People are waiting to be more financially secure and to see if their marriage lasts," ventured another respondent. These considerations have significance not only for the parents themselves but for their children as well.

Indeed, the most frequent explanations for delaying marriage

193

and childbearing were that more women want to pursue careers and that it is economically more difficult to support a family in one's twenties today. But men and women differed notice-ably—and predictably—in their answers: Forty-nine percent of the women, compared with 28 percent of the men, said that people are postponing because women are opting first for careers. The more general catchphrase—"economic reasons"—was sug-gested by 45 percent of the men but only 29 percent of the women.

A common thread underlying many of these responses was that older parents today are purposefully putting off childbearing, whereas older parents in the past generally did not do so by choice. "I think we are two completely different groups that should not be thrown into one pot," argued a Northern California woman. "Childhood and society are very different then and now. Older parents today are putting themselves first, not their chil-dren."

This perception that the new generation of older parents and their children are different from their predecessors was given a somewhat different slant by a middle-aged woman from Mount Kisco, New York. "Many older parents of people my age had lived through two world wars and the depression. This created a very special group of older parents. I would imagine that self-confident career couples in a fairly affluent peacetime society would be very different."

The reasons for postponing were viewed differently by those who emphasized changing values about personal fulfillment and the family. As one respondent succinctly put it: "Family relation-ships are seen as less important than personal success." Desires for personal growth or freedom were mentioned by 20 percent of the survey sample, and 16 percent said that couples are delay-ing childbearing in order to be more professionally or emotionally secure. The availability of birth control, changed social attitudes about the "appropriate" timing of parenthood, and selfishness were each noted by 7 to 8 percent of the respondents.

The idea that older parents and prospective parents are essentially self-centered—making their timing decisions for rea-sons that fail to consider the long-term best interests of their children—was surprisingly common. "Yuppie selfishness" and "prolonged adolescence" were phrases used by several later-born children, and one attributed the trend to "the Me Generation, which is still trying to get nurtured."

"Children are no longer the priority or symbol of status or fulfillment that they used to be," said a Virginia woman. "Everybody wants to do their own thing first. Kids are an economic liability, whereas they used to be an asset."

"Improved birth control allows people to postpone until they are forced to decide and have last-minute, now-or-never children," added a young New York woman. "It's almost as bad as the old 'accident' babies."

And a New Jersey man, who also felt that today's postponers seemed unable to accept family responsibilities, wryly suggested, "Having children late in life is bad for all parties if it's put off in the same manner as paying income taxes."

Good for the Parents

Given such comments, it is not surprising that postponed childbearing was generally considered good for parents by 43 percent of the respondents. Only 22 percent said the parents would not benefit. It is revealing, however, that answers to this question depended heavily on the respondents' age. Those in their twenties—who may delay parenting themselves—expressed this positive sentiment most strongly: Fifty-five percent thought that putting off childbearing was beneficial for couples. People over sixty had very different ideas: Only 19 percent said it was good for parents.

"It's very wise that women are putting off having kids," said a young Wisconsin woman. "Those women are terrific mothers. They have more time, more money in the bank, and more work experience. I don't think we'd have nearly the problems with youth today if it weren't for all the young parents and unmarried parents."

Others emphasized that "people will live longer and be 'younger' longer," as a Rhode Island woman put it. This notion—that older parents today are younger in spirit than those of even a generation ago—was frequently advanced.

Consequences for the Children: A Mixed View

Respondents were much more divided, however, about whether postponing would have good or bad effects on the current crop of children of older parents. One-third said that the children would generally be better off having older parents; one-third felt they would be hurt by the consequences of their parents' ages, and another third said it "depends" on the specific circumstances. These answers closely paralleled the responses to earlier questions about whether having older parents had been a net positive or negative influence on their own lives.

Older respondents, only children, and men were most pessimistic in their predictions. Interestingly, the over-sixty respondents forecast the experiences of the new generation of latecomers in a more negative way than they had reflected on their own experiences as children of older parents. Half of them said that the trend toward delayed childbearing would have a bad effect on the children, whereas only one-fifth thought the offspring would benefit.

Those who felt that postponed parenting would hurt the children offered an array of familiar reasons. Many of the negative feelings were summarized by a woman from West Hempstead, New York: "Fewer children will be born, many families will have only one child—a lonely situation—and they will be less likely to have grandparents for a substantial part of their lives. Parents may lack the energy to deal with adolescents when they are in their fifties. And will the parents live long enough to become grandparents themselves?"

Some thought that the children would suffer because they would be more likely to be orphaned or lose a parent early in life. As one woman said, "It's still very selfish to have a child late if the parents have no support network for their child."

Today's older parents also were often perceived as "too intense, going at child rearing in the same way they attack their careers," in the words of a Connecticut woman. Consequently, the children were expected to face greater pressures to achieve than those born to younger parents.

"These children will probably be born into more affluent

homes, with more mature but maybe more self-centered parents," said a New York respondent. "They are likely to have fewer siblings and less of a family identity. And they'll be more individualistic, type-A achievers."

Different parental qualities, suggesting different family outcomes, were emphasized by other respondents. As a Midwestern woman said: "The children will benefit if their parents have consciously chosen to have them, and if the parents are happier in their own lives." Others, with similar sentiments, said that today's latecomers would receive better parenting or feel advantaged because of the stability of their parents' marriages and the likelihood that their mothers and fathers really wanted them.

Changes in the population and social attitudes were noted as likely to affect the experiences of new families with latecomers. "Children born today to older parents will experience a very different childhood, adolescence, and adulthood from children of my generation," asserted one woman. "It is much more common now, and the negative stigma I felt as a child won't be so common for these kids. But I think the health-care system and work situations will need to change as more people will be coping with aging parents at a much younger age."

"If the trend continues," added a forty-two-year-old from Lincoln, Nebraska, "the children will have more reassurance that it's not 'strange' to have older parents. I think they will also respect older people more."

Not everyone was convinced, however, that recent cultural changes would really alter the overall picture of later-born children's lives. In many ways, they felt, these new latecomers will continue to be different from their peers. Although more late births are planned, people are living longer, healthier lives, and children of older parents will be less of a rarity in many communities, they are likely to have many of the same kinds of advantages, disadvantages, and different life experiences as later-born children of the 1950s or 1930s.

Wanted children of well-to-do, mature couples will feel more secure and "privileged," but, as a Chicago man said, it may be even harder for today's conscious postponers "to change their life-styles to accommodate a child. They will be less flexible, and physically they still won't be able to keep up with their children as well as younger parents."

These opinions and predictions raise many questions for families in which parents are older. They send warnings, highlight possible benefits, and suggest options for current and future generations of older mothers and fathers.

23
Perspectives

Are there lessons to be learned from the outpouring of feelings by children of older parents? Are there issues to be considered?

Contrasts and contradictions emerged from their remembrances and self-analyses. Some latecomers had very myopic, self-centered viewpoints, while others were able to step back from their lives and take a broader perspective on what having older-than-"normal" parents may mean. Individuals' relationships with their mothers and fathers, social norms, and their own experiences as parents undoubtedly affected interpretations of the import and impact of their parents' ages. Sometimes age may have been used as an excuse for an unhappy childhood or inappropriately credited as the reason for a good upbringing.

Yet, even if the effects of parental age cannot always be separated from those of other family, environmental, and societal factors, many common themes were apparent in the disparate experiences and points of view of the eight hundred later-born children who were the principal sources for this book. Their testimony has made it possible for the first time to go beyond speculations and stereotypes about the implications of parents' ages for their children.

Their stories, thoughts, and feelings offer perspectives that may help couples make a more informed decision about when to have children. They may sensitize parents and parents-to-be to an array of issues that, by and large, have rarely been discussed or considered by couples planning their families. These recollections and opinions may also alert parents to areas of potential vulnerability and opportunity, and give them important information to help them better understand their sons' and daughters' needs, fears, and concerns, as well as the broader psychological context of their children's lives.

The most obvious factor to consider is age itself. Because they are outside some assumed norm, too-old parents seem to flag "difference" that can create distress for a child. In large and small ways, gray hair, health problems, low energy, shortened life ahead, and looming retirement may intrude as problems or differences for children of older parents. These kinds of signposts of age can influence children's pride in or shame about their parents, their anxieties, and the conflicts or distance they feel between themselves and their parents. Age is what it is: Parents and children can accept or confront it, but—if we believe the latecomers' accounts—they cannot ignore it.

Those accounts and opinions and perspectives also provide the basis for establishing certain guidelines as to how older parents can reduce the problems and accentuate the advantages that are common among latecomers.

First, parents should be candid and straightforward about their ages and willing to discuss why they had their children when they did. Certainly there is nothing to be gained from dishonesty or dancing around the subject. Lies about one's age only imply that there is reason to be ashamed. Vanity wears pretty thin when counterposed against a child's discovery that his or her parents have lied. Children learn from their parents: Honesty, openness, and trust work both ways.

Differences in age, like differences in race, religion, occupation, or ethnic background, don't mean "better" or "worse" and should not be a cause for shame or embarrassment. Indeed, if the issue of age stands out in a child's mind, the many advantages of having older parents should be treated matter-of-factly and appropriately for the child's concerns.

As the Harvard pediatrician T. Berry Brazelton joked: "Older parents should convey that their children should feel lucky to have older, successful parents rather than tortured, searching, younger ones."[1]

The number of years separating parents and children is obviously unalterable. This quantitative distance between the generations does not have uniform consequences for a child, but it does *have* them. An almost inevitable effect is the emergence of a wider-than-usual generation gap, causing misunderstandings and clashes between parents and children.

If this gap is to be bridged, parents need to be sensitive to the historical and family contexts in which they were socialized, and how these differ from the contexts of their children's lives. However, a rational assessment of these differences does not eliminate feelings about different life-styles, values, and experiences that are the substance of each generation. Certainly, at a time when social and cultural changes are rapid and enormous, differences in outlook and taste between widely separated generations can be substantial.[2]

Parents are rooted in their pasts, and children are equally rooted in their own present. Understanding both realities would seem to help in negotiating the tensions of generational differences. Parents can also try to be attuned to what is current in popular culture, fashions, or more significant concerns and norms of their children's generation. But generational span need not always be defined as a gap; instead it may mean continuity with the past, and this continuity may lead to communication that bonds rather than divides.

The health-and-fitness movement of the last decade or so has made people of all ages more concerned about staying as physically fit and youthful as possible. This should be particularly important for older parents. When couples have chosen to put off childbearing and child rearing, their greater age increases the possibility of health problems and may diminish their resources of energy for bringing up a child. Yet they owe it to their children to be able to provide not only emotional and material well-being but also the active experiences that children need. Playing ball, going hiking or camping, and sharing similar activities with children are not unimportant. Older parents should, to the degree that it's possible, insure that at age fifty or sixty they will still have the stamina and vigor to pursue such activities.

If physical problems preclude this, the children's needs still must be met. Children can be encouraged to participate in sports with peers and other adults, even if parents must root from the sidelines.

Because many older parents put off having families to pursue careers, and the demands of busy professional lives undoubtedly offer stiff competition for their time, they face the problem of carving out time for their children. Experts say it is necessary to dispel the myth among these fortyish parents that they can really "have it all"—high-powered careers demanding sixty-hour work weeks, active social lives, *and* parenthood. Latecomers and child psychologists emphasize that parents should be available to devote enough of their precious time to nurturing close relationships with their children.

If parents are deeply involved in careers, they have to be sensitive to how time can be balanced between their work lives and their children. Compromises and hard choices must be made: A meeting or deadline sometimes must give way to a child's dental appointment or to attending a school play. Children may not always be the top priority, but they should not feel that they are being shortchanged or that they are intruders in their parents' lives.

Having more commitments and responsibilities are one lifestyle consequence of being older. Being more rigid and set in one's ways often—though not inevitably—is another. People in their fifth decade generally have countless more-or-less-unconscious and remarkably fixed patterns of behavior, ranging from how they spend their money to when they read the newspaper or watch television. The entry of a child into their lives will turn their world topsy-turvy. A one-year-old isn't going to wait patiently to be fed or have its diapers changed until the sports page is read or the evening movie breaks for a commercial. Because older parents' lives may be more governed by habits and routines than those of younger parents, it is important that they be alert to these patterns and accommodate to a child.

As Solomon M. Brownstein, executive director of Jewish Family Services in Houston, observed: "Part of the tension we see with older couples involves the issue of whether they can be as open and flexible as parents need to be."[3]

Of course, people's habits aren't easily malleable. But older parents can be aware that they will have to adapt their lifestyles to meet their children's needs. Paraphrasing the old jargon of the Cold War, what's called for is a truly "flexible-response capability."

While some older parents work hard at fitting children into their hectic schedules, others seem to sweep everything else in life aside to focus all their emotional energies on their children. They may deluge their offspring with love and set impossibly high standards for them. The hazards of having parents who are too perfectionistic or overattentive are well known.

Since today's latecomers are increasingly likely to be first-borns, parents should think very carefully about their optimal family size. If they want just one child, have they considered what it might mean to that child to have no brothers or sisters? Even if older parents are committed to having a second or third child, they must face the fact that they may be unable to do so. If additional children are not a possibility, then it is especially important to enrich a child's social world with peers.

Parents can expect to field an only child's questions about why they don't have siblings. Infertility is a touchy subject, and the honest-but-glib answer is that "We are/were too old." At least until a child is older, it may be better to stress how wanted their one child is.

Having an extended-family network is also important. Obviously, one cannot manufacture grandparents or aunts, uncles, and cousins, but if they do exist, ties can be cultivated and strengthened—if for no other reason than for the children's sake. Intergenerational links can be extremely valuable, so if grandparents have died, keeping memories of them alive can contribute to children's security and identity.

When blood relatives aren't living or aren't geographically or emotionally close, a surrogate extended family can be created with one's friends and their families. Ideally, such a network would include adults and children of varying ages.

Godparents, who all too often play a perfunctory role, should not be ignored either. In times past, they fulfilled a very significant cultural function—of being there if a child's biological parents were not. That function remains important, and—like it or not—it is likely to be more important for children of older parents than for the offspring of twenty-five-year-olds.

The issues of aging—of prolonged illness and death—should be squarely faced. What if parents need extensive medical care when their child is in college or just starting a career? At least the financial and other practical burdens of caring for aging parents can be cushioned by the parents' prior planning. Unless the child was brought up without a strong sense of moral responsibility, he or she will assume considerable caretaking burdens anyway. There is no need to make things worse just because one didn't want to think about the inevitable facts of aging. Wills and life-insurance policies need to be in order, and responsible guardians whom one's children trust and love should be in place.

As we have seen, long before becoming caretakers, children of older parents may fear that their mothers and fathers will die. These fears may be openly articulated, expressed in veiled form through nightmares or the metaphors of play, or hidden and repressed. In any case, they should be recognized and addressed.

The real problems of ill health or the reality of a parent's early death can impose severe strains on a child that should not be ignored because of the other parent's own fears or grief. Such circumstances obviously require deep emotional reserves, and professional counseling for a child may well be necessary. If a parent of a young child or adolescent does die, the child will inevitably assume some heavy responsibilities, but he or she should not be put into the role of the parent who has died.

Parents and prospective parents are not necessarily the only ones who need to be more sensitive to issues facing children of older parents. Their friends and spouses should also be aware that latecomers often have different concerns at different times in their lives. School counselors, psychotherapists, and other mental health professionals also tend to overlook the psychological significance of having older parents. To do so may be to miss one of the crucial variables in an individual's life.

Being a child of older parents is usually not, by itself, cause for either sorrow or celebration. However, when all is said, it is rarely a neutral matter. Latecomers have experiences and feelings that society has ignored, but as delayed childbearing becomes more commonplace, their concerns and needs increasingly will have to be addressed.

Furthermore, the shift toward later childbearing will have an ever-more-significant influence on the character of the family and on society's views of the norm. There will be individual and social consequences: Ideas of what is "older" will change in meaning. The span of generations will lengthen. Most importantly, adults starting families at thirty-five or forty will be different parents because of their accumulation of experiences, skills, capabilities, and habits. Consequently, the nature of parenting and parent-child relationships will change.

For children, having more mature and settled parents will bring many benefits. But other developmental consequences will also remain. All along the years, from the backyard ballgames never played and the grandparents never known to the feelings of being prematurely cast into adulthood and the early encounters with caregiving and death, current and future generations of latecomers will experience family life quite differently from most American children in the 20th century.

Appendix A
Later-Life Childbearing Throughout the World

Patterns of later-life childbearing throughout the world in 1977 and 1985 (when statistics are available), are presented in the following tables; 1985 was generally the most recent year for which statistics were available, and 1977 was chosen to illustrate changes that occurred in less than a decade. They show the percentages of births to mothers thirty-five and older; the live-birth rates for thirty-five- to thirty-nine-year-old mothers (per 1,000 corresponding female population); the percentage of total births to fathers thirty-five and older, and the live-birth rates for fathers thirty-five and older (for four age brackets per 1,000 corresponding male population). Statistics are taken from (or derived from) the 1986 and 1988 United Nations Demographic Yearbooks. Countries were selected on the basis of available data and to provide geographical, cultural, and socio-economic comparisons.

TABLE A1. Percentage of Total Births to Mothers Thirty-five and Older in Selected Countries (i.e., Percent of Those Born Who Are "Children of Older Mothers")

	1977	*1985*
UNITED STATES	4.4	6.1 (1984)
		7.5 (1987/NCHS)
CANADA	4.6	6.4
EUROPE		
Austria	8.5	6.3
Bulgaria	2.9	3.1
England and Wales	5.5	7.9
Finland	7.1	12.9
France	5.9	9.1
Greece	8.7	6.7
Ireland	15.4	16.2 (1984)
Italy	10.9	9.2 (1981)
Netherlands	5.0	7.2

TABLE A1. *Continued*

	1977	1985
Norway	5.2	9.0
Poland	6.3	7.0
Portugal	11.9	9.1
Soviet Union	—	6.8 (1986)
Spain	12.5	11.8 (1980)
Sweden	6.2	11.7
Switzerland	7.5	8.6
West Germany	9.7	8.6
OCEANIA		
Australia	5.3	7.5
New Zealand	4.6	5.9
Samoa	15.5	—
ASIA and AFRICA		
Bangladesh	—	12.4 (1982)
Egypt	23.3	20.3 (1982)
Hong Kong	7.5	7.1
Iraq	16.3	—
Israel	8.3	11.9
Japan	4.0	7.1
Kuwait	12.3	14.8 (1984)
Philippines	16.1	13.9 (1982)
Rwanda	24.6 (1978)	—
South Korea	7.8	2.6 (1983)
Thailand	16.7	10.2 (1984)
LATIN AMERICA		
Argentina	—	12.5 (1982)
Brazil	11.9	10.1 (1984)
Chile	10.6	9.5
Costa Rica	9.2	8.6 (1984)
Cuba	6.5	4.3
Guatemala	14.4	15.7
Mexico	14.6	13.2 (1982)
Venezuela	11.9	11.4

TABLE A2. Live-Birth Rates for Thirty-five to Thirty-nine-Year-Old Mothers for Selected Countries (per 1,000 Corresponding Female Population)

	1977		1987	
UNITED STATES	19.2		24.3	(1986)
CANADA	20.1		23.2	
EUROPE				
Austria	21.9		18.5	
Bulgaria	12.2		10.0	(1986)
England and Wales	18.3		24.1	(1985)
Finland	25.6		31.1	(1986)
France	23.9		31.4	
Greece	31.5		21.3	(1984)
Ireland	93.9		74.5	(1985)
Italy	32.2		26.3	(1982)
Netherlands	17.2		21.2	(1986)
Norway	20.9		24.6	
Poland	30.6		27.2	
Portugal	48.0		25.9	
Soviet Union	—		33.8	(1986)
Spain	54.4	(1978)	42.5	(1981)
Sweden	20.7		33.2	
Switzerland	21.8		24.4	
West Germany	18.6		23.8	(1986)
OCEANIA				
Australia	24.0		25.0	(1983)
New Zealand	22.1		27.0	
Samoa	102.4		—	
ASIA and AFRICA				
Bangladesh	—		127.4	(1981)
Egypt	—		177.8	(1982)
Hong Kong	45.7		26.1	
Iraq	135.8		—	
Israel	81.1		73.9	
Japan	13.9		17.2	(1986)
Kuwait	166.5	(1980)	128.5	(1986)
Philippines	135.9		97.1	(1986)
Rwanda	307.8	(1978)	—	
South Korea	33.0	(1978)	7.0	(1986)
Thailand	107.9		35.2	

TABLE A2. *Continued*

	1977	*1985*	
LATIN AMERICA			
Argentina	—	74.4	(1980)
Brazil	69.6	50.0	(1986)
Chile	52.1	48.0	(1986)
Costa Rica	—	76.8	(1984)
Cuba	28.0	17.7	(1986)
Guatemala	177.9	183.0	(1985)
Mexico	104.8	82.5	(1980)
Venezuela	129.4	71.9	

TABLE A3. Percentage of Total Births to Fathers Thirty-five and Older in Selected Countries (for Fathers Whose Ages Are Known; i.e., "Children of Older Fathers")

UNITED STATES	(1984)	16.1
CANADA	(1979)	13.7
EUROPE		
France	(1981)	16.7
Hungary	(1985)	10.1
Italy	(1981)	23.2
Norway	(1984)	20.9
Poland	(1985)	14.2
Portugal	(1985)	17.2
Spain	(1980)	23.3
United Kingdom (England and Wales)	(1985)	19.5
Yugoslavia	(1982)	14.6
OCEANIA		
Australia	(1985)	20.1
New Zealand	(1985)	17.0
Samoa	(1980)	35.0
ASIA		
Hong Kong	(1985)	25.4
Iraq	(1977)	41.1
Israel	(1985)	26.3
Kuwait	(1984)	43.7
Philippines	(1982)	25.0
South Korea	(1983)	10.2

TABLE A3. *Continued*

AFRICA		
Egypt	(1982)	43.3
Libya	(1977)	65.7
LATIN AMERICA		
Chile	(1985)	21.5
Costa Rica	(1984)	22.8
Cuba	(1985)	15.1
El Salvador	(1984)	29.0
Mexico	(1983)	25.2

TABLE A4 Live-Birth Rates for Fathers Thirty-five and Older in Selected Countries (per 1,000 Corresponding Male Population)

		35–39	*40–44*	*45–49*	*50–54*
UNITED STATES	(1984)	49.4	18.5	6.6	2.4
CANADA	(1979)	45.6	15.8	5.0	1.4
EUROPE					
England and Wales	(1985)	43.2	16.7	6.7	2.4
France	(1981)	55.9	20.2	7.1	2.4
Hungary	(1985)	26.9	10.0	3.2	0.9
Italy	(1981)	51.0	20.3	6.5	1.7
Norway	(1984)	46.5	16.8	5.7	1.8
Poland	(1985)	48.0	21.8	7.6	1.9
Portugal	(1985)	44.7	19.7	8.2	3.0
Spain	(1978)	79.8	38.2	12.2	2.6
Yugoslavia	(1982)	49.1	21.1	7.0 (45 & over)	
OCEANIA					
Australia	(1983)	54.2	19.7	6.9	2.4
New Zealand	(1985)	51.9	18.2	6.8	2.1
ASIA					
Hong Kong	(1985)	60.6	28.5	11.0	5.0
Iraq	(1977)	211.8	144.8	90.5	59.5
Israel	(1985)	119.5	63.8	21.8	7.1
Kuwait	(1984)	125.9	96.7	75.9	50.4
Philippines	(1980)	153.8	109.8	56.9	22.1
South Korea	(1983)	46.5	13.0	3.6 (45 & over)	

TABLE A4. *Continued*

		35–39	*40–44*	*45–49*	*50–54*
AFRICA					
Egypt	(1982)	258.4	159.6	109.2	56.9
LATIN AMERICA					
Costa Rica	(1984)	146.6	86.4 (40 to 49)		26.7
Cuba	(1985)	48.3	23.5	9.9	4.6
Mexico	(1980)	119.6	82.2	47.4	—

Appendix B
Age and Childbearing in the United States

TABLE B1. Live Births in the United States, by Age of Mother, 1987

Age	Number	Percentage of Total
Under 15	10,311	0.27
15–19	462,312	12.14
20–24	1,075,856	28.24
25–29	1,216,080	31.92
30–34	760,695	19.97
35–39	247,984	6.51
40–44	34,781	0.91
45–49	1,375	0.04
(Total)	3,809,394	100.00

TABLE B2. Births to Women Thirty-five and Older, by Birth Order, 1987

Birth Order	Number
All births	284,140
First child	55,325
Second child	80,887
Third child	65,197
Fourth and over	81,288
Not stated	1,353

TABLE B3. Percentage of Births to Currently Married Women Not Wanted at Conception or Any Future Time, by Age and Year

	1965	1973	1982
AGE			
15–24	13.1	7.5	4.3
25–34	21.1	12.0	5.9
35–44	33.7	34.0	15.9

TABLE B4. Percentage of American Women Childless by Age, 1986

Age	Percentage
18–24	71.9
25–29	41.0
30–34	23.9
35–39	17.1
40–44	13.3

TABLE B5. Percentage of Births to College Graduates, by Age, 1987

Age	Percentage
All ages	17.6
20–24	4.1
25–29	20.8
30–34	34.7
35–39	40.0
40 and over	33.7

TABLE B6. Number and Percentage of Total Births to Women Thirty-five and Older, by Race, 1987

Race	Number	Percent
All races	284,140	7.5
White	210,970	7.7
Black	34,764	5.4
American Indian	2,554	5.8
Asian American	17,133	13.3

Sources: National Center for Health Statistics, Advance Report of Final Natality Statistics, 1987, 1986 (Tables 1, 2, 5, and 6); Population Reference Bureau, Understanding U.S. Fertility, December 1984 (table 3); and Bureau of the Census, Fertility of American Women: June 1986 (table 4).

Appendix C
Medical Issues of Later-Life Childbearing

Obstetricians have traditionally characterized over-thirty-five women as potentially "high-risk" mothers. They have been found to have a higher incidence of complications during pregnancy and childbirth, and their children have a higher probability of chromosomal abnormalities leading to such conditions as Down's syndrome.

Whereas the mid-twenties are medically the safest time for a woman to have a baby, the recent revolution in prenatal care has reduced the risks in later-life childbearing through improved prebirth medical care and better knowledge of nutritional and life-style effects on pregnancy. And the relatively recent introduction of amniocentesis—a procedure to determine the presence of serious genetic and biochemical problems in the fetus—has made it possible for older mothers-to-be to choose whether to continue a pregnancy in which a fetal abnormality exists.

Nonetheless, other medical conditions affect over-thirty-five mothers and their children more than younger mothers and their babies. Women in their late thirties are considerably more likely to have fertility problems or to lose a pregnancy through miscarriage or stillbirth. They also are prime candidates for giving birth by cesarean section, and their infants have a somewhat higher chance of being born with a low birth weight.

On the other hand, older prospective mothers tend to take somewhat better care of themselves and their unborn children than do women in their teens or early twenties. The more education a woman has (and older mothers today tend to be much better educated than the general population), the less chance she has of having a newborn die or giving birth to a low-birth-weight infant.

Fertility Problems

It has long been known that infertility tends to increase with age. Thus many later-born children have been born to parents who had tried to conceive for years and would have preferred to have had children earlier.

Today, however, women who choose to put off childbearing must confront the odds that they will have greater difficulty conceiving than they might have had in their twenties. Women thirty-five and over are twice as likely to be infertile as women in their late twenties and early thirties, and they have four times the infertility rate of women in their early twenties.[1] Drugs such as Clomid or Pergonal—part of a $1-billion-a-year fertility business—can improve the chances for some women to conceive. But the older a woman is, the greater her likelihood of having problems like endometriosis and pelvic inflammatory disease, which can cause impaired fertility.

Problem Pregnancies and Problem Births

Older women are also more likely to have miscarriages or stillbirths. In the early 1980s, excluding induced abortions, about 16 percent of pregnancies in the United States ended in miscarriages or stillbirths.[2] However, the pregnancy-loss rate for women ages thirty-five to forty-four was nearly double the national average, and triple that for women in their twenties. Ectopic pregnancies—when a fertilized egg is implanted in a part of the reproductive system other than the uterus—are also about three times as common among women over thirty-five than among women younger than twenty-five.

Perhaps because of the heightened risk of Down's syndrome or a lingering social stigma about later-life childbearing, 37 percent of pregnancies among women over forty were terminated by abortion in 1983. By comparison, 26 percent of all pregnancies, and 24 percent among thirty-five to thirty-nine-year-old women, ended in abortion, according to a study by Stephanie Ventura, Selma Taffel, and William Mosher of the NCHS.[3]

The neonatal infant mortality rate, one of the most closely monitored indicators of a society's health, was 11.0 per 1,000 live births in the United States in 1980. Newborns were at the greatest risk of dying in their first year of life if their mothers were either very young or relatively old. The rate was 31.5 for ten to fourteen-year-old mothers and 22.6 for forty-five to forty-nine-year-old mothers. Babies born to women between twenty-five and thirty-four had the lowest risk of dying, but infants born to women in their late thirties were also at somewhat lower risk than the general population. For them, the infant mortality rate was 10.8.

Not long ago, cesarean sections—in which a baby is delivered through incisions in the mother's abdomen and uterus—were a fairly uncommon medical procedure, used only in cases of problem pregnancies. Since about 1970 there has been a marked and controversial increase in cesareans—controversial because some doctors have questioned whether many of them are necessary. By the late 1980s, one in four births in the United States were by C-section.[4]

Older women are most likely to have cesareans. Among over-thirty-five mothers, 32.6 percent of births were by C-section in 1986—a much higher percentage than for women in their twenties. The higher rate is partly because older mothers are likelier to have longer, more difficult labor, their fetuses are at greater risk of being in an abnormal position (so-called "breech babies"), and they are generally subject to more delivery complications such as the premature rupture of the amniotic sac ("the water breaking"). Older women also have a higher incidence of fibroids and herpes, and women who have already had C-section deliveries are likely to have them again. Two researchers attribute the increase in C-sections to "a tendency for physicians to elect this procedure because the patient was older, either to safeguard the 'long awaited child' or to avoid anticipated complications."[5]

Although maternal death in childbirth is extremely uncommon, the mortality rate for cesarean deliveries was forty-one per one hundred thousand births in 1978—four times the rate for vaginal deliveries.

One curious fact is that older women give birth to twins and triplets more often than do women in their teens and twenties. All told, about 2.1 percent of deliveries in the United States in 1985 were multiple births. But, for thirty-five to thirty-nine-year-old women, the peak age group for plural births, the rate was 2.8 percent.[6] This difference may be because higher birth orders more often result in multiple births or because older women are more likely to take fertility drugs.

Health-Conscious Mothers

Older mothers today are somewhat more health conscious than women in their early twenties or teens, and they are likely to begin prenatal care earlier.[7] These better-educated mothers also appear to pay greater attention to eating well and reducing environmental and life-style factors that could have a harmful effect on their pregnancies. Several studies have found that mothers over thirty tend to smoke less during their pregnancies. On the other hand, 49 percent of these women consumed alcohol during their pregnancies, compared with 41 percent of those in their early twenties and only 29 percent of teenage mothers, according to the NCHS.[8]

Risks for Children

Children of over-thirty-five mothers are somewhat more likely to have health problems than the offspring of younger mothers.

The incidence of low birth weight, a key measure of infant health, is highest among children of older mothers. For first births, "the ideal age of the mother is 25-to-29 years," according to Stephanie Ventura of the NCHS. In 1979, 6.2 percent of first births to mothers in this age group were of low birth weight (defined as less than 2,500 grams, or 5 pounds, 8 ounces), compared with 9.8 percent for women thirty-five- to thirty-nine years.[9]

About one in ten American babies is born after less than nine months of pregnancy, and these premature births tend to be low birth weight and account for two-thirds of the babies who die before age one. However, the percentage of preterm births to over-thirty-five women is not significantly different from the percentage among younger women.

Age seems to be a less-crucial predictor of low birth weight than socioeconomic status as measured by educational attainment. Mothers with sixteen or more years of schooling—who now are especially common among first-time older parents— are 20 to 30 percent less likely to have low-birth-weight infants than are all women in their age groups, Ms. Ventura found. (Similarly, infant mortality rates among babies born to college graduates are less than half what they are for the offspring of women who have not completed high school.)[10]

Another way of evaluating a newborn infant's overall physical condition at birth is by something known as the Apgar score. Named after the late pediatrician Virginia Apgar, who developed it in 1954, the score assigns numerical values to an infant's heart rate, respiratory effort, muscle tone, reflex irritability, and color. Although the absolute incidence of low scores, which indicate that a baby is in some difficulty, is small, infants born to teenage mothers and mothers in their forties are more likely to have lower scores.[11]

But the best-known and most-feared outcomes of later-life pregnancies are Down's syndrome and other chromosomal defects. And as the National Down Syndrome Society bluntly states: "Since many are postponing parenting until the fourth decade of life, the incidence of Down's syndrome is expected to increase."[12]

Down's syndrome, or mongolism, is a form of mental retardation that results from a genetic defect and occurs in about 1 in every 800 births. (It accounts for nearly half the 10,000 to 15,000 births in the United States each year with some chromosome problem.) However, the incidence of Down's syndrome increases markedly among children born to women in their late thirties. It occurs in about 1 in 400 births to thirty-five-year-old mothers, 1 in 105 births to forty-year-old mothers, and 1 in 20 births to forty-six-year-old mothers.[13]

One reason that genetic problems may be more likely among older mothers is that older women's eggs, or oocytes, generally are not in as good condition as those of younger women. Whereas men produce new sperm continually, women are born with all the eggs they will ever have. Thus a thirty-eight-year-old woman has thirty-eight-year-old eggs that have had more time to be exposed to damaging influences such as drugs or radiation.

The most common form of Down's syndrome, Trisomy 21, results when either the egg or the sperm contributes an extra chromosome to the twenty-first chromosome pair. This in turn produces mental retardation that ranges from severe to mild, with the average IQ about thirty to fifty. It also produces physical problems that may include improper heart development, respiratory difficulties, immature digestive tracts, inner-ear fluid retention that can cause hearing and speech problems, premature aging, and greater susceptibility to infection, leukemia, and Alzheimer's disease. Furthermore, Down's syndrome children tend to have abnormally developed facial, hand, and pelvic characteristics. The life expectancy of Down's syndrome adults is about fifty years.

Most cases in which extra genetic material causes chromosomal abnormalities are believed to be linked to the mother, but recent research has shown that the father is the source of the extra chromosome in about 20 to 30 percent of cases. There are conflicting findings, but several studies have suggested that the risk of genetic defects increases for children of older fathers.[14]

Until a decade or two ago, most Down's syndrome children were institutionalized. Today most are cared for at home. Research and experience have shown that parental love and care, medical intervention, and continuing education can attenuate the extent of retardation and health problems. But, despite the advances and the high "social quotient" of Down's syndrome children, "the individual with Down's syndrome presents unusual and demanding problems at virtually every stage of life, beginning at birth," as a government pamphlet says.[15] And certainly most prospective older parents dread the possibility that they might have a genetically deformed child.

A number of the children of older parents interviewed and surveyed for this book indicated that they had siblings with Down's syndrome, and that it often cast a pall over their own lives. Having a sister with Down's syndrome, one woman recalled, meant that family activities and resources were limited and left her feeling deprived and lonely.

Several other, much more rare genetic defects and medical problems also occur with greater frequency among the offspring of older mothers. These include cleft lip and palate, spina bifida, childhood leukemia, cerebral palsy, congenital heart defects, and dwarfism.

Prenatal Screening

In recent years health professionals have increasingly advised over-thirty-five parents to see genetic counselors and have prenatal screening for possible genetic problems. The most-commonly-used medical procedure to determine whether a fetus has Down's syndrome or other disorders is amniocentesis.

Widely used only since the late 1970s, amniocentesis is able to detect major chromosomal abnormalities and about seventy inherited biochemical disorders. The procedure involves removing fluid from the amniotic sac surrounding the developing fetus in the womb. Cells shed by the fetus into the fluid are prepared for chromosomal analysis within about two to three weeks. The procedure, which is 99 percent accurate, is best performed between the sixteenth and eighteenth week of pregnancy. Amniocentesis is considered highly safe, although it has about a one in two hundred to a one in five hundred risk of infection, hemorrhage, or miscarriage (roughly equal to the risk to a thirty-five-year-old mother of carrying a Down's syndrome child). It usually takes several weeks for test results to be known, and many women describe this waiting period as the most traumatic time of the pregnancy.

Amniocentesis can either reassure parents-to-be that their child is free of genetic defects, or—in the rare case of a positive test result—give them the option of terminating the pregnancy. As William N. Spellacy, an obstetrician/gynecologist at the University of South Florida at Tampa, said, "Amniocentesis now ferrets out the chance of older women having genetically abnormal babies. It makes them at no greater risk than younger mothers."[16]

However, difficult psychological and moral issues surround the decision to continue or abort a pregnancy. Since amniocentesis results are not available until the fifth month of pregnancy, an abortion is then more traumatic and requires hospitalization.

A newer, alternative prenatal test, known as chorionic villus sampling (CVS), has become popular since it was introduced in the United States in 1983 because it can be performed as early as nine weeks into a pregnancy. This technique involves removing material from the outside of the fetal sac near the placenta. However, some recent studies have found that CVS may be somewhat less accurate than amniocentesis and may result in a higher risk of spontaneous abortion.

Despite the relatively greater risks associated with delayed childbearing, the absolute chances of having any of these medical problems is still small for women in their late thirties and early forties. Age, per se, is probably less important in affecting the outcome of a pregnancy than a mother's general health and well-being, her life-style, and her feelings about herself and mother-hood.

Dramatic improvements in high-risk obstetric care, prenatal tests like amniocentesis and CVS, and the improved overall health of older women today compared with those of several generations ago have led doctors to revise their assessments of the risks of later childbearing. One recent study, for example, at Memorial Hospital Medical Center of Long Beach, California, compared childbearing among women thirty-five and older with women twenty to twenty-five, and concluded that "when they are given good prenatal and intrapartum care . . . the risks to healthy women 35 years and older may be no more than the risks of the younger (women)."[17]

∞

A number of books have been published that address the medical issues of having a baby in one's thirties or forties. These include Elisabeth Bing and Libby Colman's *Having a Baby After 30*, Judith Blackfield Cohen's *Parenthood After 30?*, Clark Gillespie's *Primelife Pregnancy*, and Virginia Apgar and Joan Beck's *Is My Baby All Right?*

Tables of Health Statistics

TABLE C1. Percentage of Women (Excluding the Surgically Sterile) with Impaired Fecundity, by Age (1982)

Age	Percentage
15–19	2
20–24	7
25–29	13
30–34	15
35–39	28
40–44	28

TABLE C2. Rate of Pregnancy Loss (Excluding Abortions), by Age (1982)

Age	Percentage
15–24	15.1
25–34	16.6
35–44	30.8

TABLE C3. Percentage of Births Delivered by Cesarean Section, by Age (1986)

Age	Percentage
Under 20	18
20–24	22
25–29	25
30–34	26
35 and older	33

TABLE C4. Percentage of Total Births with Low Birth Weight (Under 2,500 Grams), by Age (1987)

Age	Percentage
15–19	9.3
20–24	7.1
25–29	6.1
30–34	6.2
35–39	6.9
40–44	8.0
45–49	10.3

TABLE C5. Incidence of Down's Syndrome by Maternal Age

Age	Incidence
Under 30	less than 1/1,000
30	1/900
35	1/400
36	1/300
37	1/230
38	1/180
39	1/135
40	1/105
42	1/60
44	1/35
46	1/20
48	1/12

Sources: National Center for Health Statistics, *Fecundity, Infertility, and Reproductive Health in the United States, 1982* (tables 1 and 2); Selma Taffel and Mary Moien, "1986 C-Sections Rise," *American Journal of Public Health* (table 3); National Center for Health Statistics, *Advance Report of Final Natality Statistics, 1987* (table 4); and U.S. Public Health Service, *Facts About Down Syndrome* (table 5).

Appendix D
Questionnaire Sample Description and Survey Results

More than 800 people participated in the research for this book. A questionnaire, which I sent to most of them, was completed by nearly 650 children of older parents.

A description of the sample and selected survey results follow. Responses to open-ended questions and other qualitative data from the questionnaire have been presented and discussed in the preceding chapters.

The survey results offer a quantitative perspective on the significance of different issues, concerns, and perceptions of parental characteristics and parent-child relationships. For example, how close were these children to their parents and how involved were their parents with them? How did they view their parents' appearance, energy, and health? Did parents influence their maturity, values, and interpersonal skills?

The questions were structured so that respondents could indicate for each issue how positively or negatively they viewed their parents' influence on each dimension, and whether that influence was perceived differently in childhood, adolescence, and adulthood. Additional questions explored such subjects as the composition of an individual's family and social world; whether the individual's birth was planned or "accidental," and the meanings of the current societal trend toward postponed parenthood. Several open-ended queries encouraged respondents to indicate other subjects of personal importance related to having older parents.

The survey sample does not purport to be representative, yet it is a large and varied swath of children of older parents of all ages from all parts of North America. To take into account the different contexts in which children of older parents grow up, their experiences and responses were examined, considering whether they were only children or last-borns, and the age of their parents (that is, children born when their mothers were thirty-five to thirty-nine were compared with those born when their mothers were forty or older, and children born when their fathers were thirty-five to forty-nine were compared with those born when their fathers were fifty or older). Answers were also evaluated on the basis of the respondents' gender and present age. Where significant differences relating to these variables emerged, they have been discussed in the text and are noted in the following tables and charts. In order to compare the experiences of children of older parents with a sample that included children of younger parents, approximately seventy students at Hunter College were also administered the questionnaire; some of the results have been noted in the text.

TABLE D1. Description of Sample

Age of Parents at Child's Birth (Percentages)[a]		
	Mother	*Father*
35 to 39	54	25
40 to 44	36	34
45 to 54	4	32
55 and over	0	5

Mother's mean age: 38.5
Father's mean age: 43.4

Distribution by Birth Order (Percentages)	
Only children	19
Firstborn children (excluding onlies)	7
Middle-born children	11
Last-born children	62

Distribution by Age of Respondent (in Percentages)	
Under 30	16
30 to 45	40
46 to 60	26
61 and over	18

Geographical Distribution of Known Cases		
	Number	*Percentage*
New England	90	12.5
Middle Atlantic	362	48.5
Southeast	55	7.5
South	28	4.0
Midwest	105	14.5
Mountain and Southwest	9	1.5
West Coast	69	9.5

TABLE D1. *Continued*

	Number	Percentage
Canada	10	1.5
Caribbean	4	
Europe, Middle East, and Africa	4	
Asia	4	
	(Overseas total—2.0)	
Unknown	50	

Planned vs. Accidental

Question: Did your parents have you when they did as:

A planned baby:	49%
An "accident":	33%
Don't know:	17%

N = approximately 800.

[a] Six percent of respondents had mothers under 35, and 3 percent had fathers under 35; their answers were excluded.

TABLE D2. Evaluation of Effects of Parental Age at Different Times in Child's Life (Percentages)

	Mother		Father	
	Positive	Negative	Positive	Negative
In childhood	34	28	30	28
In adolescence	23	53	23	47
As a young adult	31	33	29	36
Later in adulthood	30	36	29	33

TABLE D3. Positive and Negative Influences of Parental Characteristics (Percentages)

	Appearance		Energy		Health	
	Mother	Father	Mother	Father	Mother	Father
In childhood						
Positive	20	20	32	29	25	26
Negative	20	15	27	25	28	18
In adolescence						
Positive	17	18	26	24	26	20
Negative	38	27	35	36	21	33
In adulthood						
Positive	23	22	27	23	20	17
Negative	14	14	32	32	49	53

TABLE D4. Children's Appraisal of Relationships with Parents (Percentages)

	Parents' Involvement		Closeness to Parents	
	Mother	Father	Mother	Father
In childhood				
Positive	49	44	47	42
Negative	19	19	23	23
In adolescence				
Positive	37	34	31	46
Negative	32	32	26	46
In adulthood				
Positive	43	38	43	38
Negative	23	23	28	23

	Parent as Role Model		Generation Gap with Parents	
	Mother	Father	Mother	Father
In childhood				
Positive	29	26	16	14
Negative	20	18	27	24
In adolescence				
Positive	16	16	9	8
Negative	45	38	63	60
In adulthood				
Positive	27	31	19	15
Negative	35	24	37	32

TABLE D5. Influences of Parents' Ages on Child (Percentages)

	Positive	Negative
Family's economic well-being	39	17
Maturity	54	17
Personality	45	17
Values	62	8
Interpersonal relationships	31	25

Question: Have your parents' ages influenced your wishes or decisions about the age you would prefer to have, or have had, children?

No: 34%   Yes: 66%

TABLE D6. Child's Social World

Question: When you were growing up, how many of your friends' parents were about the same age as yours?

None: 44%   A few: 44%   Many: 12%

Question: Were there fewer, more, or the same number of the following adults in your life as a child than was true of other children?

Parents' friends	Fewer: 38%	More: 34%	Same: 28%
Relatives	Fewer: 39%	More: 34%	Same: 26%
Grandparents	Fewer: 82%	More: 6%	Same: 12%

TABLE D7. Comparisons of Only and Last-Born Children (Percentages)

	Onlies	Last-Borns
Planned children	68	39
"Accidents"	18	44
Parents involved with children	58	41
Did things together with father	48	35
Knew many of parents' friends	52	29
Generation gap with mother	47	35

TABLE D8. Children of Fathers 50 and Over vs. Fathers 35 to 49 (Percentages)

	Fathers 50+	Fathers 35–49
Close to father	57	39
Not close to father	16	25
Father a role model	31	13
Father not a role model	28	40
No generation gap	8	10
Generation gap	44	63
Fears about father's health	48	30
Fears that father will die	29	21

TABLE D9. Different Perspectives on Parents, by Age of Respondent (Percentages)

	30 and Under	31–45	46–60	Over 60
Positive influence:				
on maturity	71	52	51	43
on personality	59	43	42	39
Positive role models	38	25	26	35
Negative feelings about caregiving	19	36	31	20

Questions about Delayed Parenthood Today

Increasing numbers of people are having their first child after the age of 35. Do you think this is:

Good for the children:	32%
Bad for the children:	36%
Doesn't matter	32%
Good for the parents:	43%
Bad for the parents:	22%
Doesn't matter:	36%

Why do you think this is happening?

Women want careers first:	45%
"Economic reasons":	32%
Personal goals:	20%
People waiting until established and mature:	16%
Birth control:	8%
"Selfishness:"	7%
Changed social attitudes:	7%
Less pressure to have children:	7%

What is likely to be the main effect on the children?

A bad experience; parents distant, children lonely:	21%
Better parenting:	15%
Children orphaned, parents die earlier:	12%
Marriages more stable:	12%
More pressure for children to achieve:	9%
A good experience because children wanted:	8%

Notes

Preface

1. The phrase "children of older parents" is used to refer to people who were born when both their parents were at least thirty-five years old. This somewhat cumbersome locution is used interchangeably with "latecomers" and "later-born children." This is not to be confused with "last-born," which refers to the last of many children born into a family. "Older parents," "midlife parents," and so on, refer to mothers and fathers who have had children after their thirty-fifth birthdays. "Much-older fathers" is an admittedly arbitrary description of men who were fifty or older when their children were born. The rarely used female counterpart, "much-older mothers," refers to women who have had children after turning forty.

2. Results and analysis of my questionnaire are presented in Appendix D. Because of the nature of the survey, these findings may be of limited generalizability and point up the need for additional, systematic research.

Chapter 1. All But Ignored

1. Cited in Carin Rubenstein, "The Baby Bomb," *New York Times Magazine,* October 8, 1989, p. 34.

2. Names and other clearly identifying facts about people who are quoted or described have been changed to insure confidentiality. Where extended case histories are presented, written permission has been obtained from the individuals discussed.

Chapter 3. Society Knows Best?

1. Glen H. Elder, Jr., "Approaches to Social Change and the Family," *American Journal of Sociology* 84, supp. (1978), pp. 25–26.

2. Glen H. Elder, Jr., Pamela Daniels, and Kathy Weingarten, *Sooner or Later: The Timing of Parenthood in Adult Lives* (New York: Norton, 1982).

3. Cited in Phyllis Kernoff Mansfield and Margaret D. Cohn, "Stress and Later-Life Childbearing: Important Implications for Nursing," *Maternal-Child Nursing Journal* 15:3 (Fall 1986), p. 140.

4. Ibid.

5. "Parental Age and Characteristics of the Offspring," *Annals of the New York Academy of Sciences* 57 (1954), ed. Roy Waldo Miner, pp. 451–614.

6. Mansfield and Cohn, p. 141.

7. Barbara M. Newman and Philip R. Newman, *Development Through Life: A Psychosocial Approach* (Pacific Grove, Calif.: Brooks/Cole Publishing Company, 1975), pp. 420–437; and Joan Aldous, *Family Careers: Developmental Change in Families* (New York: Wiley, 1978).

8. "The Philip Morris Family Survey," conducted by Louis Harris and Associates, April 1987.

9. Donna S. Kirz, Wendy Dorchester, and Roger K. Freeman, "Advanced Maternal Age: The Mature Gravida," *American Journal of Obstetrics and Gynecology* 152:1 (May 1985), pp. 7–12.

Chapter 4. Nothing New

1. Cited in Melvin Konner, "Childbearing and Age," *New York Times Magazine*, December 27, 1987, p. 22.

2. Telephone communication with Lawrence Stone, May 8, 1988.

3. Ibid.

4. John Demos, *Past, Present and Personal: The Family and the Life Course in American History* (New York: Oxford University Press, 1986), p. 47.

5. See Edward Anthony Wrigley, *Population and History* (New York: McGraw-Hill, 1969).

6. Pamela Daniels and Kathy Weingarten, *Sooner or Later: The Timing of Parenthood in Adult Lives* (New York: Norton, 1982), p. 3.

7. Telephone communication with Paul Glick, professor of sociology at Arizona State University and former senior demographer with the Census Bureau, March 23, 1988.

8. Thomas P. Monahan, *The Pattern of Age at Marriage in the United States* (Philadelphia: Stephenson-bros., 1951), cited in John Modell and Frank F. Furstenberg, Jr., "The Timing of Marriage in the Transition to Adulthood: Continuity and Change, 1860–1975," *American Journal of Sociology* 84: Supplement (1978), 122.

9. Personal communication with Stephanie Ventura at NCHS, Hyattsville, Md., December 11, 1987.

10. Telephone communication with John Modell, May 6, 1988.

11. Telephone communication with John Demos, May 6, 1988.

12. Daniels and Weingarten, p. 14.

13. Telephone communication with John Modell, May 6, 1988.

Chapter 5. Feeling Different

1. Ross D. Parke, "Families in a Life-Span Perspective," in *Child Development in Life-Span Perspective*, ed. E. M. Hetherington, R. M. Lerner, and M. Perlmutter (Hillsdale, N.J.: Lawrence Erlbaum Associates, 1988), p. 181.

Chapter 6. A Different Adult World

1. Andrew J. Cherlin and Frank F. Furstenberg, Jr., *The New American Grandparent* (New York: Basic Books, 1986), p. 26.

2. Ibid., p. 167.

3. Arthur Kornhaber and Kenneth L. Woodward, *Grandparents/Grandchildren: The Vital Connection* (Garden City, N.Y.: Anchor Press, 1981), p. 42.

Chapter 7. Family Constellations

1. Cited in Lucille K. Forer and Henry Still, *The Birth Order Factor* (New York: D. McKay Co., 1976), pp. 6, 255.

2. Relatively recent studies on birth order include Toni Falbo, ed., *The Single-Child Family* (New York: Guilford Press, 1984); Forer and Still; Walter Toman, *Family Constellation: Its Effect on Personality and Social Behavior* (New York: Springer, 1976), and Bradford Wilson and George Edington, *First Child, Second Child* (New York: McGraw-Hill, 1981). Other recent research was reported in Daniel Goleman, "Spacing of Siblings Strongly Linked to Success in Life," *New York Times,* May 28, 1985., sec. C, p. 1.

3. Forer and Still, p. 12.

4. Falbo, p. 16.

5. Frank Sulloway, "Orthodoxy and Innovation in Science," paper presented at the annual meeting of the American Association for the Advancement of Science, New Orleans, La., February 1990.

6. A study by psychologist James J. Conley found that disproportionate numbers of onlies and last-borns in large families were alcoholics—a fact that he attributed to their presumably more permissive upbringing, and greater dependence and impulsivity. See James J. Conley, "Family Configuration as an Etiological Factor in Alcoholism," *Journal of Abnormal Psychology* 89 (1980), pp. 670–73.

7. Wilson and Edington, p. 119.

8. Ibid.; see Judith Blake, "Number of Siblings and Educational Attainment," *Science,* no. 245 (July 7, 1989).

9. Daniel Goleman, "Spacing of Siblings Strongly Linked to Success in Life," *New York Times,* May 28, 1985, sec. C, p. 1.

10. Ibid; Falbo, p. 3; and H. E. Jones in *Manual of Child Psychology,* ed. L. Carmichael (New York: John Wiley & Sons, 1959), pp. 631–696.

11. Forer and Still, pp. 8–11, 224.

12. Falbo, p. 1.

13. Ibid, p. 17.

14. See Judith Blake, "The Only Child in America: Prejudice versus Performance," *Population and Development Review,* 7:1 (March 1981).

15. Falbo, p. 2.

Chapter 9. "Accidents"

1. There is no Yiddish word *mazinta*, but the nearest translation, *mezinke*, does in fact mean "youngest," according to the League for Yiddish.

2. William F. Pratt, William D. Mosher, Christine A. Bachrach, and Marjorie C. Horn, "Understanding U.S. Fertility: Finding from the National Survey of Family Growth, Cycle 3," *Population Bulletin* 39:5 (December 1984), p. 31.

Chapter 10. Long-Awaited Children

1. Among only children, 68 percent thought of themselves as "planned" babies and only 18 saw themselves as "accidents." By contrast, 44 percent of the last-borns believed that they were accidents, whereas 39 percent felt that they had been planned by their parents. The remainder said that they did not know whether they had been planned.

2. Fifty-two percent of onlies said that they were acquainted with a lot of their parents' friends, compared with just 29 percent of last-borns.

3. Forty-seven percent of the onlies spoke of a decisive generation gap, compared with 35 percent of the last-borns. Similarly just 35 percent of the onlies said that, as adults, they were close to their mothers, compared with 44 percent of last-borns.

Chapter 12. Parents of Another Era

1. Cited in Judy Klemesrud, "Older Fathers: Becoming a Parent after 50," *New York Times*, January 7, 1985, sec. B, p. 8.

2. NCHS, *Advance Report on Final Natality Statistics, 1987*, (Hyattsville, Md.: U.S. Government Printing Office, 1989), p. 26.

Chapter 13. Children of Privilege

1. Andrew L. Yarrow, "Older Parents' Child: Growing up Special," *New York Times*, January 26, 1987, sec. A, p. 32; and telephone communication with Jerome Kagan, January 20, 1987.

2. Cited in Christine Winquist Nord, *Delayed Childbearing in the United States: Implications for Women's Lives and Family Life*, draft chapters of an unpublished dissertation, 1986, Tables 6–7 and 6–9.

3. Personal communication with Grazyna Kochanska in Bethesda, Md., July 22, 1988.

4. Pamela Daniels and Kathy Weingarten, *Sooner or Later: The Timing of Parenthood in Adult LIves* (New York: Norton, 1982), pp. 71–72, 144.

5. See Nord, *Delayed Childbearing in the United States*, Tables 6–11.

6. Arlene S. Ragozin, Robert B. Basham, Keith A. Crnic, Mark T. Greenberg, and Nancy M. Robinson, "Effects of Maternal Age on Parenting Role," *Developmental Psychology* 18:4 (1982), p. 627.

7. Eleanor A. Maccoby and John A. Martin, "Socialization in the Context of the Family: Parent–Child Interaction," in *Handbook of Child Psychology*, ed. Paul H. Mussen (New York: John Wiley & Sons, 1983), p. 48; Jane Price, *You're Not Too Old to Have a Baby*, pp. 119–120; and telephone communication with T. Berry Brazelton, January 18, 1987.

8. Telephone communication with T. Berry Brazelton, January 18, 1987.

Chapter 15. Facing Mortality

1. Claudia L. Jewett, *Helping Children Cope with Separation and Loss* (Cambridge, Mass.: Harvard Common Press, 1982), p. 106.

Chapter 18. Caregiving

1. Personal communication with Robert Butler at Mt. Sinai Medical Center, New York City, March 22, 1988.

2. Telephone communication with Mirca Liberti, Jan. 20, 1987; see also Andrew L. Yarrow, "Older Parents' Child: Growing Up Special," *The New York Times*, January 26, 1987, sec. A, P. 32.

3. Cited in Elaine M. Brody, "Parent Care as a Normative Family Stress," *Gerontologist*, 25:1 (1985), p. 21.

4. Ibid, p. 20.

5. American Association of Retired Persons and The Travelers Companies Foundation, "A Working Caregivers Report," March 1989.

6. Cited in Tamar Lewin, "Aging Parents: Women's Burden Grows," *New York Times*, November 14, 1989, sec. A, p. 1.

7. American Association of Retired Persons and The Travelers Companies Foundation; and "Juggling Family, Job and Aged Dependent," *New York Times*, January 26, 1989, sec. B, p. 8.

8. Amy Horowitz, "Family Caregiving to the Frail Elderly," in *Annual Review of Gerontology and Geriatrics*, edited by M. P. Lawton and G. Maddox (New York: Springer, 1985), p. 195.

9. Victor G. Cicirelli, *Helping Elderly Parents: The Role of Adult Children* (Boston: Auburn House, 1981), pp. 169, 152.

10. Lissy Jarvik and Gary Small, *Parentcare* (New York: Crown, 1988), p. 10.

11. Telephone communication with Elaine Brody, March 11, 1988.

12. Elaine M. Brody, "'Women in the Middle' and Family Help to Older People," *Gerontologist* 21:5 (1981), p. 476.

13. NCHS, *Health United States, 1989* (Hyattsville, Md.: U.S. Government Printing Office, 1990).

14. Robert R. Cadmus, *Caring for Your Aging Parents: A Concerned, Complete Guide for Children of the Elderly* (Englewood Cliffs, N.J.: Prentice-Hall, 1984), p. 27.

15. Ibid, p. 6.

16. American Association of Retired Persons and The Travelers Companies Foundation.

17. Horowitz, p. 200.

18. Brody, p. 474.

Chapter 20. Evolving Relationships and Changing Perspectives

1. Elisabeth Bing and Libby Colman, *Having a Baby After 30* (New York: Bantam Books, 1980), p. 166.

Chapter 21. A New Generation of Older Parents

1. Population Reference Bureau, *World Population Data Sheet*, (Washington, D.C., 1990).

2. The numbers are even more dramatic for women thirty or older: By the late 1980s, nearly one-third of all births, or more than a million American babies a year, were to women who had passed their thirtieth birthdays.

3. Whereas American husbands, on average, are about two and a half years older than their wives, the later a woman marries, the closer in age her husband is likely to be. In fact, NCHS statistics indicate that only about two-thirds of the thirty-five-or-older mothers had husbands who were also at least thirty-five. By contrast, in about 85 percent of marriages, the husband is older than the wife, or the spouses are the same age.

4. Personal communication with Stephanie Ventura at NCHS, Hyattsville, Md., December 22, 1987.

5. Telephone communication with Martin O'Connell, March 24, 1988.

6. For example, during the brief period from 1973 to 1982, the proportion of contracepting married couples used sterilization increased from 23 to 41 percent, according to the NCHS.

7. Cited in Christine Winquist Nord, "Delayed Childbearing in the United States: Implications for Women's Lives and Family Life," draft chapters of an unpublished dissertation, 1986, p. 42.

8. Pamela Daniels and Kathy Weingarten, *Sooner or Later: The Timing of Parenthood in Adult Lives* (New York: Norton, 1982), p. 169.

9. Gail Sheehy, *Passages: Predictable Crises of Adult Life* (New York: B. P. Dutton, 1976), p. 265.

10. Phyllis Kernoff Mansfield and Margaret D. Cohn, "Stess and Later-Life Childbearing: Important Implications for Nursing," *Maternal-Child Nursing Journal* 15:3 (Fall 1986), p. 139.

11. Letter to the editor from Naomi Segal Deitz, *New York Times*, November 23, 1989, sec. A, p. 26.

12. Molly McKaughan, *The Biological Clock: Reconciling Careers and Motherhood in the 1980's* (New York: Doubleday, 1987), p. 31.

13. Nora Ephron, "Having a Baby After 35," *New York Times Magazine*, November 26, 1978, p. 100.

14. Personal communication with Stephanie Ventura, NCHS, Hyattsville, Md., December 11, 1987; and NCHS, Monthly Vital Statistics Report, *Advance Report on Final Natality Statistics, 1987*, vol. 38, no. 3, (supplement) (Hyattsville, Md.: U.S. Government Printing Office, 1989).

15. Stepfamily Foundation Surveys; telephone communication with Jeannette Lofas, foundation president, July 27, 1990.

16. Lucille Duberman, *The Reconstituted Family: A Study of Remarried Couples and their Children* (Chicago: Nelson-Hall, 1975), pp. 31–33, 61.

17. William F. Pratt, William D. Mosher, Christine A. Bachrach, and Marjorie C. Horn, "Understanding U.S. Fertility: Findings from the National Survey of Family Growth, Cycle III," *Population Bulletin* 39:5 (Washington: December 1984), p. 31.

18. Bureau of the Census, *Fertility of American Women: June 1986*, Series P-20, No. 421 (Washington: U.S. Government Printing Office, 1987), p. 6.

19. Bureau of the Census, *Fertility of American Women: June 1988*, Series P-20, No. 436 (Washington: U.S. Government Printing Office, 1989), p. 12.

20. Personal communication with Stephanie Ventura at NCHS, Hyattsville, Md., December 11, 1987.

21. Cited in Christine Winquist Nord, p. 24.

22. Ibid, pp. 36–37.

23. Telephone communication with Paul Glick, March 23, 1988.

24. Telephone communication with Nicholas Zill, March 10, 1988.

25. NCHS, Monthly Statistics Report, *Advance Report on Final Natality Statistics, 1987*, vol. 38, no. 3, supp. (Hyattsville, Md.: U.S. Government Printing Office, 1989), p. 9.

26. Bureau of the Census, *Fertility of American Women: June 1988*, Series P-20, No. 436 (Washington: U.S. Government Printing Office, 1989), pp. 3–6.

27. California Department of Health Service Birth Records, Telephone communication, May 21, 1990.

28. Personal communication with Barbara Foley Wilson, NCHS, Hyattsville, Md., December 11, 1987.

29. Iris Kern, *No Better Time: The Choice of Parenting After 35*, paper delivered to the annual meeting of the National Association of Social Workers, Washington, November 22, 1983.

30. Ephron, p. 125.

31. Cited in Linda Bird Francke and Mary Hager, "A Baby After 30," *Newsweek*, November 13, 1978, p. 128.

32. Beverly Beyette, "Reaching the Age of Enlightenment in Parenthood," *Los Angeles Times*, June 16, 1985, View sec. p. 1.

33. Francke and Hager, p. 128.

34. Cited in Andrew L. Yarrow, "Older Parents' Child: Growing Up Special," *New York Times*, January 26, 1987, sec. A, p. 32.

35. Richard Taylor, "A Fulfillment," *New York Times Magazine*, March 29, 1987, p. 62.

36. Elisabeth Bing and Libby Colman, *Having a Baby After 30* (New York: Bantam Books, 1980), p. 121.

37. Cited in Jane Price, *You're Not Too Old to Have a Baby* (New York: Farrar, Straus and Giroux, 1977), p. 14.

38. Susan Bram and Meredith Gould, "The Psychological Impact of Parental Age on Primiparae and their Infants" (unpublished manuscript).

39. Cited in "At Long Last Motherhood," *Newsweek*, March 16, 1981, p. 87.

40. Terri Schultz, *Women Can Wait: The Pleasures of Motherhood After 30* (Garden City, N.Y.: Doubleday, 1979), p. xx.

41. Merri Rosenberg, "A Child of Older Parents," *New York Times*, September 4, 1980, op-ed page, sec. A, p. 27.

42. Russell Baker, "Grandchildless," *The New York Times Magazine*, July 25, 1976.

43. "Miss Manners," *Washington Post*, May 22, 1988, sec. G, p. 7.

44. Telephone communication with Iris Kern, January 19, 1987.

45. Taylor, p. 62.

Chapter 23. Perspectives

1. Telephone communication with T. Berry Brazelton, January 18, 1987.

2. Given the relationship between social change and the intergenerational tensions or "gaps," it would be interesting to examine the nature of parent-child generation gaps in extraordinarily stable cultures or subcultures.

3. Telephone communication with Solomon M. Brownstein, January 20, 1987.

Appendix C

1. The infertility rate for women thirty-five and older was 28 percent in 1982, according to NCHS report entitled *Fecundity, Infertility and Reproductive Health in the United States*, ser. 23, no. 14 (Hyattsville, Md.: U.S. Government Printing Office, 1987), p. 2.

2. Ibid.

3. Personal communication with Stephanie Ventura, NCHS, Hyattsville, Md., December 11, 1987.

4. NCHS Monthly Vital Statistics Report, *Advance Report on Final Natality Statistics 1987*, vol. 38, no. 3, supp. (Hyattsville, Md.: U.S. Government Printing Office, 1989).

5. Phyllis Kernoff Mansfield and Margaret D. Cohn, "Stress and Later-Life Childbearing: Important Implications for Nursing," *Maternal-Child Nursing Journal*, 15:3 (Fall 1986), p. 144.

6. NCHS Monthly Vital Statistics Report, p. 7. the percentage of older mothers with multiple births was not only one-third higher than the national average but also nearly triple that of teenage mothers.

7. Ibid.

8. Elsie R. Pamuk and William D. Mosher, "Health Aspects of Pregnancy and Childbirth," *Vital and Health Statistics*, Series 23, No. 16, NCHS (Hyattsville, Md.: U.S. Government Printing Office, 1988).

9. Stephanie Ventura, "Trends in First Births to Older Mothers, 1970–79," *National Center for Health Statistics Monthly Vital Statistics Report*, 31:2, supp. 2 (May 27, 1982).

10. Ibid.

11. According to the NCHS, in 1987, 2.5 percent of babies born to women over forty and 2.6 percent of those born to teenagers had Apgar scores (taken five minutes after birth) of less than 7, on a scale of 0 to 10. For mothers aged twenty-five to twenty-nine, the percentage was just 1.6. NCHS, Monthly Vital Statistics Report, *Advance Report of Final Natality Statistics 1987*, vol. 38, no. 3, supp., Table 34, p. 45.

12. National Down Syndrome Society, *Questions and Answers About Down Syndrome* (New York, n.d.).

13. National Institute of Child Health and Human Development, *Facts About Down Syndrome*. (Bethesda, Md., n.d.).

14. See National Institute of Child Health and Human Development; Z. H. Lian; M. M. Zack; and J. D. Erickson, "Paternal Age and the Occurrence of Birth Defects," *American Journal of Human Genetics*, (November 1986), 39:5; J. M. Friedman, "Genetic Disease in the Offspring of Older Fathers," *Obstetric Gynecology* (June 1981); 57:6; R. H. Martin, and A. W. Rademaker, "The Effect of Age on the Frequency of Sperm Chromosomal Abnormalities in Normal Men," *American Journal of Human Genetics* 41:3 (September 1987).

15. National Institute of Child Health and Human Development, *Facts About Down Syndrome for Women Over 35*, N.I.H. Publication no. 82–536, Bethesda, Md., June 1982.

16. Telephone communication with William Spellacy, January 22, 1987.

17. Donna S. Kirz, Wendy Dorchester, and Roger K. Freeman, "Advanced Maternal Age: The Mature Gravida," *American Journal of Obstetrics and Gynecology* 152:1 (May 1, 1985), pp. 7–12.

Bibliography

American Association of Retired Persons and The Travelers Companies Foundation. *National Survey of Caregivers*. Washington, D.C., March 1989.

Annals of the New York Academy of Sciences, 57 (1954). Roy Waldo Miner, ed., "Parental Age and Characteristics of the Offspring."

"At Long Last Motherhood." *Newsweek*, March 16, 1981.

Barkan, Susan E., and Michael B. Bracken. "Delayed Childbearing: No Evidence for Increased Risk of Low Birth Weight and Preterm Delivery." *American Journal of Epidemiology* 125:1 (1987).

Belsky, Jay, Richard M. Lerner, and Graham B. Spanier. *The Child in the Family*. Reading, Mass.: Addison-Wesley Publishing Company, 1984.

Bing, Elisabeth, and Libby Colman. *Having a Baby After 30*. New York: Bantam Books, 1980.

Blake, Judith. "The Only Child in America: Prejudice versus Performance," *Population and Development Review*. 7:1 (March 1981).

———. "Number of Siblings and Educational Attainment." *Science* 245 (July 7, 1989).

Bram, Susan, and Meredith Gould. "The Psychological Impact of Parental Age on Primiparae and their Infants." (unpublished manuscript)

Brody, Elaine M. "Parent Care as a Normative Family Stress." *Gerontologist* 25:1 (1985).

———. " 'Women in the Middle' and Family Help to Older People." *Gerontologist* 21:5 (1981).

Brody, Elaine M., Morton H. Kleban, Pauline T. Johnsen, Christine Hoffman, and Claire B. Schoonover. "Work Status and Parent Care: A Comparison of Four Groups of Women." *Gerontologist* 27:2 (1987).

Bureau of the Census. Current Population Reports. *Fertility of American Women: June 1986. Series P-20, No. 421. Washington, D.C.: U.S. Government Printing Office, 1987.*

———. Current Population Reports. *Fertility of American Women: June 1988*, Series P-20, No. 436. Washington, D.C.: U.S. Government Printing Office, 1989.

Cadmus, Robert R. *Caring for Your Aging Parents: A Concerned, Complete Guide for Children of the Elderly*. Englewood Cliffs, N.J.: Prentice-Hall, 1984.

Carter, Betty, and Monica McGoldrick, eds. *The Changing Family Life Cycle*. New York: Gardner Press, 1988.

Cherlin, Andrew J., and Frank F. Furstenberg, Jr. *The New American Grandparent*. New York: Basic Books, 1986.

Cicirelli, Victor G. *Helping Elderly Parents: The Role of Adult Children*. Boston: Auburn House, 1981.

Cohen, Judith Blackfield. *Parenthood After 30? A Guide to Personal Choice.* Lexington, Mass.: Lexington Books, 1985.

Cohen, Stephen Z., and Bruce Michael Gans. *The Other Generation Gap: The Middle-Aged and Their Aging Parents.* Chicago: Follet Publishing Co., 1978.

Collins, Glenn. "More Older Women are Becoming Mothers, Study Shows." *New York Times,* September 29, 1980.

Conley, James J. "Family Configuration as an Etiological Factor in Alcoholism." *Journal of Abnormal Psychology* 89 (1980).

Daniels, Pamela, and Kathy Weingarten. *Sooner or Later: The Timing of Parenthood in Adult Lives.* New York: Norton, 1982.

Demos, John. *Past, Present and Personal: The Family and the Life Course in American History.* New York: Oxford University Press, 1986.

Diagram Group. *Mothers: 100 Mothers of the Famous and Infamous.* New York: Paddington Press, 1976.

Duberman, Lucille. *The Reconstituted Family: A Study of Remarried Couples and their Children.* Chicago: Nelson-Hall, 1975.

Elder, Glen H., Jr. "Approaches to Social Change and the Family." *American Journal of Sociology* 84, supp. (1978).

Ephron, Nora. "Having a Baby After 35." *New York Times Magazine,* November 26 (1978).

Fabe, Marilyn, and Norma Wikler. *Up Against the Clock.* New York: Random House, 1979.

Falbo, Toni, ed. *The Single-Child Family.* New York: Guilford Press, 1984.

Fleming, Anne Taylor. "Babies Over 40." *Lear's,* September–October 1988.

Foner, Anne. "Age Stratification and the Changing Family." *American Journal of Sociology* 84, supp. (1978).

Forer, Lucille K., and Henry Still. *The Birth Order Factor: How Your Personality Is Influenced by Your Place in the Family.* New York: D. McKay Co., 1976.

Francke, Linda Bird, and Mary Hager. "A Baby After 30." *Newsweek,* November 13, 1978.

Gamarekian, Barbara. "Childbirth After 35: Dispelling Myths." *New York Times,* November 27, 1983.

Gillespie, Clark, M.D. *Primelife Pregnancy: All You Need to Know About Pregnancy After 35.* New York: Harper & Row, 1987.

Goleman, Daniel. "Spacing of Siblings Strongly Linked to Success in Life." *New York Times,* May 28, 1985.

———. "Historian Links Birth Order to Innovation." *New York Times,* May 8, 1990.

Horowitz, Amy. "Family Caregiving to the Frail Elderly." In *Annual Review of Gerontology and Geriatrics,* M. P. Lawton and G. Maddox. New York: Springer Publishing Company, 1985.

Jarvik, Lissy, and Gary Small. *Parentcare: A Commonsense Guide for Adult Children.* New York: Crown Publishers, 1988.

Jewett, Claudia L. *Helping Children Cope with Separation and Loss.* Cambridge, Mass: Harvard University Press, 1982.

Karp, David A., and William C. Yoels. *Experiencing the Life Cycle: A Social Psychology of Aging.* Springfield, Ill.: C. C. Thomas, 1982.

Kern, Iris. "No Better Time: The Choice of Parenting After 35." Paper delivered to the annual meeting of the National Association of Social Workers, Washington, D.C., November 22, 1983.

Kirz, Donna S., Wendy Dorchester, and Roger K. Freeman. "Advanced Maternal Age: The Mature Gravida," *American Journal of Obstetrics and Gynecology* 152:1, (May 1, 1985), pp. 7–12.

Klemesrud, Judy. "Older Fathers: Becoming a Parent After 30." *New York Times,* January 7, 1985.

Konner, Melvin, M.D. "Childbearing and Age." *New York Times Magazine,* December 27, 1987.

Kornhaber, Arthur, and Kenneth L. Woodward. *Grandparents/Grandchildren: The Vital Connection.* Garden City, N.Y.: Anchor Press, 1981.

Kuhn, Reinhard. *Corruption in Paradise: The Child in Western Literature.* Hanover and London: University Press of New England, 1982.

Lubic, Ruth Watson, and Gene R. Hawes. *Childbearing: A Book of Choices.* New York: McGraw-Hill, 1987.

Mansfield, Phyllis Kernoff, and Margaret D. Cohn. "Stress and Later-Life Childbearing: Important Implications for Nursing." *Maternal-Child Nursing Journal,* 15:3 (Fall 1986).

McKaughan, Molly. *The Biological Clock: Reconciling Careers and Motherhood in the 1980's.* New York: Doubleday, 1987.

Modell, John, and Frank F. Furstenberg, Jr. "The Timing of Marriage in the Transition to Adulthood: Continuity and Change, 1860–1975." *American Journal of Sociology* 84, supp. (1978).

Morris, Monica. "Children of Older Mothers and Fathers Face Special Challenges." *Los Angeles Times,* March 28, 1984.

———. "Children's Perceptions of Last-Chance Parents: Some Implications of Current Trends Towards Late Childbearing." (unpublished paper).

———. *Last-Chance Children.* New York: Columbia University Press, 1988.

Morse, Susan. "Clearly on the Upswing." *Washington Post,* January 16, 1984.

National Center for Health Statistics (NCHS). Monthly Vital Statistics Reports. *Advance Report on Final Natality Statistics.* 1984, 1985, 1986, and 1987. Hyattsville, Md.: U.S. Government Printing Office, Vols. 35–38, no. 3, supplements, 1986, 1987, 1988, 1989.

National Down Syndrome Society. *Questions and Answers About Down Syndrome.* New York, n.d.

Nord, Christine Winquist. *Delayed Childbearing in the United States: Implications for Women's Lives and Family Life.* Draft chapters of an unpublished dissertation, 1986.

Parachini, Allan. "Over-35 Pregnancy No Longer Termed 'Risky.'" *Los Angeles Times,* March 25, 1986.

Parke, Ross D. "Families in Life-Span Perspective," In *Child Development in Life Span Perspective.* Ed. E. M. Hetherington, R. M. Lerner, and M. Perimutter. Hillsdale, N.J.: Lawrence Erlbaum Associates, 1988

Phil Donahue Show. "Grandmothers Giving Birth," January 21, 1988.

Porter, Jill. "Better Late than Early." *Philadelphia Inquirer,* May 8, 1988.

Pratt, William F., William D. Mosher, Christine A. Bachrach, and Marjorie C. Horn. "Understanding U.S. Fertility: Findings from the National Survey of Family Growth, Cycle III." *Population Bulletin* 39:5, December 1984.

Price, Jane. *You're Not Too Old to Have a Baby*. New York: Farrar, Straus, and Giroux, 1977.

Prouty, Olive Higgins. *Now, Voyager*. Cambridge, Mass.: Riverside Press, 1941.

Ragozin, Arlene S., Robert B. Basham, Keith A. Crnic, Mark T. Greenberg, and Nancy M. Robinson. "Effects of Maternal Age on Parenting Role." *Developmental Psychology* 18:4, 1982.

Rosenberg, Merri. "A Child of Older Parents." *New York Times*, September 4, 1980, Op-Ed page.

Rossi, Alice S. "Aging and Parenthood in the Middle Years." In *Life Span Development and Behavior*, vol. 3. Paul B. Baltes and Orville G. Brim, Jr., eds. New York: Academic Press, 1980.

Schultz, Terri. *Women Can Wait: The Pleasures of Motherhood After Thirty*. Garden City, N.Y.: Doubleday, 1979.

Sulloway, Frank. "Orthodoxy and Innovation in Science." Paper presented at the annual meeting of the American Association for the Advancement of Science, New Orleans, La., February 1990.

Sussman, Marvin B., and Suzanne K. Steinmetz, eds. *Handbook of Marriage and the Family*. New York: Plenum Press, 1987.

Taylor, Richard. "A Fulfillment." *New York Times Magazine*, March 29, 1987.

Toman, Walter. *Family Constellation: Its Effects on Personality and Social Behavior*. New York: Springer, 1976.

United Nations Statistical Office. *Demographic Yearbook 1988*. New York: United Nations, 1990.

———. *Demographic Yearbook 1986*. New York: United Nations, 1988.

———. *Demographic Yearbook 1981*. New York: United Nations, 1983.

Ventura, Stephanie J. "Trends in First Births to Older Mothers, 1970–79." *National Center for Health Statistics Monthly Vital Statistics Report* 31:2, supp. 2 (May 27, 1982).

———. "Trends in Postponed Childbearing, United States, 1970–87." Paper presented at annual meeting of American Public Health Association, Chicago, October 25, 1989.

——— and Gerry E. Hendershot. "Infant Health Consequences of Childbearing by Teenagers and Older Mothers." *Public Health Reports* 99:2. March–April 1984.

Wilson, Bradford, and George Edington. *First Child, Second Child*. New York: McGraw-Hill, 1981.

Yarrow, Andrew L. "Older Parents' Child: Growing Up Special." *New York Times*, January 26, 1987.

Index